Praise for
ALASKA ON OUR MINDS:

"How do you celebrate the post-career aspect of your life when you still have the energy to remain active and the desire to visit new places? Buddy and Kathy Bethea ordered and built a new Nordhavn 55 and turned it into an underway passport to anywhere. Their boating skills took them thousands of miles, and their personalities created friendships with those people who they encountered offshore and on land. Buddy's gifted storytelling is reflected in these collected posts, offered here for the first time in book format. Thousands of inspired followers eagerly anticipated each new post, and the Betheas' engaging charisma left lasting impressions that are still felt today. Hop aboard and sail through these recollections, but be forewarned: you may be so captivated that you will want to set out on your own adventures."

—Jeff Merrill, CPYB, yacht broker turned friend

Alaska On Our Minds:
The Journey of Always Friday

by Dr. William "Buddy" Bethea

© Copyright 2023 Dr. William Bethea

ISBN 978-1-64663-909-0

All rights reserved. No part of this publication
may be reproduced, stored in a retrieval system,
or transmitted in any form or by any means—
electronic, mechanical, photocopy, recording, or any other—
except for brief quotations in printed reviews, without the prior
written permission of the author.

Published by

3705 Shore Drive
Virginia Beach, VA 23455
800-435-4811
www.koehlerbooks.com

ALASKA ON OUR MINDS

THE JOURNEY OF ALWAYS FRIDAY

DR. WILLIAM "BUDDY" BETHEA

VIRGINIA BEACH
CAPE CHARLES

*"Twenty years from now you will be more disappointed by the things that you did not do, then by the ones that you did do.
So, throw off the bow lines.
Sail away from the safe harbor.
Catch the trade winds in your sails. Explore! Dream! Discover!"*
—M. Twain

CONTENTS

INTRODUCTION 5

ALASKA 6

HEADING SOUTH 97

SOUTH OF THE BORDER 158

BACK IN THE USA 227

SOME PERSONAL THOUGHTS ON ALASKA 291

AN HONOR BESTOWED 302

INTRODUCTION

IN 2007, BUDDY and Kathy Bethea took a well-deserved break from a long and successful medical practice, bought a great boat on the West Coast, and sailed to Alaska. Doesn't everybody?

Along the way, he recorded his adventure through a blog that at one point had as many as one million followers. This is that blog.

Enjoy the trip with him and crew from your armchair, and wish you were there.

—*Eric Fox*

ALASKA

6/14/2007

WE HAVE BEEN in Juneau at Auke Harbor for several days, enjoying the local scene as East Coast tourists. We have mixed and mingled with the tour boat crowd, and in short, done many of the things that we had planned to avoid on *Always Friday*. That is not a negative. In fact, we were all pleasantly surprised with the quality of the attractions in and around Juneau.

As "touristy" as it sounds, we spent a fascinating afternoon yesterday at an abandoned gold mine on Nugget Creek above Juneau. Far from being an overly commercialized disappointment, we found it to be just what it said: a successful gold mine from the 1800s until it was abandoned in 1944. We spent several hours reconstructing in our minds what the place much have looked like during the gold rush that gave Juneau life. The electric locomotives and the cars that delivered the men into and out of the mines still sit on the rusting tracks, silent since the cost of mining the gold rose above the value of the gold gleaned from the rocks. The museum is maintained as a labor of love by a couple that genuinely enjoy strangers that show an interest in "their" mine. With the help of those who are trying to preserve the mining history of Juneau, you can feel the frustrations and occasional elation that comprised the lives of those who risked all for the possibility of easy wealth.

Among the most fascinating things to see at the mining site were the two or three men that stood out from the crowd of tourists as dozens of people panned for gold in Nugget Creek. They were heavily bearded, dressed in old dirty denims, red flannel shirts, wide suspenders, and calf-high rubber boots as if in a gold rush movie. However, they were for real! I engaged one in conversation and learned that they go there most every day of the week and pan for gold exactly as it was done years ago. They were in their fifties and looked as if they live a remarkably simple life. No watches, no wallets, and certainly no cell phones. The fellow that I spoke to said that he had been doing this for almost twenty years, and averages over $500 per month for his successful collection of gold. So, another Alaska paradox—an abandoned gold mine still supports gold miners that have abandoned the lifestyle society has forced upon most of us.

This morning was the last one for the Harts as they are to return to Virginia today. To make their trip even more memorable, Alaska had one more trick up its sleeve. Two whales in the harbor, not more than 100 yards away! We watched in fascination while the two giants rolled and lunged among the schools of Herring that surrounded our boat. The show lasted longer than we had to watch them, so after dozens of pictures that we will share with you as soon as possible, we reluctantly left them for our next appointment with

Alaskan grandeur: Mendenhall Glacier. Another pleasant surprise in the world of Juneau attractions.

When in downtown Juneau, you see bus after dilapidated bus with signs proclaiming, "Ride to Mendenhall Glacier—$6 Each Way!" Such blatant commercialism would suggest that disappointment should wait at the end of the bus ride. But nothing could be further from the truth. Upon arrival at the Mendenhall Glacier National Park, just a few miles outside of Juneau, we were met with another Alaskan visual feast that must not be missed by anyone near the area. The glacier itself is beautiful, and the waterfalls among the most impressive we have seen so far. We took advantage of the hiking trails that allow you to get close enough to the falls to feel the water on your face and waded the streams that in a few weeks will be filled with salmon on the last run of their lives. Just another natural wonder there for the taking in this beautiful state.

Then back to the boat to prepare for Tom and Marian Shuttleworth's visit next week. When we arrived in Auke Harbor, the boat attracted the usual number of admirers, including two young Navy men who had been impressed with our use of the remote controls for the bow and stern thrusters. After showing them around the boat, one of the sailors, Greg Cazemier, graciously offered to take Kathy shopping to reprovision the boat for next week. Today she took him up on the offer and we spent the day (and many dollars) at the Juneau Costco. Just another example of how friendly and thoughtful the locals are here in Alaska. Upon our return, Greg accepted our invitation to join us for dinner on board *Always Friday*, and I accepted his offer to go salmon and halibut fishing with him. Guess who won out in that deal! Greg's plans were to become an outfitter after his retirement from the Navy in about three years. That makes perfect sense to me.

Tomorrow morning, we are going to give king salmon fishing a try in a cove near here. To get my strength up for the battle, Kathy just served Alaskan king crab legs and fresh grilled salmon for our dinner.

6/15/2007

Kathy and I went fishing today.

Your automatic reaction is certainly, "Did you catch anything?"

Well, it shouldn't be, because up here, fishing is so much more than just catching a fish.

It all started even before we left the dock where the boat was tied adjacent to *Always Friday*. Our guide was preparing bait (herring) when he heard a familiar blowing sound behind him. As he turned to look, a humpback whale lunged through a school of baitfish, lifting himself half out of the water before returning with a gigantic splash. All within a few feet of our boat.

Not a bad start for our trip in search of king salmon. The boat was a thirty-foot aluminum classic Alaskan fishing craft, different from any seen in Virginia but very similar to most of the serious boats that prevail up here.

As we left the harbor on dead low tide (a twenty-four-foot tide swing today), we headed towards Fritz Cove, just a few miles away and the local hot spot for kings. The panorama was composed of approximately 320 degrees of high, snow-capped mountains, with the remainder occupied by a beautiful view of Mendenhall Glacier approximately twelve miles away. The retreat of the water at low tide left us with a clear view of the mouths of several freshwater streams emptying into the cove. As we rode along, we were frequently accompanied by artic terns which migrate from Chile, as well the omnipresent bald eagles, ravens, and gulls.

Then Alaska offered us yet another gift. Off to our left, about thirty yards away, we saw what the guide said was, for him, the first fish of the year attempting to move upstream into the creek of its infancy. It was just like in the movies. The fish, weighing approximately fifteen pounds, was in water that did not cover his dorsal fin or tail. As she fought to move upstream, a bald eagle swooped down, sank its talons into its back, and attempted to lift it from the water.

Apparently, the eagle had overbought at the lunch counter. It could neither lift its prey from the stream bed nor release its grip on the fish (a characteristic of the eagle's talons, according to the guide). The fish turned back towards deeper water, taking the eagle with it! What followed was one of those fights for survival that happen so often in nature but not frequently before the eyes of man. For approximately ten minutes, the fish had the eagle in the precarious position of "can't fly, can't swim." The guide predicted that we were about to see our national bird drowned by salmon.

But then the tables turned in favor of the eagle. He flapped his wings furiously and reversed the progression of the pair into deeper water to the point that he was able to drag the fish onto land, flopping his last on the streambed as the eagle began his triumphant feast. Within minutes, a dozen or more eagles were tussling for table rights at the salmon's last stand. What a show, and we had not yet begun to fish for the ultimate Alaskan game fish, the king salmon.

For the next four hours, we trolled three rods at depths of thirty-five feet using downriggers, a flasher on each line, followed by a feathered jig in front of double hooks with a strip of fresh herring as added enticement. The accepted method is to troll very slowly while close to shore, allowing the currents to bring the baitfish, lures, and salmon together. It worked well. We hooked a total of five very nice fish and landed two beautiful kings of thirty-four and twenty-eight inches in length.

Of the fish that we lost, we got a good look at the largest but lost it outside the reach of the net. But our freezer tells the story, packed to the top with king salmon filets that ensure meals fit for a king during our next foray from port.

Yet another great Alaskan experience, made up of life and death, predator and prey scenarios that characterize this beautiful place. Today the successful predators were the eagle and us. The eagle ate well; our culinary reward will not be far behind.

We are hoping for a permit to enter Glacier National Park next Monday. We will know if we are successful tomorrow morning.

Tomorrow we will wait for the Shuttleworth's arrival, and then leave with them for Hoonah, AK, just across the water from Glacier Bay National Park! The trip will be through the heart of whale, bear, salmon, halibut, and seal country, not to mention the most beautiful scenery imaginable.

PS—If you have an interest, here is the link to the company that builds the fishing boats in Sitka, AK. Ours was the Orca 30, an excellent boat, and the one that I would buy if I were to live here in Alaska. www.allenmarineinc.com/

6/16/2007

NPS permit #5747 for *Always Friday* to enter Glacier Bay National Park for a stay of one week, cruising throughout the day, and anchoring at night.

The boat is ready, and the "crew" is on the way here. We will leave Juneau tomorrow morning after Tom and Marion arrive at midnight tonight. The word is that it will be the high point of our Alaskan experience.

We will let you know!

6/17/2007, Father's Day

Another change in plans in our very liquid schedule. The Shuttleworths' plane was delayed out of New York, and they will not arrive until later today. Since they have plans to travel through the interior of Alaska, leaving us next Thursday, we will not be able to get to Glacier Bay in time for a meaningful visit.

Therefore, we will turn in our GB permit and head north to see why they say the scenery between here and Skagway is so magnificent. Haines tonight, then Skagway the next night. That will take us through the heart of whale and bear country as well. Not a bad second choice. We hope to have *Always Friday* in Glacier Bay the following week with Phil and Susan Greene on board.

6/17/2007

We left Juneau under cloudy skies, which served up the opportunity to see the scenery in yet another beautiful lighting scheme. The low-hanging clouds obscured the mountaintops but seemed to magnify the contrasts between the water, mountains, and glaciers. Beautiful in an entirely different way from the blue-bird days that we have enjoyed recently.

Our plans were to cruise northward to Haines for the night, and then proceed to Skagway on Monday after exploring whatever Haines had to offer. Skagway will represent the northernmost penetration of Alaska that we anticipate completing, about sixty degrees of northern latitude.

The initial course to Haines took us by Shelter Island, which we had been told always seems to be a favorite haunt of the humpback whales. We had been gone for about an hour when I saw a whale roll about a half mile from us. Marion was less than impressed since she declared the roll to have been a porpoise, which we see very frequently in Virginia. About that time, Moby Porpoise cleared the water about 200 yards from us, rolled over in mid-air, and returned to the sea with a splash that activated the stabilizers on the boat. It was as if the fat lady at the circus had done a perfect cannonball from the top of the Empire State Building . . . but with the style and grace of Nureyev.

No more claims of porpoises were heard. We watched in amazement as 50,000-pound whales cavorted in front of us, clearing the water on multiple occasions, rolling in midair, and once showing the classic pattern of lunge feeding when one came straight out of the water with its whale-sized mouth wide open, straining herring from the sea into its stomach! That jump occurred about ten yards in front of our bow.

As we watched, we initially thought that there was at least one baby whale in the group, but the binoculars revealed a surprise when they confirmed that seals were swimming among the feeding whales, taking the seconds that fell from the cavernous mouths of the sea giants. Soon the sea gulls were enjoying the fruits of the feasts initiated by the whales, adding yet another chapter to the fascinating saga of the marine food chain that begins with plankton, then progresses to the tiny herring and ultimately to the largest mammals on earth. If you would not enjoy this magnificent show of nature, you come from a planet with which I am not familiar.

We had an interesting example of slow versus fast cruising when we met the motor vessel *Fairweather* three times while making the trip from Juneau to Haines. The *Fairweather* is one of the catamaran fast ferries that makes the same trip we took today but does so at nearly forty knots. It completed the course three times to our one, blazing by us each time at almost five times our speed. Two approaches: slow and unhurried versus fast and hectic. I'll take the former every time. I doubt if anyone on the ferry saw the interaction between the whales, seals, and seagulls as we saw it. For their sake, I hope that they don't know what they missed.

Tom has shown an amazing ability to transition from landlubber to sea captain. After only minimal instruction, he was able to both navigate and drive the boat for the entire trip. With no error at all, he followed the order "Don't touch a thing. It's on autopilot" for hours at a time!

We arrived in Haines about 6:30 PM with five more hours of daylight before us. The tide of twenty-one feet today was approaching its maximum low, making the hike up the ramp from the dock quite a challenge. That might sound like an overstatement, but look at the angles of the ramps in some of our pictures and you will see the physical challenge that makes going up or down them so daunting. As I sit here now, the breakwater rises high above the boat as if we were at ground level inside a castle, protected by high stone walls above us. However, in about six hours, we will be floating level with what is now a wall of over twenty-five feet. There are no small bites in Alaska. Everything is on a scale not often seen in the lower forty-eight.

Our "late-afternoon" excursion from the boat led us to a waterside restaurant called the Lighthouse. (It is now 11:20 PM as I write this, and you can not only still read outside but also clearly see the details of the mountains miles away.) At the restaurant, we were treated to great dinners of broiled halibut and black cod, preceded by some of the best calamari that any of us had ever had. How can the cruise ships say that they take you to Alaska when they skip everything that we have found so rewarding here? Tomorrow we will further explore the town before leaving for Skagway after lunch.

So, the Alaskan adventure continues. Every day offers another unique memory that only time, and cholesterol, can dilute. Another reason to take your Lipitor and live every day to the fullest.

I intend to do both tomorrow.

Stay with us!

6/18/2007

We awoke this morning to a cloudy day in Haines. After breakfast, we wandered among the stores in town before leaving for Skagway about 11:30 AM. Haines was well worth an overnight visit and offered a very nice Alaskan experience, with the added attraction of an excellent meal at the Lighthouse Restaurant.

The short ride of about two hours to Skagway took us through beautiful, snow-covered mountains with frequent, dramatic waterfalls along the way. Our search for mountain goats was without success today. As we neared Skagway, the winds that are characteristic of this area began to build from the south, funneling through the mountain pass. Docking a Nordhavn (NH) in twenty-knot, ninety-degree gusty winds make you happy that you have thrusters on both ends!

Skagway Harbor was filled with five cruise ships upon our arrival, and the people from the ships were everywhere. We had an excellent lunch at a harborside restaurant, with clam chowder the clear favorite. Afterwards we wandered the streets of Skagway for several hours, confirming that the place is everything you want to avoid when you have the flexibility to pick your visits in your own boat. Dozens of places selling T-shirts, tanzanite jewelry, "native" carvings, and totem poles, always at "cruise ship discounts," degrading the Alaskan experience to the point of our rededicating ourselves to avoid anywhere cruise ships go.

Since the Shuttleworths are not staying long enough for us to get to Glacier Bay on *Always Friday*, we plan to take a plane ride there tomorrow from the Skagway airport, before returning slowly to Juneau through whale country, with an overnight stop in Barlow Cove where the halibut fishing is world class. We will remember Skagway as the northernmost point of our Alaskan experience, and as a place we went once, with no desire for a return visit. Tomorrow, it is back to our kind of Alaska, which exists a mere 100 yards outside of the Skagway Harbor.

6/19/2007

We have just accomplished the first half of the two best things you can do in Skagway: leave by air and leave by water! The second half we will knock off in the morning.

Today's weather has been beautiful here, in sharp contrast to yesterday's wind and rain. It is now about seventy degrees with a light breeze from the north. The mountains, still significantly covered in snow, now stand out vividly against the blue skies and puffy white clouds. A perfect day to charter a plane and go "flight-seeing."

So we did just that!

We chartered a Piper Archer, a six-seat, retractable-gear, variable-pitch prop plane, and headed into the mountains. We hired an instructor pilot to go with us, as flying here is quite different than in Virginia. We stayed up for two hours, flew over Haines, through the mountains and glacier fields, and into Glacier Bay National Park. Incredible beauty on a scale that defies the imagination. From the air, the interaction of the currents with the outflow from the glacial melting was dramatic. Blue-green waters of the bay merged in sharp interfaces with silt-laden, almost muddy-looking effluent from the glaciers, reflecting the active destructive process still ongoing after millions of years of restructuring the surface of the earth by brute glacial force. The mountains have been caught in the web of the glacier, with the same outcome that follows the entrapment of the fly by the spider. The mountains are simply being digested by the glaciers in a feast that has lasted millions of years and is destined to continue for ages to come.

As we walked through the town this morning (just a short walk from the boat), it was obvious that the five cruise ships that had arrived last night had regurgitated another throng of souls into the carnival atmosphere that pervades the Skagway scene. When you mix that crowd with the Hollywood facades of a "reconstructed"— i.e., fake—gold rush town, you have perpetrated a travesty on the natural beauty of Alaska. As I see it, the main effect the cruise-ship industry has had on this mystical place is the denaturing of a natural treasure. Gold may have been the father of Alaska, but the dollar is the abusive husband in the relationship.

Tomorrow, we leave on board *Always Friday* for the return trip to Auke Bay. We plan to go slowly, as the trip takes us through the heart of whale country. Our good fortune in having them jumping all around us on the trip here has all of us hoping for more of the same. After our arrival in Juneau, we plan to take Tom and Marion to the Mendenhall Glacier National Park, which was one of the Harts' highlights when they were here, then off to downtown Juneau so they can say that they have been there. If you want a tacky T-shirt, let us know. They are everywhere down there!

6/23/2007

The last several days have been quintessential Alaska. The weather has varied from sunny in the seventies to today's cloudy and chilly in the fifties. Tom and Marion left on Thursday for Denali, and Phil and Susan Greene took their stateroom on Friday. After the routine Alaskan Airlines search for their lost baggage and its arrival a day later, we spent the day catching herring from the dock and then offering them up to the king salmon jumping constantly around us. Although we got several strong strikes, none resulted in fish in the net for us. Two twenty-five-pounders were landed by those fishing just next to us, confirming that the fish can be caught successfully from the dock to which we are moored.

Today, Phil and I went king salmon fishing in a cove adjacent to Auke Harbor. The scenery was its usual extraordinary entertainment, with eagles constantly flying among the boats, seeking the salmon.

We landed four beautiful fish (Phil caught three of the four by virtue of being quicker to the rod), the largest being a thirty-four-inch, twenty-five-pound king salmon full of roe for its final trip of a lifetime. The refrigerator is now brimming with fresh filets, and two of the salmon are at the fish house for smoking. The king salmon run is nearing its end, with the coho salmon expected here in great numbers within the next several weeks. We have been told that upon their arrival, we will be catching beautiful fish on almost every cast from the back of *Always Friday*. It's hard to believe that there could be more fish here than there are right now, but everyone tells us that we haven't seen anything yet.

While we were fishing, Kathy and Susan squandered a beautiful day by wandering aimlessly through Costco and other assorted spending opportunities before returning with such treasures as bear-, moose-, and salmon-shaped cookie cutters, even though in thirty-five years of marriage, I have never known her to make such cookies. It is amazing what that second X chromosome does to rational thought!

The boat continues to attract interesting visitors daily. Yesterday we met Dennis Nolder, a retired Alaskan Airlines captain (he couldn't help with the luggage) who came to see the boat. He and his wife live here, and he has his boat here in the harbor. We plan to get together after our return from our next trip, and he has offered to show us some of the prime fishing and crabbing areas around Auke Harbor.

Today we were admiring a beautiful, thirty-foot, classic aluminum Alaskan cruising boat when the owner came out to tell us more about the boat he obviously loves. As we talked, we learned that he was a military aviator, originally with the Marines but more recently a C-130 Hercules pilot with the Coast Guard here in Juneau. His association with the Coast Guard has led to many exciting rescues on the high seas of Alaska, one of which was so dramatic and heroic that it led to a book relating the events of that rescue. When Bill leaned that the Nordhavn in the harbor was ours, he asked if he could bring his family to see it since he has long been an admirer of these boats. Just another example of how our boat has opened so many doors to adventure and fascinating people of the northwest.

Yesterday we had the pleasure of meeting Craig Loomis (http://www.firstoutlastin.com) while we were eating fried halibut and chips at a local marina restaurant. For years Craig has been living the life that I always dreamed of as he ran his charter and guide service from Haines. He took us on a tour of his boat and entertained us with hunting and fishing stories—along with albums of pictures documenting his successes—that I could have listened to for hours. He is taking a charter group out for the next week, but we plan to get together after our mutual returns to the harbor the following week. He taught us several tricks of the local fishing trade, and gave us several rigs for salmon that we plan to put to good use this week. Then he not only armed us with several locations for slam dunks on Dungeness crabs but also offered to get us a trap that he knew would be very productive for us.

The most unexpected encounter was with a local travel broker who sought us out as the owners of the "yellow Nordhavn" to ask if we were interested in chartering the boat here in Alaska. Although we clearly stated that we were not even remotely interested, he presented an interesting proposal of a net return of $25,000 per week if we chose to list the boat for local Alaskan trips. An interesting confirmation of the public's perception of the value of the Nordhavn cruising experience.

We have found Alaska to be full of very nice people who love their state and are more than willing to make those of us not fortunate enough to be native Alaskans feel very much welcome while in their wonderland. They have added immensely to the enjoyment of our trip and are playing even more important roles in our enjoyment daily. Clearly, the best is yet to come.

Tomorrow, Phil and Susan have chosen to spend the next three days with us on a slow trip northward around Shelter Island, the humpback whale's favorite haunt, then southward to Tracy Arm, the Sawyer Glaciers, and Endicott Arm with its highlight of Dawes Glacier. That will entail two or three nights anchored "on the hook" in quiet, secluded coves, enjoying great meals from the ship's kitchen thanks to Susan and Kathy.

Every day is better than the day before in Alaska!

6/24/2007

What a pleasure it is to have no schedule. We left Auke Bay Harbor this morning with intentions of rounding Shelter Island to the north to show Phil and Susan the whales and then heading south to Tracy Arm. Alaska showed all of us another beautiful side, as the mountains were covered with clouds, the temperature was a comfortable fifty-three degrees, and there was essentially no wind. The flat seas made seeing the spouts of whales quite easy, and see them we did. At least twenty different sightings kept us enthralled for hours. They were everywhere: in front of us, behind us, and on both the right and left! Rolling, spouting, showing us great tail shots—all the things whales can do to make Alaska even more fascinating, they did for us.

We rode the fly bridge for hours, watching the show while listening to XM Radio music as a background to the greatest show on earth. Everyone said at least once that life doesn't get any better than this, and it doesn't. Four people, the best of friends, on a beautiful boat, in a beautiful place, with Mother Nature putting on a show as if she were trying to impress us. How do you improve upon that?

The result was that we spent several hours playing with the whales, making Tracy Arm by nightfall a challenge. An easy fix—we changed our destination to Taku Harbor. It is a beautiful, secluded cove about three hours north of Tracy Arm that was an old canning factory many years ago. It has been abandoned to the bears, weeds, salmon, and Dungeness crabs, but the state of Alaska has built unattended mooring spaces there that are available for visiting boats. That's us! So here we are, in Taku Harbor, with a beautiful view of the mountains, water, and the abandoned cannery.

As an added surprise, we found that Richard and Lorna Maybin had preceded us into the cove in their Nordhavn 76, *Spirit of Ulysses*. We met them in Dana Point where we shared the Nordhavn commissioning experience for our boats. They invited us to their boat, allowing Phil and Susan to see how good the Nordhavn experience can be in their flagship yacht. Moored near us was Louie from Juneau, who grew up in Alaska, drove a truck here for years, then bought a tavern. He is now retired and enjoying the Alaska that the cruise ships have not ruined. Taku Harbor is his kind of place. After engaging him in conversation, he accepted our invitation to see "the boat." As always, *Always Friday* was a catalyst to great insider information from "Louie the local." We are now armed with a new list of must-see places that the cruise books never mention.

Tonight was another great meal on board *Always Friday*. King salmon that Phil and I caught yesterday was the centerpiece of a meal that would easily make the Food Channel. When Kathy and Susan get together in the galley, a culinary delight soon follows. Tonight was no exception, topped off by a Skinny Cow ice cream sandwich.

It is now 10:20 PM, an hour before sundown. The clouds are obscuring the mountaintops, and the calm waters serve as a reflecting pool for the mountains, forests, and shoreline. All is calm and beautiful in Alaska, and we are off to bed—after one last search for bears with the FLIR (forward-looking infrared).

More tomorrow. A lot more tomorrow: the waterfalls, glaciers, icebergs, eagles and seals of Tracy and Endicott Arms for Phil and Susan!

6/25/2007

It rained all night last night. That was one of the few ways the night's sleep could have been made even better. For those of you from the south, you may have heard of "rain on a tin roof" to describe the most relaxing sleep scenario one could imagine. Well, that can be equaled by raindrops hitting on the deck of *Always Friday*. All night long, the natural sleeping pill of falling rain ensured a quality of sleep only brought about by complete relaxation, a total absence of stress, and the welcome fatigue that follows a great day in the wilds of Alaska. The sun rose again about 3 AM, but the skylights and portholes of *Always Friday* can be blacked out at night, ensuring a cave-like solitude that usually keeps you captive in the bed for at least the first five hours of daylight.

We arose to a scene of Alaskan beauty that I had not experienced before. The clouds were under a thousand feet, wrapping every mountain in a white, fluffy blanket that was reflected upon the still waters in a way no artist could ever capture. Stepping outside, the first breath of the crisp, fresh air of about fifty degrees introduced us to another invigorating day in the natural wonderland of Alaska.

By 9 AM, after Kathy's apple walnut coffee cake and Starbuck's best, we were off to Tracy Arm, about two and a half hours south of Taku Harbor. The trip in calm seas was a constant travelogue of Alaskan beauty, punctuated several times by whales announcing their presence with spouts that seem to persist in the air long after the laws of dispersion would have predicted their disappearance

Tracy Arm begins to announce its upcoming arrival by the unexpected presence of progressively larger icebergs as you approach its entrance. As you make the ninety-degree turn from Stephen's Passage into Holkham Bay, you enter another world more suggestive of the Arctic than the United States. The radar, FLIR, and your eyes reveal a field of icebergs ranging from several yards across to the size of a ship. As if these obstacles to navigation were not enough to get your heart rate up, the infamous confluence of opposing currents raises its head to redirect the boat in any direction it so desires. Add to that the fact that the channel markers are frequently dragged around by the icebergs to places that NOAA never intended them to be, and you will get a sense of the nautical challenge of safely entering this frigid, magnificent wonderland. Once you have successfully completed this challenging entry, you are guided by a back-course range to an onshore marker that presents you with the appropriate entry to Tracy Arm.

From that point on, you are traversing the path of ancient glaciers that have left you with the luxury of depths measured in hundreds or even thousands of feet, right up to the edge of the water. If you avoid the well-charted rocks, the threat from beneath the water is minimal. But that is not to say that the rest of the trip is a picture of relaxation. The icebergs rise from the water to constantly remind you of the "unsinkable" Titanic.

The further you go into Tracy Arm, the more the surface is occupied by icebergs. They are themselves things of beauty. The shades of blue and green, dictated by the pressure of the weight of thousands of years of accumulated ice, defy the imagination. Even the structure of the ice is fascinating. The constant motion of the flowing river of ice generates crystals that resemble Rubik's Cubes, movable in multiple directions without further fracturing of the ice. The icebergs are giant, loose jigsaw puzzles made up of millions of ice crystals arranged in ways simply impossible for man to recreate but mastered by nature millions of years ago.

The waterfalls today took on a totally different appearance from our prior visit with the Harts. The several-thousand-foot mountains were now capped by clouds at less than a thousand feet, allowing the waterfalls to originate within the clouds. The patterns of condensation yielded wispy clouds that looked more like the lightest brush strokes of an artist than the random interaction of humidity and temperature. As we approached the glacier, the air temperature dropped from fifty-one to forty degrees, the water temperature from fifty-two to forty-two, and the chill factor fell to the mid-thirties. Still, the beauty of the scenery kept us on the fly bridge, camera in hand. Not many could resist the opportunity to see, hear, and feel this beautiful place, even in three layers of clothing!

The beauty of Tracy Arms is best represented by its waterfalls. As you can see from our pictures, they come in every size and configuration that nature could devise. To truly appreciate the magnificence of these falls, you must add their sound to the more obvious visual opportunity. The sharp walls of the fjords cut by the glaciers afford you the opportunity to take the boat to within feet of the base of the falls where the sounds of the cascading waters add another dimension to the experience.

By late afternoon (still with over seven hours of daylight), we were safely anchored in Tracy Arm Cove beneath Meigs Peak. We shared the beauty of the cove with four other boats, three power and one sail.

After several mesmerizing hours of fascination with the scenery, we grilled steaks on the back of the boat after appetizers of smoked salmon dip, courtesy of our visit with Bill and Mary Pfiefer in Ketchikan. It is now after 11 PM, and the scenery outside is as pretty as we have seen all day. The mountains remain starkly visible, and details on shore are clearly discernable (no bears with us right now).

The anchor lights glowing from the tops of the four boats around us add another dimension to this beautiful cove—one of the few times that a man-made addition adds to the charm of Alaska.

Tomorrow, we plan to explore Endicott Arm all the way to Dawes Glacier at its end. The area is close to a slam dunk for seals, whales, eagles, and great natural beauty. Phil and Susan seem to be enjoying this as much as I am, so off we go into another day in heaven, Alaskan style.

PS: For any of you that might be contemplating a trip here to Alaska, I will tell you of one thing that I failed to recognize in our preparations for this trip. We came prepared to document our trip with a top-of-the-line Nikon point-and-shoot pocket camera. It has served us well, but I can tell you that it is totally inadequate for the multiple photographic opportunities that Alaska presents. This place is so photo rich that Ray Charles could have been an accomplished professional photographer. You can drop your camera here and get a great picture. You should not come to Alaska without a first-class digital SLR camera equipped with lenses (telephoto and otherwise) capable of capturing the opportunities that nature offers, sometimes hundreds of yards away. To watch 50,000-pound whales jumping 100 yards in front of our boat but out of effective range of our camera justifies our rethinking the camera equipment we have brought to this cathedral of nature.

6/26/2007

We had bright-blue skies with puffy white clouds and temperatures in the sixties until we got to Dawes Glacier at the end of Endicott Arm. As was the case with our trip to Tracy Arm, this was our second trip there. What a difference two weeks makes!

In contrast to what we found last visit, the icebergs were far less frequent, and the path to the glacier passable right up to its face. In fact, we were able to get two miles further into Endicott Arm on this trip than on the last. Our deepest penetration was dictated not by obstructing ice but by appropriate caution for the avoidance of calving ice—the dramatic shedding of large icebergs into the water. In fact, we got inside 400 yards from the face of the glacier. The occasional shotgun-blast-like sounds of calving ice added to the excitement of the experience. Again, seals were everywhere, yielding some of our best pictures. Although Tracy Arm and Sawyer Glacier get more publicity, all of us felt that Endicott Arm and Dawes Glacier were the prettier of the two. Tracy is better known simply because cruise ships can't get into Endicott Arm. If they could, they would, and Endicott's fame would rise exponentially.

The return trip presented different views of the same terrain we had seen before, made unrecognizable by the changing light and cloud patterns. There is no such thing as boring repetition in Alaska. Every day, even every hour, is different from the one before. Once again, we were visited by the whales, not only rolling and spouting but now also jumping to further impress the Greenes before their departure. When you look at the pictures, note our depth sounders on the monitor. You will be looking at two whales right under the boat! They rolled right in front of us, and then dove under the boat, allowing us to be sure that the massive return on the screen was truly of two whales.

We plan to fish for king salmon this afternoon, and then eat our victims tonight. Sounds like a cheap horror movie, but I assure it is anything but that. The Dungeness crabs we caught in our traps last night in Taku Cove will serve well as appetizers for the goodbye feast for Phil and Susan. Plans for the coming week include multiple king salmon fishing trips with locals I have met because of their interest in our boat, as well a planned day on board an Alaskan commercial fishing boat with a new friend I met on the dock.

The more I see of southeast Alaska, the more certain I am that I will spend more time here in the future. We have now begun to pick up real estate booklets and make imaginary purchases daily in preparation for the future years. So far, I have "bought" thirty acres on Shelter Island for $85,000, found a log cabin builder who will build whatever you ask for, and specked out a thirty-foot, classic aluminum Alaskan boat for my future enjoyment. It will have downriggers for salmon, electric reels for halibut, and winches for Dungeness and king crabs. And a diesel heater for Kathy, Raleigh, and Binky. Life remains good, both in reality and dreamland!

6/28/2007

A lazy day in Auke Harbor today. Our guests left early this morning, and Kathy and I have the boat to ourselves for a few days.

As nature seems prone to do up here, the Greenes were treated to a final Alaskan treat last "night" when we looked into the western sky to see a rainbow at a little past 10 PM. You would not think that dusky skies of an hour before darkness and less than two hours before midnight would be the home of such a sight, but there it was: the entire spectrum of light right before our eyes, adding a new and unexpected chapter to the beauty of snowcapped mountains, calm waters, rolling salmon, and circling eagles.

Today, being the gregarious little devil that I am, I met a new and interesting friend. Craig is a retired commercial fisherman, hunting guide, and general handyman who has bought an old fishing boat of approximately seventy feet and is converting it into his dream home to live on after his wife retires from the school system. I showed him around *Always Friday*, and he showed me around his boat as well.

After telling him of our plans to cruise and fish Glacier Bay, he invited us to his hometown of Gustavus at the mouth of Bartlett Cove (the entrance to Glacier Bay National Park), where he would outfit our boat with his traps, lines, and other paraphernalia needed to successfully pursue the sea critters residing in and around Icy Straits and Glacier Bay. He then gave me a chart with all the local-knowledge hot spots for crabs, salmon, and halibut (and bears) marked clearly for our use. As if that were not enough of a welcome for a tourist, wannabe Alaskan fisherman like me, he then took me to Western Auto and Marine (the local source of fishing gear for the commercial fisherman) and guided me through the isles as we loaded my tackle box with the "right stuff." I now own a pair of short, green rubber boots just like his, and I am considering investing in a pair of suspenders. I have now bought everything it takes to look like a local (although I did turn down the unfiltered Camels). By the time Lauren and Nathan get here next week, I should be an accepted "local" Alaskan (at least in my own mind).

Earlier today, three local policemen were walking the docks and asked us about our boat. As you may have guessed, I invited them on board for a tour. They were fascinated with the boat, and once again, *Always Friday* served as a catalyst for prolonged conversations about their home state. By the time they left, they had marked my charts with their favorite fishing spots for halibut in Tracy Arm, all of which I had passed over numerous times in ignorance of what lurked beneath our keel. Next time, I will drop a few rigs to them and see what follows. I have been forewarned that the biggest challenge there is that there are no small ones. The halibut frequently top several hundred pounds in that area, at least in part because no one fishes there. Until now!

So, the beautiful experiences of Alaska continue to accumulate. I suffered a slight pang of depression today when Ken Williams and I discussed the appropriate time to abandon Alaska for the trip south, necessitated by the onset of winter weather. Prudent advice seems to be "Be south of Ketchikan by September 1." We had always planned on just that, but I hate the thought of being forced to leave this wonderland, even if our anticipated exit is still almost two months away.

It's 4:30 PM; only six or seven more hours of sunlight today, so I am off to cast for king salmon right here by the boat.

See why I don't want to leave?

6/29/2007

You may remember that I said we had a few lazy days planned around Auke Bay Harbor while we waited for Lauren and Nathan (our daughter and her husband). Well, maybe not. Several days ago, we had the good fortune to come across a local (green boots and suspenders) while he was cleaning his fish on our dock after a successful trip to a nearby cove. He had a cooler full of beautiful king salmon of fifteen to thirty-five pounds that would be the envy of any fisherman. As we watched over his shoulder, he asked if our boat was a Nordhavn.

The door was now open. I confirmed that it was and offered

him a tour of *Always Friday*. He was already an admirer of the boats and had always thought that he would like to have a NH 40 after he retired. Greg declined our offer for a tour at that time but said that he might bring his wife by for a visit later. In parting, he asked if we would like a salmon filet to take to the boat. Guess what I said! As he cut into "our" fish, he was pleasantly surprised to find that it was a white king. A white king salmon is a variant of the species that can't be identified until you cut into the meat. It is a delicacy that never hits the lower forty-eight because it is so rare. The meat is the best fish you can put in your mouth, and the flesh is white, moist, and flaky. You would never guess it to be salmon, and you would never forget its taste if you had it just once. So, the last meal for Phil and Susan before their departure for Georgia was a highlight of the trip: broiled white king salmon with a sauce of butter and capers. If there is an enjoyable way to leave Alaska, that must be it!

Last evening, we were pleasantly surprised to see Greg and his wife, Terry, coming down the dock to see us and the boat. After a tour of every inch of *Always Friday*, we sat down for several hours of golden Alaskan stories over a glass of wine. Greg is an old Alaskan king crab fisherman, just like the TV show *Deadliest Catch*. His earlier days personified the commercial fisherman's life of danger, adventure, quick money, and quicker spending.

Eighteen years ago, he settled down, got married, and took a job on the Inland Passage ferry. He is nearing retirement but now works every other week. His week off is spent on the water pursuing everything that is wet down there. Now comes the good part! He is going to show me what he does, and how he does it. My green boots are going to get dirty (I can't decide if I am going to buy red or orange suspenders; maybe I'll see what Greg wears). Best of all, he is going to get a king crab permit (available only to locals) and show me how they catch those critters that live in waters of about 600 feet. Try to buy that trip on the cruise boats! Terry, his wife, is an accomplished artist and an ardent shopper. She and Kathy are going to utterly waste a day of their lives in the local shops while Greg and I make the most of life's opportunities in the wilds of Alaska.

I am considering putting myself up for adoption. I hope for shared custody—Greg when I am in Auke Bay, and Craig when we are near Gustavus. What more could an adventure-orphan ask for in beautiful Alaska?

The potential dangers of this land were brought to light yesterday when Raleigh discovered that she could go onto the bow of the boat if we left the Portuguese bridge door open. We inadvertently did so, and Raleigh proceeded to go to the anchor and bark her head off to show her displeasure at being left behind while we went fishing. Binky refuses to climb the starboard outboard stairs, so she was left behind in the aft cockpit, or "back porch" as Kathy calls it. When we returned, one of the locals was standing guard over Raleigh to protect her from a threat that we never considered ... a bald eagle attack!

That's right! Our national symbol considers Raleigh to be in the food chain. Raleigh's protector told us of a recent attack in which a pet cat was taken off the deck of a sailboat here in this harbor right before the eyes of the owners. Relax—there is a happy ending to that story: the husband hated the cat.

So now I am charged with protecting Raleigh and Binky from eagle attacks. The doggy doors have been erected, and the dogs are confined to the back porch where there is no room for the swooping attack that eagles must make to capture their prey. Can you imagine anything worse than seeing Raleigh soaring into the sunset in the talons of an eagle? How about Kathy being carried into the woods by a thousand-pound brown bear? You can see the awesome responsibility that I must carry for the safety of my family. Somehow, I will carry on.

Life is tough out here, even in green boots and suspenders.

6/30/2007

Today was rainy. Kind of a lazy, but still beautiful, day here. An air of excitement permeates even those who are not directly involved, for tonight, at midnight, the seining season opens for the commercial guys. The harbor is teeming with the seiner boats with their nets either carefully rolled onto the large drums near their sterns, ready for dispatching around schools of salmon, or laid out on the docks for last-minute repairs before leaving for the fishing grounds. The atmosphere reminds me of my Navy days when our aircraft carrier (*John F. Kennedy* CVA-67) was being made ready for our overseas deployment. A mixture of excitement and apprehension that I would guess has characterized the scene of deploying ships since man first went to sea. When they return in several weeks, they will have harvested literally millions of pounds of salmon from waters that we have traveled frequently over the past several weeks.

Over the last week, there has been a noticeable increase in the number of salmon jumping all around us as the nautical equivalent of the swallows' annual return to Capistrano materializes right before our eyes. Soon the local waters will be thick with salmon meeting their obligation to the next generation with their doomed journey to their birthplace. Between them and their final commitment lie the fisherman, the bears, the eagles, the salmon sharks . . . and me. Although the odds may be against the individual fish, the species makes it up in numbers so vast as to defy the imagination. Alaska will be the destination of hundreds of millions of fish in the next six weeks, and we are here to both witness this spectacle of nature and catch a few ourselves.

A spectacle of man arrived here yesterday. The yacht *Ulysses* pulled into our harbor and instantly changed the skyline with its impressive size. It is 192 feet long but appears far larger than that. In fact, it dwarfs the 152-foot Delta yacht, *Mr. Terrible*, which is here on its maiden voyage. Although *Ulysses* is only three and a half times the length of *Always Friday*, its displacement is almost seventeen times that of our boat! It looks more like a freighter than a luxury mega yacht.

Ulysses was built by Trinity Yachts in New Orleans but caught fire two weeks before completion and burned for nine hours before it could be extinguished. The prospective original owner, one of the richest men in New Zealand, bought the damaged ship from the insurance company and repaired it in another yard. It is now completely rebuilt and touring the world. The picture of Kathy standing by the bow will give you some idea of its immense size.

For anyone that enjoys boats, both commercial and private, Auke Bay Harbor offers endless entertainment, requiring nothing more than strolls down the docks packed with boats of every size and description (except cruise ships, thankfully).

Today was a high point in my transition to self-proclaimed "local" status. Another new friend, Eddie Kelly, a local fishing guide, has been graciously teaching us the techniques of salmon fishing from our boat or our dock. Today, he took us to Kathy's favorite grocery store for reprovisioning, followed by a return visit to Western Auto and Marine, my new "favorite store" since all of the local fisherman, both commercial and sport, know it to be the place for serious fishermen. While there, I succumbed to the obvious need to blend in with the locals as I become more proficient as a gatherer of sea creatures from the local waters. So now I have the requisite rubber-faced bib overalls, brown Carhart fishing pants, and red suspenders.

Kathy says that I look like a fool. I say I look like a local fisherman. She is right, and I am happy. We both win! I have my eye on a wool stocking cap—I just need it to be a few degrees colder. The first time I see one of the "real" fishermen with one on, I'll be back at Western Auto, Visa card in hand.

There is one advantage to all my recent purchases—I won't need anything else for Halloween next year.

Tomorrow, another of those wondrous schedule-free days. Something good will happen—always does!

7/04/2007

More good news from the docks of Auke Bay! This one was Binky's contact.

As we were walking Raleigh and Binky down the dock, as we do several times a day, Binky went into one of her hysterical barking spells that signaled her recognition of a dog that must be played with. In front of us, peeking over the rails of F/V (fishing vessel) *Hadassah*, was Gracie, a beautiful, three-month-old yellow lab. After the usual undignified doggy hellos were completed, Binky and Gracie began to entertain the dock people with unending chase scenes, punctuated by playful barking, nipping, and quick reversals of field that would make a Heisman winner look sluggish.

But the best was yet to follow. Gracie was owned by Glen and Jean Carroll, lifelong commercial fishermen (fisherpersons?) from Homer, Alaska, who were following the salmon here in Auke Bay. Their boat, a fifty-eight-foot seiner, was built about twenty-five years ago by Delta Marine before they converted their production to luxury yachts.

The 154-foot *Mr. Terrible* (moored here, and pictured several times on our site) represents the new generation of Delta Marine, but you can see the dedication to quality that permeated their company years ago when you look at the construction of *Hadassah*. It is a beautifully built, efficient fishing machine that is destined to ply the seas for many more years to come. They recognized us as the crew from *Always Friday*, and as you can guess, I offered to show them our boat in the hopes that a reciprocal offer to see theirs would follow.

It did! Yesterday morning, Glen, Jean, and their chief crewman,

Ian, came to visit. While Kathy and Jean talked knitting, Glen, Ian, and I went over every foot of *Always Friday* in a tour that only a professional mariner would find interesting. "Stem to stern" would best describe the tour. They were as impressed with the quality and seaworthiness of Nordhavn boats as I was with Delta fishing vessels.

Then came the homerun. They invited us to join them for dinner last night on board *Hadassah*. Not just any dinner, but sockeye salmon caught the day before in their nets, and prawns (really *big* shrimp, up to six inches) from their traps. A meal fit for royalty was served up in their galley for one of the most enjoyable nights of our Alaskan adventure.

Even better than the food was the company. Glen and Jean entertained us with stories of their fishing years that would easily justify a book. We learned about the uncertain economics of fishing that revolve around the costs of IFQs (individual fishing quotas) that must be bought at sky-high prices from those awarded them years ago based upon prior catch histories, the vagaries of pricing that leaves the fisherman vulnerable to uncertain returns on certain expenses, and the variables on the cost side as uncontrollable as a whale dashing through a $25,000 net. Glen, like many other fishermen, is still waiting for restitution after the Exon Valdez disaster. Although his annual income has been adversely impacted every year since the massive oil spill, he has yet to receive a penny in settlement.

Yet you could see their love for the lifestyle of commercial fishing in every story they related to us. As we have seen so often up here, when you show a respectful interest in the lifestyle of these wonderful people, they take you into their "homes" with a warmth that makes you feel instantly accepted into their fold. But just to be sure that they knew I was for real, I wore my Carhart pants and red suspenders.

So, now we have new friends on the dock, and both we and Binky could not be more pleased.

Just when I thought things could not be any better here, Glen invited me to join him for a salmon seining trip on board *Hadassah*.

That's right, me on board a classic Alaskan fishing vessel as they pursue the sockeye salmon invading Alaska in numbers that defy the imagination. The average boat (and there are several hundred of them) will take over a million pounds of fish from these waters every year and not make a dent in the population!

What we will do on our trip is run about sixty miles to a prominent point that historically funnels fish into a relatively small and very predictable area. Those points are well known by the fleet, so there will usually be three to four vessels taking turns with their nets. The boat next in line pulls the net from the stern of their boat with a powerful tender of about twenty-eight feet with an engine designed to produce tremendous torque (something like a seagoing tractor). The net is pulled toward shore and left there for about twenty-five minutes. Then the tender pulls the net in a circle back to the main boat with the salmon hopefully entrapped by the net. That boat then pulls away to load their catch on board while another takes the active spot to duplicate their efforts as salmon in the millions run up the coast towards their spawning area, not unlike lemmings to the cliffs.

Each boat continues this "fisherman's waltz" of setting the nets, waiting twenty-five minutes for the fish to accumulate, hauling the nets, loading the fish, and moving back in line for another run, ten to fifteen times per day. The results are hopefully 100,000 pounds or more of fish for their efforts in a good day, which are then off-loaded by vacuum machines onto market boats where they are sorted by species, and then run to Ketchikan for processing and shipping all over the world.

If I were a cat, at least one of my nine lives would be spent doing exactly what Glen, Jean, and Ian have done for years. The opportunity to join them for a taste of their lifestyle will be as good as it gets in Alaska.

Lauren and Nathan join us in several days for what we hope will be a week of successful fishing for salmon, halibut, prawns, and Dungeness crabs in surroundings that exceed your imagination.

7/07/2007

I went salmon fishing July 4; just got back last night. Caught a little over 2,000 of those beautiful fish. That obliterated my previous freshwater personal high of thirty-three bream and blew by my saltwater personal best of forty-six blue fin tuna. That's right! About 2,000 salmon brought on board, encompassing all five species of salmon found in Alaska.

Wednesday about noon, I left Auke Bay with the crew on board *Hadassah*, bound for Tenakee Inlet. Our course took us up Saginaw Channel into Lynn Canal, then south through Chatham Strait to Chichagof Island, split by Tenakee Inlet, a trip of about seventy miles. That area is well known for its predictable confluence of massive numbers of salmon as they return from the sea to spawn. The Game and Fish Commission (G&F) had announced a fifteen-hour opening for seining based upon their assessment of the numbers of fish in the area and the probabilities of successful spawning in the face of fishing pressure. After cruising along at 7.5 knots for about eight hours, we arrived in the evening in time to place a king crab pot in hopes of capturing the next night's dinner.

The brief salmon season opened the next morning at 5 AM, so we were up bright and early to full daylight at 4 AM. By 5 AM the net was in the water. I've previously described the process of seining for salmon, but now I got to see it for myself. Ian, the skiff man, dragged the net from the back of the boat by the tractor skiff, then we gave the fish about twenty-five minutes to swim into the net. After that short wait, with the wonder of hydraulic systems that could seemingly move the earth, the rig was then retracted into the boat where Jamie and his son stacked the net before the salmon payload was dumped on board for storage in the chilled seawater tank that will hold 100,000 pounds of fish. The process of setting the net, waiting for the fish, retrieval of the net, and storage of the catch takes about an hour.

In the fifteen-hour window of opportunity, the process was repeated nine times, with an opportunity lost when a rock cut the net, requiring skillful repairs for about an hour. It is now early in the season, and the catches vary from minimal ones of about 1,000 pounds in a day to acceptable ones of 10 to 12,000 pounds per day. Within the next several weeks, as the salmon pour into Alaska in numbers that defy the imagination, the catches will rise to single sets (a set is a cycle of deployment and retrieval of the net) of 30,000 pounds, and a day's catch of a tenth of a million pounds in a single boat the size of the *Hadassah*!

There are approximately 200 "limit seiners" in Alaska for the salmon run, and each will take a million or more pounds of salmon from the waters this season, yet the total haul represents less than 20 percent of the fish passing through here to spawn and die. The term "limit seiner" refers to G&F regulations that limit the size of the salmon seining boats to fifty-eight feet in length. To gain more size in the boats, the beam has been stretched to more than twenty feet, yielding the beautiful look of the classic Alaskan fishing vessel. The G&F carefully watches the catch of salmon and alters the season and legal locations for fishing on a daily basis. Glen just found yesterday as I left the boat that he can fish limited areas again on Sunday, based upon the catch of the fleet on Wednesday. It was nice to hear that the commercial fishing industry has a great respect for the job G&F is doing to regulate the natural assets of Alaska.

Back to "our" fishing trip. In the nine sets that we ran, about 2,000 salmon weighing 10,000 pounds were put into the holding tank. The catch included all five species of fish, each of which brings a different price on the market. We caught only two king salmon, the largest twenty-three pounds. Kings make up a small segment of the Alaskan salmon population and are more important in the hook-and-line arena than in the commercial netting market. The coho salmon, very desirable sport fish, are just beginning their run and were caught in small numbers. The most valuable species present in significant numbers at present is the sockeye, cherished for its rich red meat and great taste. Chum salmon, which run up to thirty pounds, are here in numbers, and valuable to the food industry. The predominate fish soon will be the pink salmon, caught in numbers that are amazing.

Every species of salmon makes great table fare; however, the prices paid to the fisherman vary based upon foreign demand, numbers of available fish, and the tolerance of the fish to the freezing process after capture. Glen was pleased with the day's results, even though the numbers pale in comparison to what they expect to catch over the next several weeks as the big run arrives. We dodged a big bullet when two whales swam right by our nets without entering them. If they get into the nets, they simply swim through them as if they were not there, leaving a mess that takes days to repair, at a cost of incredibly significant lost fishing opportunities.

Throughout the day, the crew functioned as a well-oiled machine, with Jean, Glen's wife, serving as valuable deck crew, as well as chef for everyone else on board. She is amazing. She knows fishing as well as anyone on board and runs the hydraulics as well as she runs the galley. The meals, centered around the ultimate in fresh seafood, would qualify *Hadassah* as a first-rate restaurant if it never caught a fish. Fresh sockeye salmon, crab salads and salmon wraps all flowed from the galley between hauls of the net. She is one amazing woman of the sea. The best catch of Glen's life was Jean!

When the thirteen-hour "season" closed at 8 PM, we were off on a six-hour run to the south to rendezvous with the tender ship for transfer of the catch to Ketchikan. About 3 AM, we met the 120-foot tender at Pearl Straits where the next chapter in the story unfolded. The *Theresa Marie* works as a king crab boat out of Dutch Harbor in the winter. We may see her on *The Deadliest Catch* next season.

In the middle of the night, in a chilly drizzle, we anchored and waited for the tender to raft up with us. After securing the two vessels together, the tender passed a long vacuum hose to our boat where it was placed into the hold for removal of the fish to the tender for sorting and weighing. The hose pumped the fish onto the tender's sorting table on the deck, where the crews of *Hadassah* and *Theresa Marie* separated the fish by species before weighing them. Upon completion about 4:30 AM, Jean was given an itemized receipt by species and weight, the fish became the property of the processor, and we were off to bed after an exceptionally long day.

The next morning, we left to the north to return to Tenakee Inlet for Sunday's anticipated G&F salmon opening there. As we left Pearl Straits, we were given a private showing by five whales as they surrounded a school of herring with bubbles, then plowed through them with mouths open in a highly effective fishing method well known in whales. After about four hours of pleasant travel up Chatham Strait, we were back at our king crab trap in Tenakee Inlet where seven beautiful crabs had dropped in. Three were females, so they went back in to replenish the stock. The other four suffered a terrible fate that will make our lunch today another memorable Alaskan event.

A quick walking tour of Tenakee Springs convinced me that I would not want to live in a town of sixty-five people and almost as many bears, with no streets and one store. But enough people go there to fish, hunt, or retire to make it a scheduled stop of the Alaska Seaplane Services. So yesterday afternoon, after profusely thanking Glen, Jean, Ian, Jamie I, and Jamie II for one of the greatest experiences of our Alaskan adventure, I boarded a de Havilland Beaver float plane in Tenakee Springs, goody bag containing sockeye salmon, fresh halibut, and king crab legs in hand, for my return to Juneau and *Always Friday*. The flight was over beautiful coastlines dotted with cottages and fishing/hunting camps surrounded by thick forests and snowcapped mountains that look like never-ending postcard scenes.

Lauren and Nathan, our daughter and her husband, are now here with us in Auke Bay. We are off today for a ten-hour cruise through the heart of whale country to Icy Straits, then to Hoonah for the night in a quaint little fishing village that is home to the family of

Bill and Mary Pfeiffer, whose company and hospitality we enjoyed in Ketchikan. Tomorrow, we have a permit to enter and stay in Glacier Bay National Park for three days of fishing, crabbing, bears, whales, glaciers, and general sightseeing in one of the most beautiful places on earth. We will be anchoring each night in different coves that redefine natural beauty. A local fisherman who befriended us here in the harbor, Craig Forgaard, is going to meet us there in his boat and show us some secret spots that should improve our probabilities of fishing success dramatically. Just another example of the genuinely warm reception we have been given by the local Alaskans.

The next three days should be among the best of our trip. Everything is the experience of a lifetime. Such is Alaska! Don't croak before you see this place (and *not* by cruise ship).

7/07/2007–7/11/2007

Our trip to Glacier Bay began on Saturday, July 7, after my return from my once-in-a-lifetime commercial fishing experience on board F/V *Hadassah* with Glen and Jean Carroll. Since Lauren and Nathan had whales high on their list of hopeful experiences, we turned north out of Auke Bay to cover the high-whale-probability area of Shelter Island. We have never been through there without being thoroughly entertained by the humpback whales that seem to accumulate in significant numbers to feed upon the herring thrown out of control by the prevailing currents in that area.

Less than an hour after leaving the harbor, we found them again. On the west side of Shelter Island, the whale party was in full swing. Groups were rolling, diving, and jumping every few minutes for the hour we dedicated to nothing more than enjoying this great show of nature.

With the whale experience now successfully checked off our list, we turned south for Hoonah where we planned to spend the night before entering Glacier Bay with a five-day permit in hand. It was a beautiful day on the water, and Mother Nature's show never stopped, with whales, both singles and groups as large as six, constantly near us, both in and out of the water. As salmon by the millions moved into the straits, their presence was reflected by dozens of "jumpers" (a self-explanatory commercial fishing term recently learned in my travels) in every direction.

As if there were not enough action in the waters visible around us, the depth sounder revealed the secrets of what was happening beneath us. The depths of up to 1,200 feet were seemingly filled with enormous, thick schools of herring there to serve as lunch for the whales. Salmon constantly appeared on the screen as smaller, more diffuse groups seemingly moving as one towards their spawning grounds. Although not clearly seen on the depth sounder, halibut in all sizes up to 400 pounds are known to move inshore from the Pacific, in part to feed upon the dead salmon after they complete their suicidal mission to their home creeks.

About 6:30 PM, we pulled into the harbor at Hoonah, one of the oldest native villages still extant. As a tourist attraction, it would score rather low, but when you meet and greet the locals, it takes on a new flavor. We did just that, and met an interesting couple deeply involved in rebuilding a beautiful old commercial fishing boat that began its fishing career in the mid-1930s. Their labor of love is about to culminate in the reactivation of a beautiful vessel once relegated to a fate of gradual degradation by the elements. The world will be a slightly better and clearly a prettier place once its old diesel pushes it back to sea again. If you ever see M/V *Compassion* on the water, you'll know what I mean!

My next conversational stop was an old pickup truck where several locals were cooking on a butane grill resting on the hood. It was obvious from the odor that something good was in the pan. They had just caught a sixty-pound halibut from just off the dock, and the term *fresh fish dinner* was happening to the max. We talked long enough for me to learn that the fisherman who caught it is a hunting and fishing guide who works just enough to keep well fed and happy. Not a bad career path.

Early the next morning, in full light at 5 AM, we began the trip across Icy Straits to Glacier Bay National Park. The three-and-a-half-hour trip through calm waters was again characterized by nonstop spectacular, natural shows by the whales (up to ten in one group), salmon, otters, ducks, and eagles. Prior to our entry into the park, we confirmed our impending arrival by VHF radio and received our entry instructions. As first-time visitors, I was required to attend an orientation lecture pertaining to protective restrictions for the wildlife, and bear precautions for the dangerous carnivores eagerly awaiting fresh meat (usually salmon, but they are not picky about their meat source).

Next came the rewards of a new friendship. In a previous update, I wrote of meeting Craig Forgaard, a retired commercial fisherman from Gustavus who is rebuilding an old boat (the *Jonathan*) to serve as their home upon his wife's retirement. Craig came through! With the added pleasure of the accompaniment of his partner in guiding services (Ripple Cove Charters), Suzi Daniels, we took to the waters of Glacier Bay.

By the evening of our first day on the bay, we had over twenty gigantic (by Chesapeake Bay standards) Dungeness crabs on board, and Nathan had caught his first halibut ever. On the following day with Craig and Suzi, we added five beautiful sockeye salmon to our catch list. Then, to top it off, we set a string of his shrimp traps, waited two hours, and collected two dozen lively shrimp for our dinner. Why would Craig and Suzi do this for strangers from a foreign land? I am left with only one rational explanation, supported by multiple experiences in this wonderful place and which I'll probably repeat numerous times: Alaska is the home of some of the nicest people I have ever had the pleasure to meet in my life. If you show an interest in their state and lifestyle, they quickly take you under their wing and make your experience even more unforgettable.

The next day, we were off to the north to enjoy the phenomenal beauty of the park. Our anchorage for the night was perhaps the most beautiful one we have enjoyed since leaving California. North Sandy Cove is a quiet, calm anchorage surrounded by snow-covered mountains partially hidden by low-hanging, white fluffy clouds. One of the many memorable moments occurred when we heard a cacophony of primal howls coming from the wilderness near us. Apparently, a pack of wolves had an experience that they felt warranted telling the world about! For a minute or two, we heard every sound that could come from a pack of wolves; then it was quiet again. What happened we will never know, but it was a privilege to share the news with the wolves, whatever the event. Words cannot convey the beauty of that wonderful place. Don't miss it if you are ever here.

The park rangers' warning about bears served as an attraction rather than a deterrent to our visit to this magnificent place. All visitors are prohibited from going ashore there because of the high concentration of Alaskan brown bears. And did we see one! Shortly after leaving the cove, we spotted a *big* male Alaskan brown bear (also called a grizzly when found any place other than the Alaskan coast) sauntering down the shoreline. In my hunting days in Alaska, I have seen quite a few bears, but this was by far the largest I have ever seen. I would guess him to be about nine feet tall on his hind legs and close to 1,000 pounds. If you were a trophy bear hunter, you would chase this one to the ends of the earth.

We watched him for about a half hour as he confidently strolled down the water's edge, probably contemplating the pending arrival of the salmon. His physique exemplified power in nature to the extent that he has no true equal in North America. So, we checked "bear" off Lauren and Nathan's list of things to see in Alaska and moved to the next entry: "glacier."

I had heard from some of the locals that Margerie Glacier was putting on a great show in terms of calving. So we cruised by the more popular Johns Hopkins Glacier (named for the school that sponsored the expedition that named the glacier) without stopping and continued upstream to drop by Margerie's place. It was a beautiful sight with the sun playing on the blue-green and white ice as it completed its several-thousand-year journey to the sea. The natural function of a glacier was evident in the deeply scoured walls of the canyons, sculpted by the slowly moving ice. John Muir, for whom one of the glaciers was named, said it well many years ago when he wrote, "The Master Builder chose for a tool, not the thunder and lightning to rend and split asunder, not the stormy torrent nor the eroding rain, but the tender snowflake, noiselessly falling through unnumbered generations."

Every machine the Caterpillar has ever built could not duplicate in an eon the work done by nature's heavy-duty contractors, her glaciers. And today, she was working overtime! We pulled *Always Friday* to within a quarter mile of the face of Margerie and watched as she shed gigantic pieces of ice into the sea, spawning icebergs that float down the straits until melted by the sun. Every few minutes, a shotgun-like blast would alert us to the impending birth of another iceberg, followed by the dramatic separation of chunks of ice the size of large houses.

One of our goals was to get pictures of *Always Friday* in front of a glacier, and this was our chance. So up came the davit and down came *Friday Nite*, our tender. We spent the next hour or so running the tender through the ice fields, over to the cliffs filled with birds, and finally back to *Always Friday* after we had pictures of the boat from every imaginable angle. After again securing *Friday Nite* on the boat deck of *Always Friday*, we were preparing to head south when the VHF came alive from the passenger ship *Noordham* of Holland-America Lines. She was pulling into the area as one of the two ships allowed into the park daily. The captain (or officer of the deck) asked if we were a Nordhavn! We then talked about the boat, and his hopes of owning one for himself one day, for several very enjoyable minutes before signing off.

Wait a minute . . . this gets *a lot* better! As I was setting the boat up to leave the area, I heard Lauren and Nathan scream in a way that clearly conveyed excitement, amazement, and some degree of fear. I heard an explosion magnitudes above what we had heard previously as I looked up to see a truly gigantic piece of the glacier, about the size of a twenty-five-story office building, explode with a boom and fall in seemingly slow motion into the sea, not more than a quarter mile from us. Simultaneously I heard my new acquaintance on the *Noordham* exclaim over the VHF, "Nordhavn, you had better turn in to that one!"

I had already begun to do so with opposing thrusters and was spinning on our own axis to meet head-on the mini tsunamis spawned by the calving glacier. I distinctly remember three waves of ten to fifteen feet rolling under us, slowly pitching the 120,000 pounds of *Always Friday* up and down in a thrill ride compliments of Mother Nature! It was no threat to our boat, but I would not have wanted to be there in some of the smaller trawlers we have seen up here, and certainly not in a kayak.

After things settled down, the VHF again came alive from the *Noordham*. With an inflection reflecting the excitement of one who had just witnessed something special, the voice from the cruise ship said, "That was the biggest show I have seen in the twenty years of my career here!"

And we were there to see it on *Always Friday*. The lesson to be learned here is that this happened with no warning whatsoever. The quarter mile we kept between us and the glacier is the minimum acceptable separation in my minimally experienced opinion. When you read of these warnings in the books, it is natural to assume that it won't happen in your presence, but believe us, it can! Thus, we were able to check "glaciers" off the wish list with a world-class checkmark.

Next stop Blue Mouse Cove for another night at anchor. Kathy planned a break from seafood (not my idea) with rack of lamb on the menu. Lauren and Nathan's wish list of whales, seals, otters, puffins, salmon, halibut, crabs, shrimp, bears, and glaciers had been successfully completed. A leisurely dinner, followed by a Kaleidoscope movie was the plan—but guess who came to dinner! As we were dropping the anchor in Blue Mouse Cove, a humpback whale announced his presence about a quarter mile away with a spout not only easily seen but also easily heard. I had noticed that the sounder showed almost wall-to-wall herring as we entered the cove, and apparently the whale had noticed that too.

As he rolled and lunged through herring, we launched *Friday Nite* for Lauren and Nathan to ride around the cove (avoiding the whale's territory as per the national park directive). Rather than leave the territory, the whale moved towards our anchorage . . . and stayed there for three amazing hours. After dinner, we stood on the deck of *Always Friday* and watched in amazement as he demonstrated the whale technique of bubble feeding.

For some reason the whale found our spot in the cove to be a very desirable one. He was so close for hours that we could not only see his net of bubbles but also hear them when they popped to the surface. As soon as he completed the circle of bubbles, he would lunge through the surface for a natural show for which you cannot buy a ticket at any price. We took many pictures, but the shutter delay in our cameras made it almost impossible to capture the magic of the moment. We witnessed his performance dozens of times before going to bed near midnight. What a day in Alaska!

The next morning, I awoke early with plans to cruise south the almost forty miles of the park, then check out of Glacier Bay with the Park Service by radio before entering Icy Straits for the trip back to Juneau. But Mother Nature threw a monkey wrench into those plans. We would have hit Sitakaday Narrows near the entrance to the park on a raging incoming tide of almost six knots. That would knock quite a hole in a cruise speed of eight knots. So, I devised plan B.

Craig had told me of a very productive halibut spot near North Marble Island. There, the bottom rapidly rises from about a thousand feet to fifty, and the halibut love it! So, I plotted a course for that spot, fed it to the autopilot, then sat back and watched the sounder announce our arrival about ninety minutes later. The anchor held well in fifty-two feet of water, and in no time, we had circle hooks about the size of your palm baited with fresh fish bellies, weighted with twenty-four-ounce lead sinkers, and suspended just off the bottom. In a little over two hours, we caught six beautiful halibut that taxed our fifty-pound test tackle, as well as our backs. We kept only three (those yielded over seventy pounds of beautiful, white filets) and returned the rest to the depths. It is hard to believe that we were throwing thirty-pound halibut back into the sea. The three we kept weighed fifty, thirty, and twenty-five pounds, and they were not even the three largest that came on board *Always Friday*. People pay a fortune for Alaskan halibut fishing trips, and we had a world-class one just waiting for the tides to change! This place is unbelievable.

We left Glacier Bay National Park with the tide now behind us, making almost ten knots rather than a net two knots had we not "gone fishing." Tomorrow we will be back in Auke Bay Harbor in preparation for Nathan and Lauren's departure on Thursday. Time goes by way too fast up here.

Sunday, our friends from Lynchburg will join us, and we will be off to new adventures. It would be hard to ask more out of life than what Alaska and its people offer.

PS: The sockeye salmon are sleeping peacefully in our cooler under a blanket of ice prepared for our use thousands of years ago, compliments of Margerie Glacier.

7/132007

I received the following email this morning from the source of the friendly voice on the *Noordham* that shared our experience of the birth of the monstrous iceberg at Margorie Glacier this past week:

—Original Message—
Subject: Glacier Bay/*Noordham*

Good day Buddy,

I was the Alaska Pilot on the *Noordham* in front of Margerie Glacier who talked to you on the VHF the other day. Great odyssey of yours. I have checked out your website and I think, how strange that I have been a pilot in Southeast Alaska since 1986 but my time is nearly always spent on the "Golden Highway" on main ship channels, and you are seeing places that I only wonder about. (Blue Mouse Cove? Passed it hundreds of times but never been in it.)

Good luck on the rest of your voyage. I have an intense schedule for the rest of July, but I will be in Ketchikan until the morning of the 17th when I fly up to Elfin Cove and get on another ship and then I will be underway here and there until the end of the month. If you come into town, feel free to give us a call.

Doug MacPherson

My response follows:

Thanks Doug!
Great to hear from you!
I had mistakenly assumed you to be permanent ship's company and had planned to take a handheld VHF the

next time we were in Juneau in hopes of raising you on the *Noordham*. Hopefully, we can meet up somewhere along the way home, as we will be heading south, ultimately to Virginia, in mid-August.

There is certainly an advantage to our 6 ft draft, as we can go many magical places in Alaska that the big boats can only peek into while passing. North Sandy Cove is perhaps the most beautiful anchorage that we have ever seen, but obviously impassable to you on the *Noordham*. Please stay in touch and call anytime you see *Always Friday* on the AIS. We will always answer with pleasure!

Hope to see you in person soon!

Thanks, Buddy

So, the pleasures of Alaska continue to fall upon us. Doug becomes another friend of *Always Friday* and adds to the great memories of this trip of a lifetime. Tonight, the crew of the F/V *Hadassah* will join us for a fresh halibut dinner on board *Always Friday* before heading out to sea tomorrow (without me) for the next opening of the salmon season. Today I got word that the salmon have hit the streams in the area, so the bears will soon discover the same news. That means that they will be congregating at streamside in full view of my new camera.

Stay with us! Wonderland is in full swing, and I am Alice!

7/15/2007

Jim and Lisa Walker arrived on schedule and with baggage in hand at 1 AM. The first on time and intact delivery of guests and their luggage yet for Alaska Airlines! The next morning, Kathy and I teamed up to get the only visitors slot into Glacier Bay for the seventeenth by simultaneously calling the park's reservation office at their precise opening minute of 7 AM. I got a busy signal . . . but she got through! So, we have that invaluable permit #6090, our ticket to show Jim and Lisa Alaska at its best. But we were in Auke Bay, and Glacier Bay is about eight hours of beautiful travel away. I plotted a course that would take us closer to our Tuesday-morning appointment with Glacier Bay, adding yet another wonderful experience in our Alaska travels: Elfin Cove. It is across the straits from the park and is on the "must-see" list of everyone who has been there.

Off we went, down Chatham Straits to Icy Straits, then west through some of the most beautiful scenery you could imagine. The weather was perfect (fifty-five degrees), the winds nonexistent, and the water flat as a mirror. Jim and I stood on the bow and watched as *Always Friday* split the salmon to either side as we plowed through the water at eight knots. The water was clear but dark. We could clearly see the salmon as they darted out of the path of the bow in every direction. You cannot imagine how many fish have made their way from the Pacific for their rendezvous with destiny.

Lisa was one of those ideal guests whose only goal for the trip was to fulfill a lifelong dream of seeing *a* whale in the wild—which, in Alaska in August, is akin to seeking a pigeon in Trafalgar Square. Shortly after leaving Auke Bay, her easily fulfilled dream came to fruition in the form a spout a mile away. Her excitement was tempered by my suggestion that we not divert for a closer look since it was a certainty we would get better opportunities later. With a degree of concern that her long-awaited opportunity to see Mr. Whale up close might have been squandered, she reluctantly agreed to cruise on. As we passed through the Inian Islands, preparing for our approach into Elfin Cove, there they were! A pod of humpback whales numbering over ten, cavorting in front of us several miles away. Their location was divulged by multiple spouts constantly visible and punctuated by occasional splashes that, even from several miles away, could only mean whales.

We turned towards them and spent the next several hours literally surrounded by these magnificent animals as they devastated the schools of herring our sounder confirmed to be in the wrong place at the wrong time. It is always my hope to see one of these monsters leap from the water, roll, and return with a splash that could only be generated by a 50,000-pound mass meeting the water. My hopes for Jim and Lisa were met in trumps. These whales jumped, rolled, squealed, spouted, and splashed as if they were auditioning for the National Geographic Channel! Perhaps the most impressive show was a formation double jump, roll, and slash that would have made the Blue Angels proud.

After being thoroughly entertained for several hours, we resumed our trek towards Elfin Cove. As Alaska often does, she had a surprise for us.

We were riding a fast-moving ebb tide of approximately five knots (meaning low tide was on the way) into a narrow passage with a channel thirty feet wide at low tide. Having never made that trip, it was a challenging navigation under the best of circumstances. But we found the circumstances to be anything but good. Look at the amazing picture that looks as if a 500-foot breaking wave is coming at you from between two mountains. That is an isolated fog bank obscuring the passage into Elfin Cove.

I am not sure what confluence of temperature, humidity, and wind came together to produce this weather phenomenon, but there it was: the most daunting weather system that I have seen in my aviation or nautical experiences. With a combination of a falling tide, racing current, unfamiliar passage, narrow channel, and zero visibility standing in the way of a night's sleep in Elfin Cove, everything about this scene screamed the aviation phrase "Divert to an alternate!" The easy decision was made to delay our entry into Elfin Cove until better weather and drop the anchor somewhere else for the night.

In aviation, diverting to an alternate airfield almost always carries with it a degree of disappointment and inconvenience. But not on the waters of Alaska. Here it is just an opportunity to add another experience to your memory book. A check of the chart and the bible of Alaskan cruising (Douglass's *Exploring Southeast Alaska*) suggested that Idaho Inlet would serve our needs for the night quite well. We turned ninety degrees port and headed into one of the most picturesque spots you could imagine.

The inlet is surrounded by thick wilderness made up of giant Christmas trees towering more than a hundred feet into the air with snowcapped mountains on either side. A deep channel runs down the middle, thanks to the work of glaciers thousands of years ago. But as is so often the case up here, Idaho Inlet presented us with its own unique characteristic. Apparently, this is the high-rent district for otters. They were everywhere! When we have seen them before, they have been either solitary or in groups of at most three. Not in Idaho Inlet. These fun-loving creatures were there in groups of twenty or more, backstroking their way through life without an apparent care in the world, entertaining us as we moved through the seven miles to the head of the inlet and water shallow enough to anchor.

Around every bend was another scene worthy of the cover of any book on nature. Then, off the starboard bow, there he was: a big Alaskan brown bear strolling through the grassland beside the inlet. Our four sets of binoculars watched him in awe until he disappeared into the trees, confirming that the beauty of this place also hides the potential threat of animals that might on occasion find white meat preferable to salmon.

As we prepared to anchor in this beautiful, isolated area, the VHF came alive with "*Always Friday*, haven't we talked before?" We were sharing Idaho Inlet with the beautiful seventy-four-foot Nordlund yacht *Hanalei*. Steve and I had shared a night's anchorage before, far from here in Taku Harbor, just north of Tracy Arm. He suggested that we anchor near him and join him for a visit on *Hanalei*. His hospitality was immediately accepted, and we were off by tender to join them there.

Steve had accumulated a who's who of Idaho Inlet. The occupants of the two onshore cabins we had passed were there, true "locals" in every sense of the word. The honorary mayor of Idaho Inlet informed me of the property taxes now due upon our arrival there, but I explained that I was exempt by virtue of my ever-present Carhart pants and red suspenders. With such convincing evidence that I too was a "local," I easily prevailed on my appeal. Paul, living the life of my dreams as a hunting and fishing guide, tentatively accepted my offer of our boat for his cabin, with the understanding that he teaches me everything he knows about Alaska.

Steve and I have the same idea about how to enjoy this magnificent place. It has nothing to do with cruise ships and everything to do with getting to know the great people who have been lucky enough to grow up in this great land. Tomorrow morning, we are going to delay our entry into Elfin Cove long enough to go ashore with the real locals to see how they live in this wonderland of nature.

Today's lunch of king crab with drawn butter was followed tonight with a thick steak cooked outside on the grill with otters, eagles, and terns watching the process from the sea and air. So, our unplanned turn into Idaho Inlet for the night turned out to be not a disappointment but instead another highlight of our trip. It just seems that nothing ever goes wrong in Alaska.

7/16/2007, Monday

This morning I was up at 6:45 to enjoy the view from *Always Friday* at anchor in Idaho Inlet. It was raining lightly with the soft sounds of raindrops permeating the pilothouse as the otters floated on their backs around the boat like squirrels in Central Park. Thankfully, that is all this place has in common with NYC. The mountains were partially cloaked in layers of white clouds stacked upon each other like separated layers of a cake. I can't convey in words the beauty of this place.

About 9 AM, we weighed anchor and followed the reciprocal of last evening's pathway in to retrace the same path outbound. The eagles, salmon, and otters were joined by the whales to ensure our entertainment as we again headed for Elfin Cove. We hoped to catch Paul and Tami Johnson of Gull Cove Guide Services at their home to take them up on last night's offer to drop by on the way out.

Their home is in a beautiful cove that personifies the Alaskan experience. Paul is a respected brown bear and fishing guide in the area, and he and Tami have hunters and fishermen booked with them throughout the year. Look at gullcove.com to see what a real Alaskan experience can be. Paul had a real interest in seeing the boat, so we invited them on board later that day for a visit in Elfin Cove.

After leaving Gull Cove, we again made our way into the challenging approaches of Elfin Cove. The impenetrable fog bank of yesterday had diminished to a level that allowed a careful radar run culminating in our passage into the harbor between rock walls separated by only thirty yards in eleven feet of water! We tied up to the dock for the night, free of charge, and wandered around this quaint little village built into a mountainside, with walkways on stilts serving as the town's streets. There is little here other than fishing, but it is world class. We saw several charter boats come in loaded with coho salmon, halibut up to 215 pounds, and a salmon shark of over 300 pounds. Salmon sharks are yet another species that follows the migration of the salmon, but with sinister plans for their namesakes. Alaska is a complicated, tightly intertwined ecosystem that appears to be thriving at every level, from the lowly plankton to the magnificent whales.

At Tami's direction, we hit the high spots of this town with a winter population of eight citizens in about fifteen minutes. Then they joined us on board *Always Friday* for a tour. Paul seemed impressed with the quality and seaworthiness of Nordhavns, and coming from a man of such experience, that was quite a compliment.

We exchanged contact information in hopes of crossing paths again while we are here in their world. Any time spent with such nice people is more than a pleasure.

Tonight, it was fresh halibut in the center of the table, and tomorrow it is off to Glacier Bay for the next five days. Craig Forgaard, my local hero who dressed me in my Alaska togs at Western Auto and Marine, is going to meet us at noon for lunch at the Glacier Bay Lodge. Between breakfast and lunch, we will again traverse the whale-laden waters of Icy Straits with great friends, in a boat perfectly suited for exactly what we are doing here in the most beautiful place on earth while most of the world gets up and goes to work. No wonder I am always smiling in the pictures!

7/20/2007

Unfortunately, when we awoke after a pleasant, rainy night moored at the Elfin Cove dock, it was low tide, and there wasn't enough water in the outbound channel to float an outboard. The seventeen-foot tides were to dash nothing more than our plans on the rocks. A request for local knowledge yielded the advice to stay put until the tide rose to near the base of the dry dock, about three hours down the line.

A quick call to Craig and Marylyn Forgaard delayed our lunch plans with them at Glacier Bay Lodge until midafternoon. About two and a half hours later, a boat delivering a pilot to one of the cruise ships returned to Elfin Cove and reported five feet of water at the channel. We needed six and a half feet, so we waited until our telltale tidal level of near the dry dock base was a reality, then off we went at idle speed with the sounder yielding no more than one to two feet under the keel and the lateral walls of the entry channel to Elfin Cove no more than two feet away on either side. It was one of the most intriguing harbors we have visited on our trip, but don't go there without checking the tides.

We caught the currents across Icy Straits just right and saw a maximum speed of 13.7 knots over the ground, which pushed us into Glacier Bay around 3:30 PM. Craig and Marylyn were waiting for us, but the lunch option at the lodge had long expired, so we exchanged that missed opportunity for dinner with us that night on board *Always Friday*. Craig had again put his Dungeness crab pots out in anticipation of our arrival, so we climbed on board their boat and pulled only three traps before we had all the crabs we could possibly use. Jim and Lisa got the chance to see the process that again filled our cooler with crabs nine inches wide across their backs, making the largest Chesapeake Bay blue crab look puny in comparison. Alaska has a way of doing that on many fronts. That night, we enjoyed more of Craig and Marylyn's Alaska tales over grilled flank steak while anchored in Bartlett Cove.

The next morning, Craig picked us up in the fuel truck to give us a tour of his hometown of Gustavus. Another site not on the cruise ship agenda but reflective of what Alaska is genuinely like outside the tourist routes. After accepting his offer to crab, fish, and shrimp together in two weeks when Kathy's father is here, we were on our way north to the "halibut hole" in hopes of catching one each for Jim and Lisa, since we didn't have room for any fresher fish on board. We anchored in fifty-five feet of water at a point that rose abruptly from a depth of several thousand feet and dropped the lines over the side. Shortly thereafter, they both were successful halibut fisherpersons, and Lisa's fish of thirteen pounds had matched her hopes and physical abilities perfectly. With her fish filleted and in line for star attraction status on the *Always Friday* dinner table, we weighed anchor and headed for one of the most picturesque spots in Glacier Bay, South Marble Island.

The island is the home of not only a large sea lion colony but also thousands of one of Alaska's prettiest birds, the puffin. It was to be my first try at long-distance photography with my new Nikon

D2Xs SLR camera. I had spent far more time than I usually do with the instruction manual, trying to understand the basics, since putting this camera in my hands is somewhat like learning to drive in a Ferrari. I know absolutely nothing about photography but am an eager learner when amazing photo opportunities are found in such abundance in Alaska. Both the puffins and sea lions put on shows that would entertain anyone with a respect for nature.

Our next stop was home for this night: North Sandy Cove—in my opinion, the prettiest anchorage in Glacier Bay! The run into the cove was marked by dozens of jumping salmon; the hundreds of marks on the sounder were confirmation of the salmon run in full swing. As if that were not proof enough, as we turned the last corner into the anchorage, we were met by a brown bear standing by the shore, even more interested in the salmon than we were.

Remember the crabs we got with Craig yesterday? Kathy performed her magic and turned them into crab cakes that could not be equaled in any restaurant. Remember how I said there was more meat than we could eat? I was wrong; Kathy and Lisa had one crab cake each, Jim had two, and I had seven! Didn't mean to—they were just too good to stop! After dinner, as we sat around the table, Lisa looked out the window, and standing on the shore about fifty yards from us was a moose! It stayed in the twilight for about thirty minutes as we took pictures at every conceivable camera setting to get undeniable confirmation of its visit.

After the moose left, we were off to bed with plans for Marjorie Glacier the next day. By 7:30, we were on our way, staying close to the shore to see the bears down at the water's edge in search of an easy meal. We turned into Tidal Inlet and were so mesmerized by its beauty that we did not turn around until we had reached its origin. This place has it all! Roaring waterfalls, virgin forests of 200-foot-tall Christmas trees, streams gurgling into the inlet, and a beautiful wolf that trotted along the shore with us for half a mile before disappearing into the forest. From several hundred yards away, we got his picture in such detail that you can see individual teeth and even the groove in his tongue.

Margerie Glacier was again a highlight of Alaska. Its visual beauty was enhanced by nature's soundtrack of thunderous cracks as the glacier broke at its edge, producing icebergs the size of houses. No one could witness such power and not be awed by nature. Then it was southward for sixty miles to the night's anchorage. Berg Bay was the sight of the camp of Muir and the other original explorers of Glacier Bay. Now we were following them with none of the trials and trepidations they must have experienced as the first non-native explorers.

Since the ride to Berg Bay was about eight hours, we enjoyed our dinner on the bridge where we said both hello and goodbye to Lisa's halibut caught the day before just a few miles from the supper in which he had a starring role. But the day was far from over. What could you add to a day that included moose, bear, wolves, otters, eagles, glaciers, and natural surroundings beyond belief? The answer is . . . . orcas. That's right! Two beautiful killer whales were waiting for us at the entrance to Berg Bay. Their six-foot dorsal fin arising from a body of black and white makes it impossible to confuse them with humpbacks. All four of us got good looks at perhaps the premier natural attraction in Alaska. It was too dark for pictures, but the scene is permanently embedded in the minds of all four of us.

After calling in their location to the park staff, we entered Berg Bay and dropped anchor near the footsteps of Muir and his fellow explorers. Another wonderful day in Alaska. Tomorrow, we head back for Juneau. Never has the saying "It is not the destination but the trip that counts" been truer. We will be there for several days after Jim and Lisa leave for Virginia. Then Bill and Mindy Young will join us for Kathy and Mindy's mutual birthdays in Tracy Arm. It should be quite a party (of only four). Can't wait!

7/24/2007

Today is our last day in Auke Bay Harbor for a while, as we leave with Bill and Mindy Young for this long-awaited reunion with our great friends with whom we've had many travels over the past twenty years. Our plans include Tracy and Endicott Arms with their respective glaciers, Sawyer and Dawes. We will be anchoring in Tracy Cove and Taku Harbor, both on our list of Alaskan favorites. The freezers are filled with freshly caught halibut, salmon, king and Dungeness crabs, as well as Costco steaks and lamb chops. The scene is set for another great week in this beautiful place.

But that is not to say that the last few days have been dull. Kathy chose to spend her time in the "city," while I took the opposite approach. Two days ago, I had the pleasure of coho salmon fishing with Dennis and Donna Nolder and their dog Prada on board their boat, *Red Lady*. (You guessed it! Donna's hair is red.) Dennis is the retired Alaska Airlines pilot I met by way of the boat when he was wandering the docks and expressed an interest in *Always Friday*. He and Donna later joined us for a visit on board, and they reciprocated with an invitation to fish with them.

We went about twelve miles from Auke Bay to a place famous for the accumulation of coho salmon this time every year called Hand Trollers Cove. It got its name many years ago when that was an accepted form of commercial fishing, now superseded by more modern power-trolling and netting techniques. But that day, our trolling methods were highly effective. We put six beautiful cohos (also called silver salmon) in the boat, destined to reside in our freezers by nightfall. Apart from Prada taking a brief dive into the sea from the docks, everything came together for a beautiful day of Alaskan salmon fishing.

Last night was another new recipe for halibut gleaned from a new cookbook on Alaskan game fish that Kathy turned up during her shopping day. Then off to bed for a night of sleep made easy by the sound of rain on the deck of our Alaskan home.

This morning, another new Alaskan friendship led to an invitation to join Greg Gallant and his friend Josh for a day of halibut fishing. Greg and Josh are crewmen on board the Alaskan ferries that take as many as 500 passengers at a time throughout the state by way of the inland (mostly) passage. Their passengers are true "local" commuters, as well as vacationers from all over the world. You may recall that I first met Greg when he was cleaning a cooler full of king salmon last month during their run. He gave us the treasure of Alaskan fish, a filet of white king salmon, and we have stayed in touch since. It was Greg, a retired king crab fisherman, who took us to his king crab pots for a firsthand experience in catching those tasty critters of the deep.

Today he and Josh showed me all the secrets of halibut fishing, and before long, we had our limit of two apiece, even after throwing back "small" ones twice the size of citation flounders in Virginia. To show you where the expertise lies, Josh caught five of the eight, and Greg caught the largest at about thirty pounds. To top off the experience, Josh reeled in what he thought to be a small halibut, but much to our surprise, wrapped in his line was a king crab of over seven inches across the body with a span of over three feet. You can imagine my pain when they threw him back into the sea since the season had just closed about ten days ago.

In a few hours, Bill and Mindy will be on board, and we will be on our way to Tracy Arm, crown jewel of Alaska. The salmon are everywhere, you can't miss on whales, the eagles are keeping an eye on us, and Binky will soon be barking at otters.

7/25/2007

Mindy and Bill arrived on time and ready to sail. Within an hour of their appearance on board *Always Friday*, we had introduced them to our good friends on the *Hadassah*, again moored next to us after a very successful fishing trip (again without me), checked them out on life jackets and raft location, and tossed off the lines from the dock. The day was cloudy, but the mountains were still majestic as they surrounded Mendenhall Glacier from all sides. The whales were uncharacteristically scarce for the early portion of the trip, but they were replaced by the presence of dozens of commercial gill netters along the shore, reflecting an opening in the salmon season of at least that day. The boats were stationary with their nets of around 1,500 feet trailing behind their sterns like the tail of a tiger.

As we passed through the allotted fishing area, we could see several boats retrieving their catch, with salmon coming over the stern every ten feet or so of net. The number of fish in the area, shown by the netter's success, as well as our sounder, continues to amaze me. They are here by the tens of millions, and the tremendous number of fish taken by commercial fishermen represents less than 20 percent of those moving into Alaska!

Our late start necessitated our stopping short of Tracy Arm for the night, and Taku Harbor was the perfect opportunity for a pleasant night. Taku Harbor is a beautiful natural harbor with modern, unattended floats built by the state of Alaska from Fish and Game license money. There is space for five or six boats to moor, and for many more to anchor out. It is the site of an abandoned cannery with remnants of its prior history everywhere. Kathy and I had been there before with Phil and Susan and at that time shared the harbor with four other private boats (including *Spirit of Ulysses*, the seventy-six-foot Nordhavn of Richard and Lorna Maybin).

But this time, the salmon season changed the residents of the harbor from pleasure boats to working fishermen. By nightfall, the harbor was a temporary home for about a dozen of the classic Alaskan gill netter's boats, yielding a scene usually reserved only for a painting on the wall. Tied up next to *Always Friday* was a beautifully kept gill netter's boat by the name of *Oracle*. Doug, its owner, explained that the name came from the source of its funding, a wise purchase of Oracle stock years ago. After seeing his boat, we invited him on board *Always Friday*, but he declined since his successful day of fishing had left him with more in common with the fish than he was comfortable in bringing on board our boat.

In keeping with the warm welcome that we as visitors to this beautiful place have seen so often from the locals of Alaska, Doug then presented us with two beautiful salmon from his fish hold, a sockeye and a coho—two prizes of Alaskan waters. The sockeye that awoke that morning in the icy waters of Alaska found himself on the hot grill of *Always Friday* that night! Our table fare for Bill and Mindy's first night in Alaska was fresh Alaskan king crab, compliments of Greg Gallant, and Doug's sockeye salmon!

The next morning, I was up about 7 AM to an empty harbor, as all the working boats were long gone to the fishing ground. As we turned south for Tracy Arm, we found the fishermen congregated around Limestone Cove, cashing in on the tremendous presence of migrating salmon. There, just off the port bow, was *Oracle* with its net strung off its bow exactly like the web of a spider. By the pilothouse was Doug, camera in hand, taking pictures of . . . *us*! Then channel 16 came alive with his voice. After switching to 68, we thanked him profusely for his fish the night before and renewed our offer to host him on board *Always Friday* in the future. At his request, we exchanged email addresses, and he promised to send us copies of the pictures of our passing the fishing fleet after he returns to port.

Upon arrival in Tracy Arm, we were again greeted by a welcoming party of whales, always a high point for our guests. For the next three hours, we cruised by waterfalls, eagles, whales, and jumping salmon until we reached Dawes Glacier. After carefully picking our path through the ice field, we were within a quarter mile of its face, witnessing up close and personal one of the great sights of nature. By 9:30 PM we were back in Tracy Arm Cove for the night's anchorage, sharing the cove with a beautiful sixty-two-foot Nordhavn, *Tesla*, and a sailboat. Kathy and Mindy served up another five-star meal of fresh halibut in lemon chive butter on a bed of couscous while anchored in a beautiful cove surrounded by snowcapped mountains and serenaded by a gurgling creek just off our stern.

The days are becoming progressively shorter, with near darkness by 10:30 PM, significantly different from the "midnight sun" of five weeks ago. The mountains blocked access for the satellite TV, but the Kaleidoscope nevertheless yielded an enjoyable night at the movies with *For Love of the Game* playing in the *Always Friday* salon. Tomorrow is Kathy and Mindy's joint birthday. We will leave the anchorage in the morning for a trip down one of Alaska's most famous passageways, Tracy Arm, in hopes of making it a memorable birthday for each of them.

7/26/2007, Thursday
(The Birthday of Kathy & Mindy!)

Their birthday began with late arisings by the birthday girls. A beautiful day in Tracy Arm Cove even though the weather forecast was for rain. We have found the weather forecasting in Alaska to be no better than a good guess, wrong as often as right. Their most common error is to call for bad weather and get a beautiful day instead. At least no one gets mad when that happens.

After a breakfast of poached eggs on English muffins, we weighed anchor and cruised up Tracy Arm by some of the most beautiful waterfalls imaginable. Having had a perfect view of Dawes Glacier from less than a quarter mile away the day before, we chose to skip Sawyer Glacier since it usually is blocked no closer than a mile by pack ice. Instead, we cruised back to the entry of Tracy Arm to try for some halibut for Bill. The chosen spot was recommended by Blaine, a Juneau policeman who visited our boat last month. He told us of catching big halibut there for years, although no one else fished for them there.

The deal was one fish since the freezers are filled to the brim with fresh fish. The chosen bait was the belly of last night's sockeye salmon from Doug of the *Oracle*. We dropped the bait onto a rising at fifty feet surrounded by much deeper waters. The whales had the place surrounded, and the birds were scavenging what the whales could not keep in their cavernous mouths. After a few minutes, Bill hooked a big halibut that took the bait slowly, then shook his head vigorously as he felt the hook. After losing line to the fish multiple times, Bill asked for some relief from the rod butt stuck in his stomach. While putting the belly belt around his waist, the line went slack . . . and he was gone. The hook-up and fifteen-minute fight suggested a fish of about fifty pounds—a nice fish, but one that we would have released had we landed it since there was no room in the freezer.

Having experienced what it felt like to meet halibut on his home ground in Alaska, Bill and Mindy were ready to start the trip back to Auke Bay, with plans to anchor out someplace along the way. I assumed that Taku Harbor would again be a popular spot for the commercial fishermen we had seen there two days ago, but Limestone Inlet, the center of gill netting activity when we last passed, was devoid of fishermen. Apparently, the Fish and Game Department had closed the area for further fishing, and the fishermen had gone elsewhere in their pursuit of salmon.

About that time, the VHF radio came alive with a report of a pod of orcas moving into Taku Harbor. We were less than two miles from the reported orca site and headed that way, so we all came to the bridge of *Always Friday*, binoculars and cameras in hand, to search for the elusive black-and-white creatures with the six-foot dorsal fins. Just as we reached the mouth of Taku Harbor, I saw an aberration in the surface of the water seconds before the telltale dorsal fins of at least four orcas broke the surface. Kathy and Mindy got for their birthday a visit from the most sought-after seasonal visitors to the waters of Alaska, a family of killer whales! Quite a party.

After a birthday dinner of rack of lamb, followed by cheesecake given to us by Eric and Kim of the *Abyssinia* to make room in their freezer for their freshly caught fish, we were off to bed, surrounded by the indescribable beauty of Alaska. Tomorrow we will cruise back to Auke Harbor for dinner in Juneau before Bill and Mindy return to Florida. The guest rooms on *Always Friday* will next host Kathy's father, sister, and her husband for a week in Elfin Cove and Glacier Bay. Nathan's *Always Friday* record of a sixty-pound halibut will be in serious jeopardy that week.

7/28/2007

Two of the usual updates follow this unusual entry. Jim and Lisa Walker, who shared our adventure with us last week, emailed to us the following note, and asked that it be included on the website.

> Thanks, Buddy
> July 26, 2007, Lynchburg, VA
> **We were treated like dogs on *Always Friday***
> Many of us have fantasized about the next life and what we might like to be. The most frequent fantasy I have heard is "I want to come back as my children." From July 14 to 21, Lisa and I concluded that coming back as Raleigh and Binky might be an even better future. What a life! Sleep, eat, and play. It suits us!
> **The Boat**
> Buddy has described the boat in detail on his site, but like Alaska, words can't really capture the essence of it. It is a meticulously engineered vessel that is packed with redundancy, all with a view to saving your life if there were

an "event" on a transoceanic crossing. Very utilitarian; not really. This boat is elegant, comfortable, and soothing. The workmanship is well beyond anything built in the Carolinas. I am most familiar with the typical eastern sport fishers, and from the gelcoat to the joinery, this Nordhavn is well beyond what I am used to seeing. So, it's luxurious, yes, but it is technically overwhelming. NASA would be envious of the computing power floating on this baby. Dual auto pilots, dual radars, triple chart plotters, more compasses than I could count, infrared night vision, satellite radio, satellite telephony, satellite television, GPS receivers to monitor GPS receivers, and cameras to monitor all parts of the boat from the pilot house or the sky bridge, except my stateroom, of course. I'm sure I've left something out, but if you know Buddy, you know he didn't. If you're fearful of the water, there is no need to fear a passage here. Buddy could pilot this boat around the world from his desk in the Wainwright building.

Alaska

The license plates say, "The Last Frontier." It must be. I imagine Virginia was somewhat like this 300 years ago. It is pristine with very little evidence of the spoils of man. We saw a moose, two brown bears, a wolf, countless bald eagles and humpback whales, harbor seals, sea lions, otters, and two orcas.

The depth sounder was constantly alive with schools of salmon and herring, a fisherman's dream. We caught two halibut (dinner) in just a few minutes of fishing. The air is clean, the sky clear, the water as God meant it to be. As we sat and watched Margerie Glacier shed herself into the bay, I wondered why it had taken me fifty-eight years to get here. The most beautiful place I have ever been.

In beautiful downtown Gustavus, population a few

hundred, the general store sign reminded all of a healthy fine if the rental DVD was late. I asked the clerk if there was forgiveness during a snowstorm. She very politely told me they don't have snowstorms. "It starts snowing in October and stops in March." The total was twenty-odd feet in the '06/'07 season, and this is southern Alaska! It must have been beautiful. At 85 degrees north, twenty-foot tides are the norm, so currents and depths can be challenging. No worry; Buddy has a piece of software that calculates the perfect time to leave to minimize the effects of tides and currents!

The Hospitality

If the measure of a great resort is the staff to guest ratio, then *Always Friday* must set the record. I felt at times like there were two guests, Lisa, and myself, and two staff, Buddy and Kathy. We had a private cruise ship for our personal Alaska vacation. Gourmet meals, elegant accommodations, and an experienced crew that was anxious to see that we enjoyed every moment.

Buddy has never met a stranger, so we found ourselves pulling crab pots with Craig, a local (Dungeness crab cakes for dinner, thank you Kathy), or having a drink with Steve, the founder of Red Robin, in a cove 100 miles from civilization. Only Buddy can meet people in the middle of nowhere. He collected more dinner invitations while I was there than he could ever honor.

Rereading this I see how hopeless it is to capture all that we did or that was done for us. This may capture it: While I was rinsing the boat at Elfin Cove, a lady walked by and asked if the boat was mine. I replied, "No, it's my doctor's." Her reply: "You must have really been sick." No, but I do have a great doctor! It may be too late for you to see Alaska the way Lisa and I, did but it's not too late to spend some time with this fabulous couple on this incredible boat. Just do it!

Jim & Lisa

7/29/2007

Yesterday was supposed to be a reprovisioning day at Costco prior to Kathy's family's arrival, but the airlines struck again. A cancelled flight out of North Carolina delayed their arrival by a day, so we made chicken salad out of chicken poo poo! Bill and Mindy had another day in Juneau, so we decided to go places not frequented by those from the lower forty-eight. There are only forty miles of roads in all of Juneau, and none of them lead very far out of town. Juneau is the only capital that can't be reached by road, only by air and sea. The roads are for local traffic only, but that doesn't mean that they can't take you to wonderful places! Case in point: Sheep Creek.

If you drive through Juneau, avoiding the opportunity to load up on tanzanite or T-shirts, and don't stop until the end of the road about five miles later, you will find yourself a witness to one of the greatest spectacles on earth. The salmon are going back to their birthplace to spawn and die, and all those in nature that share an interest in their plans are there to play their role in natures grand scheme. We were there too! What we saw was nothing short of amazing. Salmon of ten to fifteen pounds were literally lined up nose to tail to move from the sea to the fresh water of their hatching four years ago.

We saw two different systems in play. The chum salmon, looking ragged beyond words shortly before their deaths, were actively spawning in pools right in front of us. The males were using the last of their energy to jockey for position with the egg-laden females as their last act before death. The sockeye salmon, dressed in their bright-red suits with grotesque faces that would win most

Halloween contests, were fighting to go upstream against not only the current but also the bears and eagles. The fish are no longer eating, and in fact are dying from the inside out. The flesh that was so cherished by the sport and commercial fishermen just a few weeks ago is now soft, mushy, and unfit for human consumption, but the bears and eagles have been waiting in line at this restaurant for this meal for months.

We watched in amazement as the scene unfolded as if we were watching, rather than reading, *National Geographic*. The fishermen were there not for the decrepit salmon, which are no longer interested in any fly or lure, but to catch the Dolly Varden trout there to eat the salmon eggs when ejected by the doomed females.

Now for the bears! Drawn to the shallow streams by the presence of the hapless and helpless salmon, they forgo their usually shy personalities and present themselves with little regard for our presence. For an hour, we had the privilege of watching a mother bear and her two cubs as she caught sockeye salmon for their meal right before our eyes. We watched her romp down the stream and return with a red, thrashing sockeye in her mouth for her cubs. When a male bear approached the feast, she ran her cubs up a tree and followed them there to protect them from the males, which are infamous for killing cubs. All this just a few miles from "downtown" Juneau with its thousands of cruise-ship customers oblivious to the show right under their noses.

That was how our bonus day was spent in this unbelievable land. Shared with the salmon, eagles, and bears while the tourists missed it all, oblivious to one of the greatest shows on earth. In a few hours, we are off to Glacier Bay, park permit #6248 in hand, for a week in as close to heaven as you will find on earth. Stay with us! We will let you know what amazing experiences nature has in store for us this week upon our return to Juneau in eight days.

7/30/2007

We left Auke Harbor yesterday about 2 PM with plans to get as close to Elfin Cove as possible before stopping for the night. The weather was beautiful, and Kathy's father, sister, and her husband were with us for their long-awaited Alaskan adventure. Suzanne's main goal was to see a whale—not a major challenge in Alaska in July. In fact, by late afternoon, we had seen at least twenty-five humpbacks, in groups as large as ten. The birds, seals, and salmon were congregating around the whales to take advantage of their copious leftovers of stunned herring. We spent at least an hour at one site, watching the giants of the sea perform their show, the tickets for which would command sky-high prices anywhere offered.

Not far from the whales was the Gull Cove Lodge, run by our new friends Paul and Tami, whom we met a few weeks back in Idaho Inlet. We stopped by to see them, but unfortunately (for us at least) they had just picked up six new clients in for salmon and halibut fishing for the week. No chance for them to join us for dinner as we had hoped. So, the next stop, Idaho Inlet, was our stop for the night. You could not ask for a more pristine wilderness, filled with otters by the dozens, eagles, and the ever-present salmon. We watched a beautiful sunset as the fog drifted in layers among the snowcapped mountains, and then sat down for one of Kathy's halibut dinners that would make New York restaurants proud.

This morning, we left Idaho Inlet with plans for Elfin Cove by late afternoon with some salmon fishing before docking there. When we were last in Glacier Bay, while tied up at Bartlett Cove, I met Ken, the captain of one of the day boats that takes tourists to see the glaciers and other magnificent sights. He and his son, Luck, were interested in *Always Friday*, so I took them for a visit on board. Our conversation turned to fishing, and Ken related that he was once a charter captain at Elfin Cove and knew every foot of the area. When I told him of our plans to take Kathy's family there, he pulled out the chart and showed me a "sure thing" for salmon. The secret was to be "on the west side of Three Hill Island east of Cross Sound with torpedo lures two hours before high tide. The coho's will be there!" That where we were at the appointed time, and Ken was so right!

Kathy's father's wish at eighty-seven years of age was to catch salmon in Alaska. Suzanne and Hugo had their fishing licenses in hand in hopes of catching "something" (not sure what). Within minutes, Charles (her father) had a tail-walker on, and a few minutes later, a ten-pound coho salmon, one of the true prizes of Alaskan waters, was in the net! Over the next two hours, we caught ten more, returning five of the beautiful fish to the sea simply because of full freezers. Charles's first coho salmon was the guest of honor for dinner tonight, but he was not around for dessert. We now have a unanimous request from all three of our guests for much more fishing during the coming week.

This place generates genuine excitement in even the most "citified" visitors from the lower forty-eight. All this happiness was the result of great advice given to an outsider by one who has made Alaska his home for years. You can't imagine how many of the highlights of our trip have come to us in just this way. I can't say enough good things about the friends I have found here in Alaska.

Tomorrow we will leave Elfin Cove at 5 AM to hit the tide at a time when *Always Friday* will float through the narrow entry channel. Don't try to bring anything with the draft of a Nordhavn in here at any time other than near-high tide! Our destination is Glacier Bay with a one-week permit in hand. Craig, Marylyn, and Suzi, *real* locals from Gustavus, will join us for those things in Glacier Bay known only to those who have lived there for years (as well as for dinner on board *Always Friday*). Whales, salmon, eagles, and otters have been checked off our guest's lists of hoped-for Alaska sightings. Bears, puffins, calving glaciers, moose, and sea lions remain unseen so far, but the week is just beginning.

7/31/2007

As planned, I was up at 4:45 AM to leave Elfin Cove with enough water under *Always Friday* to float us out of the harbor. Hugo, my brother-in-law, who, like me, doesn't want to miss anything up here, was with me on the bridge as we easily cleared the harbor with an extra four feet under the keel. With Cross Sound to port, and the Gulf of Alaska just beyond that, we steered north towards our next planned course change into South Inian Pass.

As it came into view, an error on my part became quite apparent. The last time we left Elfin Cove, we did so on a rising tide with the prevailing currents of seven knots pushing us *towards* our destination, Glacier Bay. This morning we departed on an ebbing tide, which now surged through South Inian Pass at 8.4 knots directly *against* us! Such a current would propel us not towards Glacier Bay but rather *in reverse* towards the Gulf of Alaska. So, it was back to the charts for plan B. If we were to continue northward, leaving the Inian Islands to starboard, the islands would shield us from the current, allow time to elapse (thus mitigating the adverse current), and allow us to traverse North Inian Pass towards Glacier Bay. Since that pass is considerably wider than the southern pass, I surmised that the currents would be less dramatic.

All worked as expected, and we made our way along the new course, even cashing in on some local advice that I had once been given by one of my Alaskan idols. "When the currents are strong, move towards the shore, and catch an eddy in the opposite direction" was the lesson that now became pertinent to the circumstances. I did so, moving inside of 100 yards from shore where the depths remained around 500 feet or more, and watched our speed over ground increase from 4 to 9.5 knots. But that was not the whole story.

As so often happens in Alaska, the change in plans yielded an experience superior to the one originally planned. The southern shore of North Inian Pass was a wonderland different from any that I have seen anywhere up here. The side of the mountain making up the shore looked like one of those beautiful Japanese bonsai gardens with rocky shores rising to groups of majestic trees interspersed with wispy clouds and light morning fog. As the waters moved with visible turbulence along the shoreline, sea lions by the dozens frolicked in the water or slept on the rocks.

As if that were not enough, groups of humpback whales rolled and spouted in constant entertainment as bald eagles watched from the trees. You cannot visualize the beauty of this scene if you were not there to witness it. My navigational misdemeanor led to one of the most memorable experiences of our adventure. If I am fortunate enough to ever cross this path again, I will always take North Inian Pass in hopes of again witnessing this masterpiece of nature dressed as she was this morning.

Our arrival in Glacier Bay was shrouded in thick fog necessitating a radar approach and Binky's curse, the foghorn. Since we were to join Craig and Marylyn Forgaard, our friends (and my local hero) from Gustavus, for dinner at Glacier Bay Lodge, we planned to stay around Bartlett Cove and fish for halibut there. Nathan, my son-in-law, caught his first halibut near there, but not his fifty-pounder that was the current record holder on *Always Friday*.

We anchored in about sixty-five feet of water and dropped our salmon-laden hooks into the chilly world of the funny-eyed flatfish, Mr. Halibut. After about an hour, we had two nice ones of about fifteen pounds each tied to the back of the boat. Then Hugo got into a *big* one! It took line over and over as Hugo struggled to bring him towards us. As new fishermen almost always do, he attempted to use the reel as a winch rather than use the rod as a lever. After trying this unrewarding method for about twenty minutes, he asked for some relief from the battle being won by a fish that acted as if he was well over a hundred pounds.

There being no other volunteers on board, I took the rod and began working him towards the boat while explaining the more effective technique of using the rod to subdue the fish rather than the reel. Just as I expected a gigantic halibut to come into view . . . and then the line went slack. He was gone! No equipment failure, no bad technique—he just stayed in the water too long and the circle hook dislodged. Not at all an uncommon occurrence with big fish of any kind. But all was not lost. Hugo and the rest of our crew had seen the techniques of using the rod as your most potent weapon against the fish and were ready for the next opportunity, which was not long in coming.

About fifteen minutes later, with Hugo again on the rod, a strong strike followed by violent headshakes signaled the presence of another big halibut now hooked by a much more knowledgeable fisherman. The fish took another 100 yards of line and uncharacteristically came to the surface with several rolls well behind the boat. After about twenty minutes of perfect rod and reel technique, Hugo had the fish at the stern of *Always Friday*. I popped her with a well-placed harpoon dart, and the sea erupted with piscatorial violence reminiscent of a big tuna or marlin at the stern. The dart now tied the big fish of almost five feet in length to the back of the boat with one-inch rope, ensuring that she was going home with us. Another big gaff mid fish, and she was at the stern but still far from dead and potentially dangerous to both fishermen and the boat. Several blows between the eyes with a weighted club ended the battle, and Hugo was the new holder of the halibut record on board *Always Friday*. Sixty-five pounds is now the weight to beat!

After cleaning the fish, we docked at Bartlett Cove to meet Craig and Marylyn for dinner at Glacier Bay Lodge and another chance to hear real Alaskan tales from true Alaskans. Tomorrow, we plan to explore the canyons of Muir Inlet with their unique mountain beauty and copious wildlife.

8/01/2007, Wednesday

We awoke this morning to thick fog that made seeing anything more than thirty feet away impossible. Our exit from the cove was entirely on instruments, with the radar, chart plotter, and AIS acting as our eyes and ears. As the fog lifted, we saw a very unusual sight when a cruise ship, which we had been monitoring on radar as well as talking to their bridge to arrange safe passing parameters, appeared from the fog with the superstructure visible but the hull obscured by fog.

As we moved north, conditions improved to the point that the unparalleled beauty of Glacier Bay was once again ours to enjoy. We first stopped at South Marble Island and enjoyed the sea lion and puffin show for almost an hour, capturing amazing pictures of that never-ending show. As we entered Muir Inlet, we were surrounded on both sides by mountains higher than we had seen elsewhere in the park of 4,400 square miles. Within a few miles of the entrance of the inlet, high on the side of a mountain off our starboard side, were mountain goats! About twenty of them grazing contentedly in places no one could visit without a true fear of falling off the face of the earth.

Not far from Marble Island was our home for the night, North Sandy Cove. We had anchored there before and were always impressed by its beauty and wildlife. That is the place that is off limits for going ashore because of a high bear population. And that was a good decision, because there awaiting our arrival was a large male black bear, contentedly eating berries within 100 yards of our stern. On the opposite shore, protected from the large male by the inlet, was a young black bear oblivious to our presence.

After a delicious halibut dinner, we were off to bed after a great day on the water. Tomorrow it will be Marjorie Glacier, reached by a long, enjoyable ride through bear and whale country. What a way to spend a day . . . or a lifetime!

8/02/2007, Thursday

We awoke in North Sandy Cove to the presence of two more black bears sharing the anchorage with us. We watched them for an hour as we ate breakfast and prepared to leave for Marjorie Glacier, about forty nautical miles up the bay. As we left the cove, a milestone of my Alaskan transition from tourist to local occurred when Ken, the captain of *Fairweather Express II* who has become a friend since we met several weeks ago on the dock, called me on channel 16 to ask my advice on his course through the area. Imagine that! The captain of an Alaskan tour boat asking *me* my opinion on where the action was in Glacier Bay. In my mind (only), I had arrived!

A few minutes later, as we passed Sebree Island at the mouth of Muir Inlet, off the port side of *Always Friday* appeared one of the visual treasures of Alaska, a group of orcas. Although considerably smaller than humpback whales, they occasionally kill them for sport. Several weeks ago, a dead humpback was found in Icy Straits, intact apart from the tongue—the calling card of the orca. We have heard from several locals a famous story of two moose caught by orcas swimming an inlet and killed, apparently for fun. Seals are often their victims, with many pictures in the local tourists' shops of the unfortunate animals being thrown into the air by the orcas.

But now their presence was characterized by fluid majesty as they rolled and dove with their tall dorsal fins clearly identifying them as the ultimate predator of the sea. It is not unusual to spend weeks in Alaska and never see an orca, but we have been fortunate enough to see them on three occasions, with today's close and prolonged encounter the best opportunity yet to enjoy their company in this magical setting.

As we moved on, we took a side trip down Tidal Inlet, one of the most beautiful spots in the area with waterfalls, landscapes, and wildlife that would alone justify a trip to Glacier Bay. When we were last there with Jim and Lisa, we got great pictures of an adult wolf that are now on the website. Today, another surprise: at the mouth of the inlet were four wolf pups playing as if it were recess at wolf school. We watched in fascination for half an hour and recorded the event with the magic camera for the website before moving on towards Marjorie Glacier. But there are few routine trips in Glacier Bay.

As we passed through Russell Cut, just onshore were three Alaskan brown bears, a large female and her two silver-backed cubs! If you were on land, this would represent the most dangerous bear situation you could imagine, but from the safety of *Always Friday*'s fly bridge, we enjoyed the privilege of sharing their day in the wilderness from a distance that would be foolhardy otherwise. Several hours later we were at Marjorie Glacier, one of the most beautiful places in Alaska. Kathy's family got to see the glacier from a quarter mile away, as close as safety allows (remember the massive iceberg that fell in our presence when we were there with Lauren and Nathan). The night was spent in Kathy's favorite anchorage, Blue Mouse Cove, with a sunset that was a nice final touch for the day. Tomorrow we are to join Craig for more fishing in his secret places. I think Kathy's family now sees why I hate to think of leaving this place.

8/03/2007, Friday

Boy, do I have a fish story for you today! But first you must hear the bear story.

We awoke in Blue Mouse Cove to another beautiful but cloudy day in Alaska. Our plans were to cruise to Bartlett Cove and meet Craig for halibut fishing, but two beautiful bears changed our plans. Just outside of Tidal Inlet, a mother brown bear and her two-year-old cub were standing in a stream, fishing for the salmon moving into the fresh water for spawning. The mother soon disappeared into the wilderness, but the cub stayed around for at least thirty minutes, moving rocks by the shore, looking for sea creatures left high and dry by the low tide. We were amazed by his strength as he moved boulders that weighed at least 200 pounds with no difficulty at all. As we watched him, time slipped away from us to the extent that the currents were rapidly building against us in Sitakaday Narrows.

Our cruise south to meet Craig became a losing battle against the currents, with our speed cut from our usual eight knots to something less than two knots. When it became obvious that we could never make our rendezvous with Craig as planned, I called him on the radio to make him aware of our circumstances. He suggested that we stop short at Ripple Cove and try for halibut there, but the currents made even that short detour a two-hour battle. So, it was back to the charts for plan C.

A small creek emptied into the bay just a short distance north of us near Rush Cove and was easily reachable since the current would now be with us. I saw hundreds of birds in the area, suggesting that they were feeding on salmon eggs spawned in the creek. If spawning salmon were there, then halibut should be there too. We reversed course, saw our speed go from 1.9 knots to 14.7 knots, ran less than a mile, and dropped the anchor in sixty-five feet of water. We baited the hooks with half a salmon each in hopes of enticing the big ones without catching smaller ones, a trick taught to me by a guide in Elfin Cove. We were out to break Hugo's sixty-five-pound halibut record of yesterday.

The big bait trick worked well, as shown by the fact that "small" halibut of about twenty pounds followed the bait back to the boat, trying in vain to get the salmon in their mouths. We had fished only a short time when both Charles and Hugo hooked up on very nice fish. Charles fought his very efficiently, and in fifteen minutes we had him alongside the boat. After checking his weight, we released him to swim again since there was absolutely no room in our freezers. Charles, at eighty-seven years of age, had successfully landed a seventy-five-pound halibut and taken the lead in *Always Friday*'s biggest fish contest. His performance will not surprise you once you learn that he was a Ranger in WWII, serving with Merrill's Marauders in Burma, with a Bronze Star and Purple Heart on his chest when he returned from the war.

But Hugo was still fighting a fish that he thought to be considerably stronger than his sixty-five pounder of the day before. The fish shook his head violently on many occasions and made several long runs, taking line off the reel at his discretion. But after about thirty minutes, Hugo had him at the stern. All agreed that he (actually she—halibut over fifty pounds are always females) was the new record for the biggest fish caught on *Always Friday*, so we decided to take it on board. A harpoon through the midsection tied it to the boat. Then a gaff went into the jaw before running a rope through the gills. It took both of us to get it onto the boat, but when we did, we confirmed its length to be sixty-four inches, and its weight 135 pounds! Hugo's fish was more than twice as large as his record of the day before, and forty pounds heavier than Charles's transient holder of the biggest-fish award. An amazing fishing experience serendipitously brought about by a bear that canceled our original plans to meet Craig in Bartlett Cove!

Upon return to the Bartlett Cove docks, *Always Friday* and Moby Halibut drew quite a crowd of both boat and fish admirers. Ken, the captain of *Fairweather Express II*, not only joined us there but brought his daughter, Amy, who is a fishing guide here. Amy picked up a knife and cleaned Moby in a flash, yielding about seventy pounds of beautiful filets that went to all who had gathered at the dock since *Always Friday* was full of fish.

We met Keith and Nancy Douglas from Austin, TX, while they were wandering the docks. After a tour of the boat, they joined us for dinner at Glacier Bay Lodge. And who was there to also join us but Paul Johnson of Gull Cove, with John, the guide we met in Idaho Inlet. Paul is my kind of man, and any time spent with him is time well spent. I am thinking of splitting that joint custody three ways when I am adopted up here—Craig, Greg, and Paul will each have me for four months of each year.

Speaking of Craig, he and Marylyn surprised us with their presence at the restaurant, adding even more to a great day in Alaska. I and my family were surrounded by my Alaskan friends in one of the most beautiful spots on earth. What more can you ask from one day of your life?

Tomorrow we are going after coho salmon with Craig and Pat. I'll bet we will have another good fishing story from that! We will see.

8/04/2007, Saturday

We awoke to another beautiful Alaskan morning, just like all the rest. Craig had scheduling problems with his boat, so we decided to take the proven fish taker, *Always Friday*, into Icy Straits instead of *River Moon*. We fished among the whales, sea lions, and otters for several hours, catching more halibut than we could use, but no salmon. To top off a great day, Craig offered to take us into the bay for Dungeness crabs, one of the delicacies of Alaska. Since neither Charles, Hugo, nor Susanne had ever seen one, they jumped on that opportunity. Within an hour, we had eight big males with no future at all on board and scheduled for dinner.

Kathy's family leaves us tomorrow in Juneau, so we said a heartfelt goodbye to our new friends in and around Glacier Bay and cast off for as far down Icy Strait as we can get tonight. We will be in Auke Bay tomorrow and will depart with Bobby and Margo on board as soon as Nordhavn can get a faulty alternator replaced. It failed without warning, but the redundancy of the boat allowed us to continue without a hitch. The insignificant hum of the generator several times a day is the only hint of the alternator's unexpected passing. Once repaired, we will be southbound for Ketchikan, the beginning of the end of one of the greatest experiences of my life: the beautiful people and beautiful places of Southeast Alaska! Stay tuned for more adventures on a slow boat to Seattle.

8/08/2007, Wednesday

We said goodbye to our family and welcomed Bobby and Margo from Norfolk, VA, onto our boat with plans for an immediate departure for Ketchikan. But delays in delivery of a new alternator dictated a delay in our plans. A valuable lesson: even when you pay for and expect next-day delivery, you still should expect UPS to take four days to get your package to you in Alaska. So, we took a rainy day that we did not anticipate spending on land and found a way to make it a great day in Alaska.

First, we retraced our steps to Sheep Creek where the chum salmon were fighting the battle nature had precluded their winning so that Bobby and Margo could see this amazing show. All the players were there: the salmon by the thousands, driven to spawn and die by that ingrained, irresistible code that has guided the species from the beginning of time; the eagles, gulls, and trout, all gathered to feed on either the eggs or the doomed fish themselves. A scene that leaves anyone that witnesses it in absolute awe of nature.

From there, we next drove to Mendenhall Glacier and were treated to a sight that I had never seen, even though I have seen the glacier many times over the last several months. The entire valley was shrouded in layered clouds that gave the scene an unearthly feeling, filled with impossible beauty. Just downstream from the glacier, the sockeye salmon were still running strong. As we watched them battle upstream, the woods on our right erupted with a large black bear running upstream to grab a hapless salmon and drag it onto the bank where it was the guest of honor at the bear's awards banquet.

Quite a sight, and what an opportunity to share the sometimes cruel reality of nature. This dedicated salmon was born here, traveled widely in the Pacific Ocean for the past five years, heard the call to renew the species, traveled 2,500 miles to meet his obligation . . . and got eaten by a bear 500 yards from his goal! Good try, but he became one of the 99.9 percent that *don't* make it back to spawn.

But our next stop in Juneau was one of the most fascinating of our trip. The DIPAC salmon hatchery was in full swing, receiving returning chum salmon by the thousands as they climbed the man-made creeks bringing them from sea level to the hatchery's elevation of about twenty-five feet in graded steps. The salmon were pressed head to tail, as tightly as sardines in a can, as they climbed the ladders to meet man's efforts done on their behalf to better ensure the perpetuation of the species.

As they reached the last level of elevation, what at first blush appears to be a horror story began to unfold. The salmon were lifted from the water on a metal screen; then a brief jolt of electricity ended their lives more quickly than the sad, slow demise dictated by nature. They were then separated by sex on a conveyer belt where workers slit the bellies and expressed the eggs into a bucket. A similar process on the male side freed the milt from the lifeless bodies of the males. Then milt (or sperm) of seven different fish were mixed in the bucket with the eggs for fertilization, thus ensuring genetic diversity in the offspring. The fertilized eggs were next taken into dark surroundings to hatch soon. Upon hatching, they will be kept in pens until they reach several inches in length, then released into the wild where they move into the Pacific for four to five years before returning to this same hatchery as participants in this process, next time as doomed parents rather than juvenile winners of a low-probability game of survival.

Once man has fulfilled the responsibility for the assured survival of salmon, the bodies of the fish, now devoid of reproductive potential, are reduced to four-inch chunks of meat in a grinder and reintroduced to the channel, 400 feet below the surface, where they are welcomed by the crabs, shrimp, and halibut into the food chain that benefits all Alaskan marine creatures. When you realize that this superficially barbaric process alters the survival rate for a hatchling from 5 to 75 percent, you see the value of the three dozen or so hatcheries now going full swing in Alaska. Something must be going well because this place is alive with salmon.

Our last day in Juneau was made even more memorable by visits from some our best Alaskan friends. Both Greg and Craig brought us mementos of our summer with them in this little spot of heaven. I sincerely hope to cross paths with them again in the future, hopefully on their home turf here in Alaska.

This morning, Mike from John Deere got our alternator back online, and we four are now in Stephens Passage, on the way to Ketchikan. Our southerly course of 152 degrees represents the first segment of our trip home. I would like to say that I view that with mixed emotions, but I don't . . . only sadness. I love this place. I love these people.

8/10/2007, Friday

Our trip south to Petersburg took place on one of the nicest days we have enjoyed recently. It was a bright sunny day with no wind and farm-pond-flat seas. The salmon were everywhere, and the gill netters were after them with a vengeance, having been given an open day for fishing by the Game and Fish Department. The fishing seasons here are not like hunting seasons back home in which it opens and closes on a specified day. Here G&F officers count fish moving into areas or specific streams. If there are more than an adequate number of fish to ensure effective spawning, the season is opened for a few days. Then the numbers are reassessed to determine the impact of the fishing. If the numbers are still adequate, another few days of fishing are authorized. The process repeats itself if salmon are in the area. The result is that about 80 percent of the salmon that arrive in Alaska escape the commercial fishermen and enjoy the opportunity to perpetuate their species.

As we turned south at Gastineau Channel, I heard a familiar voice on the VHF radio. It was Doug on the *Oracle*! We had crossed paths at Taku Harbor last month when we were moored there on our way to Tracy Arm and he was moored there for the night between fishing days. When I heard his voice, I called him on the radio, and we talked for several minutes before he wished us a safe trip south. Just another example of the great people and many new friends I have found in Alaska, and another reason why I am so sad about leaving.

About an hour later, we found ourselves amid a large pod of whales which literally surrounded us for the better part of an hour. Although we have seen several hundred whales over the past three months, I never tire of watching these magnificent creatures in the most beautiful environment one could imagine. Bobby and Margo have now enjoyed one of the greatest shows on the sea, and their excitement was obvious and contagious.

At midafternoon, we arrived in Petersburg, a true Alaskan fishing village. The harbor of several hundred slips was essentially empty, as all the boats were out after salmon, halibut, or crabs. The fish processors were going full blast, with tenders emptying their catches via vacuum hoses in the next step in the marketing process. A single sniff would tell you the primary industry of this little town of Norwegian origin.

That night, we enjoyed a fine dinner at (write this down if you are ever coming here) the Beachcomber Inn about four miles from the pier. They come to the docks in a van to pick you up, deliver you to the restaurant, and take you back home. The food was great and uniquely cooked into a truly memorable meal. Try it next time that you are in Petersburg.

This morning we arose to the prospects of again navigating one of the most famous and potentially challenging waterways in America: Wrangell Narrows. The currents dictate your departure time unless you don't mind going backwards for several hours as you challenge an opposing current. The Narrows is one of those Alaskan oddities in which the currents move in opposite directions at each end of the run. With appropriate attention to the tides, you can (and should) be able to ride favorable currents for the entire run of about twenty-one miles. We again hit it just right and traversed the over sixty channel markers without difficulty. It was a different look from what we saw in early June. The king salmon run is now over, and the lodges that had been packed with sportsmen from all over the world were now quiet and apparently closed for the season.

Our original plan was to leave the Narrows and turn towards the town of Wrangell to spend the night there. But our arrival would be in the early afternoon, and there simply isn't enough to do there to justify spending sixteen hours in Wrangell. Back to the charts for plan B again. A decision was made, and we turned south to pass Zarembo Island on the west side with plans to proceed down Snow Passage to Clarence Strait toward Ketchikan. Coffman Cove, about thirty miles away, seemed to be an appropriate anchorage for one of Kathy's great halibut dinners and a good night's sleep before completing the trip to Ketchikan on Saturday, where Bobby and Margo will leave us for Virginia.

But as we moved south, favorable currents would have put us at anchorage by 5 PM. A quick check of the charts showed Ratz Harbor, an abandoned logging camp, to be a better choice, with our arrival predicted at about 7 PM. So, plan C went into effect. We were off to Ratz Harbor, named by the Russians around 1840. I'm not sure who Ratz was, but his story probably had a sad ending for him. Craig Forgaard taught me that Alaskan lesson when we were rounding Anton's Rock outside of Glacier Bay's entrance. He said of the rock, "You don't get a rock named for you in Alaska by going safely around it!"

With about two hours of remaining light, we turned into Ratz Harbor.

You guessed it: Alaska did it for us again! A fortuitous change in plans put us into a place of incomparable beauty. The cove is about a half mile long and half that wide, surrounded by beautiful wilderness with a stream feeding into it at the southern end. That stream obviously is a spawning site for salmon, as the water all around us was alive with jumping fish. When I say alive with salmon, I mean that at any moment for the next twelve and a half hours of our presence there, there were probably two dozen salmon out of the water and in the air within 100 feet of our boat.

As we sat there in amazement, the constant slap of acrobatic fish hitting the water sounded as relaxing as rain on a tin roof. Out came the spinning rods, and in no time, we had four fish on board. They were in variable stages of coloration dictated by the spawning season, but Margo's fish was bright silver and perfect for the dinner table. Kathy altered the planned halibut feast to include fillet of pink salmon, a famous Alaskan delicacy. Fresh fish takes on a new meaning here. Our "fresh salmon" had been swimming around our boat thirty minutes before gracing our dinner table in Ratz Harbor.

This morning we were on our way by 7:30, with Ketchikan our goal by early afternoon. As we passed down Clarence Strait, the salmon seiners' boats were working the shore, cashing in on a concentration of fish I never thought possible until our time spent in this phenomenal place. Within twenty-five miles of Ketchikan, the charter boats began to show up along the shore with their fishermen as surrounded by salmon as we were last night.

But we weren't totally roughing it out there. The PGA Championships were playing by satellite TV on one of the bridge's Furuno displays, thanks to our brilliant AV system from Definitive Concepts. *Always Friday* has furnished us with everything we could have asked for to enjoy the last three months in comfort and safety. I can't say enough about how happy we are with our boat! It has been even better than we anticipated, and we have asked more of it than most boats could ever deliver. I would not hesitate to confidently take it anywhere in the world where the inhabitants are not prone to kill us!

We will be in Ketchikan for the next week or so, hopefully fishing and relaxing (as always) before turning south for a visit to Seattle. We plan to see John and Debbie, Ken and Roberta, and Don and Lilly of the Nordhavn community, as well as visit with Rod and Nancy, who recently left Virginia for Rod to become CEO of Swedish Medical Center. Alaska in my rear-view mirror makes me incredibly sad, but I will be taking home with me a list of new Alaskan friends, and memories of the best summer of my life!

8/11/2007-8/15/2007, Saturday-Wednesday

We awoke this morning to an empty guest room on *Always Friday*. Not a good feeling, and not really a bad feeling, just quite different from the nonstop excitement we have enjoyed for the last fourteen weeks. During those weeks we have enjoyed the company of our family and a dozen of our very closest friends as we shared an adventure that far exceeded my expectations.

But now the midnight sun is gone by ten at night, the course is consistently southward, and we have said goodbye to our fantastic newfound friends from the most beautiful place on earth. It is the autumn of our trip, and just like the leaves on the trees, the most wonderful parts of our trip fall behind us in the wake of our departure from Alaska. It makes me sad to know that the confluence of circumstances that melded into the trip of a lifetime will never fall into place again as they have this summer. But we are still thousands of miles from home, with more friends to join us along the way, so my melancholy mood is at least mitigated by the thoughts of adventures to come. Maybe it will be as good as Alaska.

Then reality sets in . . .

Nope. No chance anything could ever equal Alaska!

8/14/2007, Tuesday

Today Kathy and I planned to wander the streets of Ketchikan just to see what was there. Not as a tourist since I wore my Carhart pants, but not as a local either: I left my red suspenders on the boat! There is no one off the *Norwegian Princess* from New Jersey that I really want to talk to, so why wear my "locals" stuff? We walked from *Always Friday* at Bar Harbor and stopped short of downtown for the best halibut sandwich you ever tasted. Again, prior local information had left me with the knowledge that the prize-winning sandwich was a local's secret—at the Burger Queen. You would never stop there on your own, but the sandwiches are world class!

While waiting for it to be cooked, I thought that I would try a long shot and email Doug McPherson, the bar pilot on board the *Noordham* who had shared the world-class calving experience of Marjorie Glacier in Glacier Bay National Park last month with us. We had been in contact several times since and discussed the possibility of meeting in Ketchikan if he were there when we arrived.

I pulled out the Blackberry and emailed, "We are in Ketchikan. Where are you?"

Within minutes my phone rang with yet another compounded dividend from our Alaskan adventures. Doug was in town and would meet us in forty-five minutes at Salmon Landing. We were there on time, and so was not only Doug but also his wife, Jean! They picked me out of the crowd by my Carhart pants. We hit it off and enjoyed Alaskan and boating conversations until Doug had to report on board the cruise ship for his departure northward. But Jean was not leaving with him. When she asked if we would like to see where they live in Ketchikan, another local adventure was assured.

Jean took us all over the south end of the city, pointing out the sights that the tour buses never see. The last stop was their home overlooking the water with a view that would command at least $5 million in the Virginia real estate market. From their porch, you can see the main outbound channels to Vancouver, beautiful, tree-covered islands, commercial and private fishing boats, jumping salmon, and a constant presence of seabirds following the fish. Malibu Beach has nothing to compare with this place. Jean told us of one negative, which I considered to be a positive. The place is loaded with bears! In fact, one had crawled *into* her car just last night.

After spending a beautiful afternoon with Jean and her great personality, we were off to the boat. To top off the visit, as we left their home and crossed a small bridge, there below us was a bear after the salmon in the stream.

But the day was far from over. Bill and Mary Pfiefer, whom we had met and enjoyed company with on the way up to Alaska, asked us to join them for dinner at one of their favorite restaurants, Salmon Falls. The view and food were fantastic, and the company even better. More stories of Alaska from Bill, Mary, and their daughter, Natalie, home from Washington, DC, where she was serving as an intern for one of Alaska's senators, kept us entertained for a great evening. One of their stories brought home the wild side of living here when Bill related how just last summer a brown bear had attacked a friend of theirs in Hoonah, bitten her head, and detached her hip with his claws before her husband shot and killed it. It is understood that there are no outside social events in bear country without the protection of men with bear guns, which saved this woman's life that day. (We never went ashore from *Always Friday* without an answer to any bear's aggressive intentions.)

8/15/2007, Wednesday

Another Chamber of Commerce Day in Ketchikan. Bright-blue, cloudless skies with temperatures near eighty degrees. Bill and Mary again dedicated most of their day to our enjoyment as they took us way off the beaten path to see the sights and meet their friends. Among the most memorable were Al and Carol Johnson, who have retired to their log cabin on the waterfront overlooking the channel into Ketchikan. It is as picturesque a place as you can imagine. If I could reproduce it right down the road, I could spend my retirement in contentment. They sit on their porch with spotting binoculars and assess the competence of every skipper and vessel that passes their inspection station, unless he has taken their thirty-two-foot tug, MV *Tenacious*, to Wrangell for a day of golf. They should live to be 120 with that schedule.

For dinner, we again joined Bill and Mary, this time at their home for an outside picnic to celebrate the blue-bird day, followed by a ride into the wilderness to a mountain lake that has been a source of great pleasure for their entire family as they raised their five children. The beauty of this place never ceases to amaze me!

Tomorrow's plans are somewhat up in the air, as the upcoming weather in Dixon Entrance just south of here may dictate our taking a side trip to Misty Fjord while gale warnings blow over. If so, it will be just another example of a change in plans yielding another opportunity to bask in the beauty of Alaska.

8/16/2007, Thursday

Today, after the unexpected pleasure of a personal visit on board *Always Friday* by Doug and Jean McPherson (our bar pilot friend from the cruise ship *Noordham*), we left Ketchikan, taking the northern route to Misty Fjord, another Alaskan national park famous for its beautiful scenery, wildlife, and fishing. We plan to send the next five days or so exploring the many coves and bays that make this 2.2-million-acre, out-of-the-way place a favorite spot in Southeast Alaska. It can only be reached by boat or floatplane, so Yellowstone-like crowds are not a concern.

Just north of Ketchikan, we turned north up Behm Canal (not a realistic designation since it is four to five miles wide in most places) with thirty-knot winds directly astern. The boat and autopilot handled the conditions beautifully with very little effect on our path and no effect on our comfort. After an uneventful run of about five hours at eight knots, made even more enjoyable by a National Geographic segment on the great bears playing on satellite TV on the middle Furuno display, we turned into Yes Bay on the northwest side of Behm Canal. The seas immediately calmed, and the winds fell to insignificance as we wound past a beautiful fishing camp to a well-charted anchorage about three miles from the entrance.

Yes Bay is named for the Tlingit Indians' word for mussels, although I never saw one. The snowcapped mountains of our summer have been replaced by the temperate rain forests of southern Alaska. The luscious green forests reflect the fact that this area receives at least 200 inches of rain every year, and in fact it is raining lightly at this minute. But again, rain does not dampen the spirits here. It simply offers another perspective on this magnificent scenery.

We knew from prior conversations at the Ketchikan docks that the *Albedos*, a forty-foot Nordhavn, and *Slante*, a forty-five-foot Selene, had a float plan like ours, and there they were, anchored in the same cove. After dinner, Jim and Lynda and Van and Maureen motored over in their tenders with hot buttered rum in hand for an enjoyable visit before turning in for the night. Later in the evening, we saw nav lights gliding into the cove, and yet another Nordhavn joined us here for the night. It was *Samba*, another forty-footer. We had seen only two other Nordhavns in Alaska until now, when three of us were anchored together in a remote wilderness cove. Our home ports verified the long-distance lifestyles of these boats: Arizona, Minnesota, and Virginia!

Tomorrow we will enter the Misty Fjord wilderness with tentative plans to anchor in Fitzgibbon Cove. It should be beautiful.

8/17/2007-8/18/2007, Friday-Saturday

We slept late and got a late start out of Yes Bay on Friday. After a four-hour run in misty rain, we were in Fitzgibbon Cove for the night, with both *Albedos* and *Slante* joining us again at anchorage. A very pretty cove and a secure anchorage, but not really a destination spot. After a steak dinner followed by the family Scrabble championships, I hit the electronic charts (NobleTec) to plot tomorrow's course to one of the highlights of Misty Fjords, Punchbowl Cove. That done, we went to bed with the soothing beat of the rain on the deck as effective as any sleeping pill. Even Raleigh and Binky slept in until after eight.

This morning (Saturday) we awoke to not only steady rain but also low visibility, justifying (in fact, requiring!) all the navigational toys on the bridge of *Always Friday*. *Albedos* and *Slante* decided to return to Ketchikan rather than push through the challenging weather to Misty Fjord. So, with the chart plotter, radar, ARPA, and AIS lighting our way, Kathy and I were off to Punchbowl Cove.

But one of the advantages of going eight knots is that you have time to do things during passages other than drive the boat. As we cruised down Behm Canal, I was reading Douglass's cruising guide on the area (perhaps the most important book of our summer) when I came across their description of Walker Cove. It sounded much too attractive to simply ride by, so yet another plan B episode became a part of our summer. The book said that there are no anchorages inside the cove because of the great depths associated with the glacial origins of the waterway, so my initial plan was to make a side trip into Walker Cove, then proceed on to Punchbowl Cove for the night.

As the radar signaled our arrival at the cove on the port side of the canal, it also showed a strong return signal at the mouth of the cove. When we were about half mile from the entrance, we could see that the radar contact was a large yacht of about 150 feet, complete with a helicopter on the aft deck! The captain had heeded the words of the cruising guides and anchored outside the seven-mile-long cove while running the guests into the interior by tender. We slipped by them through the narrow entrance and headed down the deep channel and into some of the most beautiful scenery of our trip.

The glacier-carved walls are almost vertical, and as high as 4,000 feet. The origin of Misty Fjord's name is no mystery, as the entire spectrum of cliffs, sea, and sky were framed with layered clouds that appeared more the work of an artist's brush than the product of meteorological chance.

To finish off this masterpiece of nature were waterfalls by the dozens. By waterfalls, I don't mean just streams of water falling into the cove. I mean dozens of postcard-perfect waterfalls with millions of gallons of water roaring down from thousands of feet above, splitting into multiple branches, projecting from the walls like giant fire hoses and generating dramatic acoustics usually associated with the close passage of a freight train. We stood on the bridge of *Always Friday* and marveled at the fact that we were literally surrounded by not only the visual rewards of the all-encompassing presence of the falls but also the unique experience of the most beautiful surround-sound auditory experience of falling water that I could have imagined. Nothing short of running out of navigable water would have led us to turning around before we reached the head of the cove. Every foot of the way was a privileged minute spent with Kathy in the heavenly landscapes of Mother Nature.

As we completed the seven-mile run to the head of the cove,

there before us was a babbling creek with salmon running upstream as hard as they could. As usual, the efforts of the salmon did not go unnoticed by the other residents of the wilderness. The gulls were there by the dozens, probably for the eggs that escaped from the salmon's creek-bed nests. And the eagles were well represented as well, with as many as five at a time wading into the creek, standing by the shore and waiting for an unfortunate fish, or sitting in the trees in apparent majestic indifference. What more could you ask for? Well, how about a brown bear that, as we approached the creek, ran into the stream, caught salmon, and sauntered off into the wilderness with Raleigh and Binky watching from the bridge window.

Then the coup de grâce. A humpback whale spouted and rolled no more than a hundred yards from the boat.

Back to Douglass's guide that said that Walker Cove is too deep to drop the anchor for the night: as I write this, we have been securely anchored through two tides in sixty to seventy feet of water right at the mouth of the creek described above. We will sleep tonight literally surrounded by the songs of the waterfalls, the nests of eagles, and the tracks of grizzlies. If you ever pass this way, you should consider shadowing our path through this beautiful place.

Tomorrow we are off to Punchbowl Cove, supposedly the crown jewel of Misty Fjord. If it can match Walker Cove, I will be pleasantly surprised.

Addendum at midnight: FLIR (forward-looking infrared) did it again! As I often do at wilderness anchorages, just before going to bed I went to the bridge to check the water and shoreline for signs of life using the FLIR camera. It looks for heat sources of any kind and has so far discovered in the darkness around *Always Friday* seals, a whale, deer, and otters. As I turned it on, right off the bow, about 100 yards away, was a large, bear-shaped, bright-white (warm by IR) heat return that by its size could only be a big brown bear. You could see its individual legs moving as he walked, and its head as he moved along the shore.

I called Kathy to see it, and we watched it walk along the creek before entering the black (cold by IR) water, probably for salmon. Obviously, he had no idea that we were there ... until I briefly tapped the air horn! With that, he stood up on two legs, dropped to the ground, and scurried into the trees. He didn't go far into the brush, as we could still see his heat signature for a few more minutes as he contemplated returning to the stream. But he decided against it and disappeared into the wilderness. An exciting way to end a beautiful day.

8/19/2007-8/20/2007, Sunday-Monday

The last two nights have been spent as deep into Misty Fjord as you can get. No one around—just pure wilderness and its citizens! At almost every stream that is not essentially vertical, the salmon are moving into the fresh water with their celebratory entourage of eagles, seals, gulls, and bears following in their wake. We watched as a large tricolor brown dropped by the creek for a salmon lunch, then after eating, casually walked down the beach shoulder and deep in the water, less than a hundred yards from us on *Always Friday*. A beautiful sight, if you are on board a boat. A sobering sight if you share the land with him.

By the way, grizzlies, Alaskan brown bears, and Kodiak bears are all essentially the same bear. The only difference is their geographic distribution, which contributes to size differences. If a brown bear is born and lives in the lower forty-eight states, and grows up primarily on a vegetarian diet, he is called a grizzly bear. If he is born and raised in Alaska on the coast where he has access to an inexhaustible source of fish in the summer and fall, he grows even larger and is called an Alaskan brown bear. If he happens to be an Alaskan brown bear born on Kodiak Island where the gene pool favors very large bears, he is called a Kodiak bear.

It's all quite academic; any of them can (and will) eat you alive and enjoy it. Anyone who believes the Walt Disney rendition of the brown bear may as well sprinkle salt and pepper on his head, for there is a chance he is going to be some bear's lunch. Nonetheless, they are truly magnificent animals when enjoyed from a safe distance. Kathy refuses to even get in the tender after seeing so many bears so close to the boat. On the other extreme, Binky wants a piece of one—any time, any place.

So, good night from the northern end of Rudyerd Bay. Drop by if you are ever in the area!

8/21/2007–8/22/2007, Tuesday-Wednesday

We ran approximately 50 nm south from Misty Fjord to Foggy Bay yesterday. The anchorage there is a complicated entry but well protected once you are in there. Pretty, but we are more difficult to impress after three months in Alaska. A Sitka blacktail deer greeted us upon arrival, but no bears were seen. That doesn't mean that they didn't see us, though! On the shore were crudely painted "Trap Line" signs reflecting a warning that local trappers had a string of traps out for martens, a mink-like animal important to the local fur market. Kathy topped off the day with grilled sockeye salmon that was as good as any meal she has made us this summer.

This morning (Wednesday the twenty-second) we got an early start for the run to Prince Rupert, BC. Bill Calliott is to meet us there on Friday for four days of the Inside Passage.

As I write this, sadly we are in Dixon Entrance, crossing the Alaskan border into Canada. Frankly, I feel like a steel bar in a magnetic field. Craig, Greg, Paul, and Glen are forcefully pulling me back northward, but reality, commitments, and Kathy are dictating a southerly course.

It has been the most wonderful summer of my life, but now the greatest show on earth is over, and Elvis has left the building.

HEADING SOUTH

8/22/2007, Wednesday

WE ARE NOW in Prince Rupert, awaiting the arrival of Bill Calliott before continuing our southerly course towards Seattle, and ultimately home to Virginia. It is a well-accepted fact that you should be south of Dixon Entrance before the end of August, as the weather patterns then begin to shift to the more unstable and potentially deadly patterns of Alaska's fall and winter. In fact, our departure from Alaska had been delayed by five days by gale warnings and ten-foot seas in the areas we just traversed yesterday. The wait for better weather was well rewarded.

We left Foggy Bay in weather that gave it its name but soon had excellent visibility as the fog burned off. It was a blue-bird day with bright, sunny skies and *no* wind! That is a rare set of circumstances for Dixon Entrance, as the Gulf of Alaska and all its infamous weather flows unimpeded into that channel. All summer I have been reading horror stories of the many shipwrecks that now adorn the bottom of Dixon Entrance. But today it was like a lake. Only an occasional gentle swell suggested that we were anywhere other than thoroughly protected waters. The shoreline was alive with commercial fishing boats, with both seiners and gill netters cashing in on the final trip for the millions of salmon now here.

As we cruised along, I noted the first sign that we were back in British Columbia: a large, tree-length log floating on the surface. But as we got closer, its identity became clear. It was a humpback whale apparently enjoying a Posturepedic moment on the surface. This was the second time we had seen sleeping whales. The first was in Tenakee Springs, but those two awoke and moved on. This one did not seem aware of our presence at all.

As we moved closer to Prince Rupert, we saw close to a dozen more whales rolling lazily in the water, with the presence of hundreds of birds suggesting that they both were feeding on unfortunate schools of herring. We took the long way into town since the shortcut through Venn Canal was described as a "local knowledge only" passage. Another hour on the water was an acceptable price to pay for the peace of mind associated with a well-marked, big-ship channel into a port we had not entered before.

Prince Rupert during salmon season is a tough place to find dock space, and in fact all three marinas were at near-maximum capacity with transient commercial fishing boats. As we were sitting in neutral off Rushbrooke Harbor, contemplating potential anchorages, a crewman on board a docked seiner yelled to us, "Beautiful boat!" My tongue-in-cheek response to him was that it would be even prettier if we had a place to dock it. His response made our day: they were about to leave the dock, and we could have their space! So, fortune smiled upon us, and we are now tied up at one of the best slips in town.

The night's dinner was an unusual one for British Columbia: Japanese food at a sushi bar. I made it a little more local with a sockeye salmon concoction in addition to an eel roll. The clocks moved ahead an hour with our exit from Alaska, so we are now only three hours behind Virginia time and will be in that time zone until Central America.

So, off to bed in a quiet little town of 18,000 with infinitely more stars visible in the sky that we ever see at home. Tomorrow, we plan to rent a car and find out what else there may be to see here.

8/23/2007, Thursday

A lazy, beautiful day in Prince Rupert spent seeing the sights. We rented a car and went to the old cannery about ten miles outside of town. A fascinating visit into the history of commercial fishing and the big business that carried the fish to international markets. Well worth the short trip to get there. We have been catching big Dungeness crabs off the stern of *Always Friday*. The water is 300 feet deep at our slip, and it's quite a haul to get the traps up, but the crabs are ample rewards for our efforts. Last night, Eric and Kim from *Abyssinia* and Clark and Nina from *Rikki Tikki Tavi* joined us for dinner at one of the local pubs. A perfect example of what the cruise-ship industry does to these small ports—a mediocre oyster sandwich for each of us runs $60! But the company made it a good deal, as we talked about the Alaskan experiences we had shared this summer.

Bill Calliott will join us tomorrow afternoon, and we will be off to Lowes Inlet, about 65 nm south of here early Saturday morning, with Seattle the goal in the next couple of weeks.

The scenery remains beautiful, the wildlife plentiful, and the trip very enjoyable, but it's not Alaska.

8/24/2007, Friday

Bill arrived safely by de Havilland Beaver floatplane from Ketchikan this afternoon in classic NW Passage weather: low ceilings and light rain. No lower-forty-eight pilot in his right mind would fly in what these guys call "routine conditions" up here. The flight of approximately seventy miles was never above 1,000 feet, and visibility always under a mile. They navigate by GPS and depend heavily upon transponder-based collision avoidance systems. Still, it is an unforgiving environment for man and his flying machines.

Just last week, Craig, my hero from Gustavus, lost his friend in a plane crash in the Brooks Mountain Range of northern Alaska when he and another friend were sheep hunting there. They left one of the men's fifteen-year-old sons in camp while they scouted the surrounding mountains for sheep by float plane. Two days later, a plane saw the emergency signals of the son, landed, and learned that they had not returned from that flight two days earlier. Search planes later found the wreckage at 4,000 feet on a mountainside. Neither had survived the crash. When you see the amount of floatplane traffic up here (they're like cabs in New York), you wonder why there are not many more accidents. They are excellent pilots, but the combination of challenging weather, immovable objects, and gravity creates an unrelenting foe!

After dinner at a Greek restaurant in "downtown" Prince Rupert (which will generously go unnamed), we said goodbye to Clark and Nina on *Ricky Tiki Tavi*, moored next to us, and went to bed with a light rain rhythmically tapping on the deck, ensuring a good night's sleep. Tomorrow we are off to Lowe's Inlet with Bill, one of the most beautiful anchorages on the Inside Passage!

8/25/2007, Saturday

We left Prince Rupert this morning at about nine in cloudy but still quite good weather. None of us had been down this part of the Inland Passage; our northbound trip last May was outside from Port Hardy to Ketchikan. At that time, we were running in calm seas before a gale, necessitating fifty-four straight, nonstop hours for Frank, Kathy, and me. Our return trip has been and will remain day runs of about seventy miles, with stops every night at small towns or at anchor.

The scenery in British Columbia is quite different from Alaska, and strikingly beautiful. It is more reminiscent of Hawaii than Alaska in our opinions. Densely treed mountains with thickly foliated valleys punctuated with frequent waterfalls looks more like Kauai than Glacier Bay. Eagles are not as plentiful, but whales and salmon continue to surround us. Bill saw his first humpback whales just outside of Prince Rupert and added many more to his list of experiences before Lowe's Inlet.

The inlet is set several miles back from the main waterway, with a beautiful waterfall at the head. We chose to anchor with the bow several hundred yards off the mouth of the freshwater stream's entrance, with its current constantly holding the bow upstream. I had been concerned that Bill might not see the kind of scenery in British Columbia that would justify his trip here from Virginia, since almost all our fantastic experiences this summer were in Alaska, but we were off to a good start. BC had already shown him beautiful scenery, the romance of the fishing fleet, bald eagles, humpback whales, and, of course, salmon by the thousands. The magic chariot was still rolling along! *Always Friday* was moving south through beautiful British Columbia with a happy crew.

After a good night's sleep, we left early to meet Bill's return plans next Tuesday. Lowe's Inlet certainly deserves its reputation as a well-protected, beautiful anchorage that should be high on anyone's list of favorite stops in BC.

8/26/2007, Sunday

After a strong recommendation from Craig in Gustavus, we had planned to stop in Butedale, but upon arrival, it looked as if a tornado had hit it! Every building was not just dilapidated but literally in ruins. There was a handwritten welcome sign on the logs used as a dock, and a sign in a crooked window read, ICE CREAM, but neither served as enough enticement to get *Always Friday* to spend the night there (although the ice cream promise made me think twice). Back to the charts for yet another plan B!

Swanson Bay, an old, abandoned sawmill, was not far down the way and could be easily reached for an anchorage before nightfall. So off we went. About ninety minutes later, there it was—a quiet little cove with remnants of a brick chimney and an old wharf kindling thoughts of what must have gone on here in its heyday, early last century. Upon arrival, two bald eagles were waiting for us in classic postcard poses. The salmon jumped incessantly in their attempt to go upstream against all odds. Seals dove on the salmon, generating unseen underwater carnage.

After an excellent steak dinner, we were interrupted by the sounds of two whales feeding around the boat. For the next thirty minutes we watched and listened to them bubble feed through schools of herring, with the action clear to our eyes as well as the FLIR camera.

I went to bed feeling much better about the quality of Bill's Inside Passage experience with us on *Always Friday*.

8/27/2007, Monday

Another early start sent us down the well-protected waterway for a smooth ride to Bella Bella. We had picked that destination not only to show Bill the "local economy" but also because the book said it had internet and cell coverage—neither of which we had seen for almost two weeks. After about 65 nm, we were there, with strong internet and cell signals confirmed by all three phones and the computer, but the facilities for the night seemed much better in Shearwater, just a mile or so further. So, after confirming by VHF radio dock space for a starboard-side tie with fifty-amp power availability, we pulled up at the Shearwater Marina.

As is often the case, we were met with a half dozen people asking to see the inside of the boat in return for having taken our lines upon arrival. I conducted a boat tour while Kathy took Raleigh and Binky for their first walk in grass in two weeks. Then, a surprise—Shearwater does not share the cell or internet signals with Bella Bella. We were back in the communication blackout that frankly is not a total negative to me. Having been a doctor for thirty-six years, there is something quite relaxing about knowing that the phone is not going to ring.

It doesn't take long to see all that Shearwater has to offer. Bill and I wandered with interest through the small shipyard filled with many old and dilapidated wooden commercial fishing boats that could tell a million fascinating stories. A lumberyard was filled with massive logs that appeared to have been salvaged from the waterway, which was infamous for the abandoned trees lost from floats used by the lumber industry to carry their products to market. Significant damage to numerous boats occurs every year from logs strewn the entire length of the BC waterway. On a more positive note, they would make a beautiful log cabin on Shelter Island just outside of Juneau!

After Bill treated us to a salmon dinner at the Shearwater Dock Restaurant, we were back to the planning charts for tomorrow's leg southward. Bill leaves us for home from Bella Bella, with his trip again confirming how much great friends add to any experience. A full-scale gale is brewing in the area, so our plans will be driven by a great respect for what the weather can do here where we will be exposed to the open Pacific between here and Port Hardy. The same rule that should drive every airplane pilot applies equally here on the sea—you never *have* to be anywhere!

8/28/2007, Tuesday

Bill left us this morning for Vancouver, and ultimately home to Virginia Beach. We had considered staying in Shearwater for another night, but the dock mistress made a fatal business error: she had the audacity to suggest that Binky was wearing out her welcome there, simply because she briefly barks with wild excitement every time we return to the boat, relieving her lifelong nightmare that Kathy might have inadvertently left her behind. We can't understand why anyone would not enjoy witnessing that touching moment of canine ecstasy, relived about five times every day, so we decided to punish them for their lack of appreciation for Binky's feelings by leaving!

We were off again, with brief internet and cell service allowing us to call family and update our position on the website as we passed Bella Bella. Heading down Fitzhugh Sound in heavy rain and essentially no visibility, *Always Friday* plowed through the twenty-knot winds on the nose and four-to-five-foot seas as if it were a bathtub. No roll, no pitch—just a smooth ride at nine knots. At the Kwakshua Channel, we turned almost due west for Pruth Bay, consisting of several safe anchorages in which we could wait out the gale that is building. Two hours before dark, in thirty-knot winds, we were safely anchored in ten fathoms with a 5:1 rode of half-inch chain on the southeast side of Keith Anchorage, with gale-force winds expected out of the south for the next twenty-four hours.

Before we went to bed, the winds had increased to forty-plus knots. The Nobeltec GPS anchor watch confirmed that we are holding the bottom firmly. As predicted, the wind is going over our heads, with much of its power absorbed by the shoreline trees. We are snuggly inside *Always Friday*, doing what Nordhavns do better than almost any other boat—comfortably weathering a storm that in other boats might be much more menacing. The rain is pouring out of the dark-gray sky, the wind is howling, and Kathy is cooking a great dinner while watching the Food Channel on satellite TV as I type this update and listen to Willie Nelson on XM Radio!

Some may think it crazy, but I really enjoy bad weather on the water. It gives nature a whole new palette and light with which to paint the scenery. Even so, we won't cross Queen Charlotte Strait until favorable weather is assured. The comfort and reassurance of being on *Always Friday* in challenging weather comes, at least in part, from our experiences last May in which she safely and comfortably took us through weather much more severe. In fact, since last May, she has taken us 4,376 nm from southern California to the 60th northern parallel without one moment of fear, trepidation, or regret. *Always Friday* has more than fulfilled our hopes for her. She has been our magic carpet . . . and the ride is not yet completely over!

8/29/2007, Wednesday

The gale blew full force all day today with constant, heavy rain being blown from the south at a forty-five-degree angle. Except for a sailboat about a mile away on the other side of the cove, we are alone in an area charted as Keith Anchorage in Pruth Bay. It was not a time to take the tender visiting, so we had a lazy, comfortable day in which Kathy watched several movies while I dug through electronic manuals, looking at little-known, and even less used, features of the radar systems.

The AIS confirmed that every boat in the area was tucked into a cove somewhere, weathering the gale. The GPS anchor watch suggests that even in forty-knot winds, we are not swinging on the anchor itself. The radius of our swing is less than 100 feet, and we have 250 feet of half-inch chain out from the surface to the anchor. Therefore, it appears that about half of the chain never leaves the bottom. If my assumptions are correct, it is a good argument for heavy chain rode as opposed to rope.

After a dinner of shrimp scampi, and *Dream Girls* on the Kaleidoscope, we were off to bed with plans for an early departure for Port Hardy in the morning if the offshore West Sea Otter buoy reports are favorable. Dixon Strait and Queen Charlotte Sound are the two major open-water obstacles on the Inside Passage. After waiting several days in Misty Fjords for a weather window, we hit Dixon Strait at a good time last week. After crossing Queen Charlotte tomorrow, we will be inside again all the way to Seattle.

8/30/2007, Thursday

I awoke at 5:30 AM to get an early start across Queen Charlotte Sound. The winds usually build by midafternoon, and that in association with the swells from the gale would make for a challenging crossing. The winds had fallen to less than ten knots, and the seas north of the sound were calm. The tradeoff for no wind was fog, but low visibility is no obstacle for *AF*. With Binky's curse, the foghorn on automatic, we entered the sound with the radar and AIS confirming that many other boats had made their moves after the gale as well.

With only a few course deviations for traffic, we completed the crossing in about nine hours. The remnants of the gale, as well as a weather system in the Aleutian Islands, yielded significant swells from the west while we were exposed to the open Pacific, but the boat was unaffected apart from occasional pitching. We docked in Port Hardy at the Quarterdeck Marina, only to find that there was no internet or fifty-amp power. After a walk through the town and a mediocre restaurant meal, my curiosity for Port Hardy had been satisfied.

On the boat lift was a reminder that these are unforgiving waters. A sixty-foot cruiser was out of the water with both props folded back by a large, submerged rock. He had attempted to leave the harbor outside of the markers and had paid the price. Luckily, the damage was confined to the props. About thirty miles north of here is a boat awaiting a salvage barge, still on the rocks after grounding last week.

Tomorrow Kathy is going grocery shopping while I wash the boat; then we are off to some point between here and Campbell River for the night. The trip through British Columbia is nice and peaceful, but it's not Alaska! I sure miss that place and all my friends there.

8/31/2007, Friday

We left Port Hardy with a full refrigerator and a clean boat.

There are several genuinely nice little towns between us and Campbell River, but none were far enough south to put us in range of Seymore Narrows at 3 PM tomorrow for slack tide. This was a perfect example of the advanced planning demanded by the currents in Alaska. If you hit the Narrows at anything other than slack tide, you will be facing currents of up to fourteen knots with turbulence that will overcome any rudder. In other words, you may find yourself on an out-of-control roller coaster, hurtling down a path bordered on both sides by shear granite! Even the cruise ships time their passages for slack water.

So, after completing my computations, it was necessary for us to get about 60 nm down the road today. Port Neville fit that bill nicely. I don't know why they call it Port anything. The dock is fifty feet long and only holds two boats. The books alerted us to that fact, so we were prepared to anchor upon confirmation that the dock was full. It was, so we went further in, in search of an anchorage at July Point. Nobletec was excellent, and we completed the rather complicated approach without a hitch. Waiting for us there was a big black bear! He and the orcas we saw en route this afternoon managed to keep the embers of Alaskan excitement glowing softly (but not blazing as they once were).

Certainly, the most exciting event of the day was a VHF call near Port McNeil. An unexpected *"Always Friday? Is that you, Buddy?"* came from John, Paul Johnson's guide this summer at Gull Cove! John had been on board his father, Steve's, boat in Idaho Inlet when we and the Walkers went over to see them in the tender. That was the start of my friendship with Paul and Terri, and John. He was with us on that bittersweet last night in Glacier Bay when so many of my new friends were present for our goodbye.

Now, more than 500 miles from Glacier Bay, we crossed paths with John again as he ran the outboard used for fishing this summer back to Washington state. He slowed from his forty-knot cruise speed long enough for us reminisce about our times in Alaska; then it was goodbye again as he dashed south. It seems that Alaska never really leaves me, even though I have left Alaska. I hope that never changes.

9/01/2007

I was up at 6 AM to set in motion the time/distance/variable current navigational challenge that I had worked out last night. It was all designed to hit Seymore Narrows at 3 PM for the slack tide. If late by any appreciable margin, a six-hour wait for the next slack tide would be required to avoid today's currents of almost eleven knots. I had inserted a thirty-minute buffer into the plan, with plans to simply slow down if an early arrival were to occur at the calculated speed. However, I had not counted on visibility of less than 100 feet, which is exactly what we found as we prepared to leave Port Neville.

Waiting it out was not an option if we were to make the slack-tide opportunity at Seymore Narrows, and *Always Friday* is superbly equipped to go anywhere in such weather. So, by 6:30, we were on the way with one radar on three-mile range and the other on twelve miles. Redundant chart plotters (Furuno and Nobeltec) ensured that our position was accurately known, and the AIS (automatic identification of ships) was again proving its essential role as it warned us of the positions, courses, and speeds of, on this day, as many as nineteen boats within twenty-four miles of our position. When non-AIS-equipped boats triggered an image on the radars, the computer reflected their course and speed as if they had AIS on board.

For the first five hours of the nine-hour trip, the fog persisted to the degree that on several occasions, we met boats passing within a quarter mile, their wake the only non-electronic hint of their presence as they glided by within the cover of the fog. The timing of our arrival at the Narrows coincided nicely with the slack tide, and we cruised right through what four hours earlier would have been a truly life-threatening and foolhardy experience.

We are back in the same marina that Kathy, Frank, and I left from on June 1 to begin our fifty-four-hour nonstop run to Ketchikan. We are now inside of 200 miles from Seattle and plan to be there in about a week. In the meantime, we plan to join John and Debbie Marshall, who commissioned their Nordhavn 55 with us in Dana Point, for a visit near their Washington state home. If Ken and Roberta Williams are still in the area, we hope to see their new Nordhavn 68, *Sans Souci*, before they head to Hawaii and all points west.

Our plans to leave Campbell River for Comox have been delayed by yet another gale, located north of us but adversely affecting our weather as well. It is Labor Day weekend in BC as well as the States. If we were to arrive in Comox on a holiday weekend with no slips available and the wind blowing thirty-five knots, it would not be a festive event! So, the rule "You never have to be anywhere!" has again been applied, and we are in Campbell River for the second night. Craig's admonition to be out of Alaska by late August was excellent advice as Dixon Entrance and Queen Charlotte Sound (both now well behind us) are living up to their reputations as major impediments to the southward trip out of Alaska. Both areas are being buffeted by forty-knot winds today!

9/03/2007, Monday, Labor Day

After a lazy, one-day layover in Campbell River, waiting for a gale to clear, we were off this morning for Comox, a short four-hour ride southward. However, when we called ahead to make sure we could get a slip, there was no answer on VHF or cell phone. Rather than risk running a rather tedious approach through a shallow bank into the town, only to find no room in the inn, we diverted to Nanoose Harbor, a US and Canadian naval base associated with torpedo testing. Of course, we can't tie up there, but the anchorage adjacent to the base is good. We have spent thirty-three nights at anchor this summer, and some (maybe even most) of our best experiences occurred while "swinging on the hook."

Actually, "swinging" is a misnomer. Apart from two nights in Pruth Bay during a major gale, there was almost no movement any night we were anchored on *Always Friday*. As a rule, we used a 3:1 scope, which gave us secure and comfortable anchorages, with the GPS anchor watch confirming that we never dragged the anchor at any time. In the gale we used a 5:1 scope, and the anchor never moved during two days of winds up to forty knots. Today we passed 720 hours on the main engine and 4,600 nm traveled since Dana Point, CA, 105 days ago. That is an average of almost seven hours of running every day since we left California last May 21. There were nine days in which we ran twenty-four hours each day (Dana Point to Victoria and Port Hardy to Ketchikan), and a few lazy days in Juneau along the way between forays out of Auke Bay, but as a rule, *Always Friday* has been doing all summer what she was designed to do: take two to six people anywhere they want to go in comfort and safety!

We are now approaching civilization again, so Kathy's excitement level is climbing, while I am threatened by catatonic depression. She can't wait to see the shopping centers of Vancouver and Seattle, while I can't wait to see the open Pacific. Even after thirty-five years of marriage, she remains confused about what is important in life! Obviously, no sane person would choose a handbag from Nordstrom's over halibut from Glacier Bay. I will keep trying, but I am not optimistic for her epiphany.

9/04/2007, Tuesday

We anchored last night in Nanoose Bay. Not a good night. There were no problems with the anchorage, the boat was perfect, the sockeye salmon dinner excellent, and the sleep sound . . . but we were surrounded by civilization at every point on the compass.

I went out on deck after dinner and was met with the sounds of trucks changing gears on the nearby roads. Houses were everywhere. The stars were diluted by the lights on the highways, and if you were to hear a wolf howl, it suggested the strong probability that he had just been hit by a car.

Craig, Greg, Paul! 911! Come get me! It's about to get worse; we just tied up in Vancouver.

9/06/2007

After two nights in Vancouver, we are on the seas again, en route to Anacortes, USA, through six-foot following seas in the Strait of Georgia. As usual, the boat is handling it well, while other cruising boats around us are probably quite uncomfortable. John and Debbie Marshall on board *Serendipity* (NH 55-20) are waiting for us at Cap Sante Marine, and Ken and Roberta Williams on board *Sans Souci* (NH 68-01) are on the way to join us there this afternoon. Hopefully, Don and Lilly Weipert will join us as well.

Don, Kathy, and I brought *Always Friday* to Victoria from Dana Point last May through the challenging weather that we documented in updates after our Victoria arrival. I had not known Don before our departure. He had volunteered to go north with us in hopes of seeing how Nordhavns handle rough weather, as he was considering buying a NH 55 like *Always Friday*. Boy, did he get his wish! Forty- to fifty-knot winds with fifteen-plus-foot seas for several days in a row. You may wonder what he thought of the boat? Well, he and Lilly have been in Dana Point for the last several days, finalizing their ownership of their own NH 55. If they can join us, it will be under their new status as Nordhavn owners. If you like the lifestyle these boats are built for, you can't *not* like a Nordhavn. Ours has been more than we ever hoped for and apparently impressed Don and Lilly just as much.

The city of Vancouver was not much of an attraction for a metrophobe like me. I'm not sure that is a word, but it should be.

It all began at Coal Harbor, in the middle of downtown Vancouver, with our being shoehorned into a slip only twenty-four inches wider than our boat. That was our home for two nights for only $270 US! We got Big Bus tickets for two days that allowed us to see all the sights, none of which would beckon me back to the city. As for culinary opportunities, the best experience was cashew chicken in Chinatown when we ordered cashew shrimp. The worst experience was $5.50 iced tea with no refills at a Greek restaurant. The best meal of the stay was steak last night on *Always Friday*. By the way, the standard conversion of US to Canadian dollars is now one to one.

As we approach Anacortes (18.5 nm out at present), I can see on the AIS *Serendipity* docked at the harbor and *Sans Souci* moving toward the harbor at 8.4 knots on a heading of eighty-four degrees true. Modern-day electronics are amazing! The winds have fallen to ten knots, and the seas aren't noticeable on *Always Friday*. The next few days should be a lot of fun with our cruising friends.

PS: I wish I had more exciting news, but Alaska is about 800 miles behind us.

9/12/2007

We arrived in Seattle in midafternoon on a beautiful day apart from fifteen-knot winds making docking in a tight slip a challenge. We got in safely thanks to thrusters on both ends of *Always Friday* and the fact that Kathy has gotten quite good at letting me know what is needed from the thrusters from her vantage point. We will be looking for duplex wireless headsets at the boat show to make docking even easier.

Seattle is a city that immediately wins you over with its beauty and the warmth of its people. The dockmaster was the most helpful one we have seen in almost 5,000 miles of cruising this summer, and the people at Emerald Harbor Marine (where our short list of warranty work is being done) could not be nicer or more proficient. The people from the Seattle Nordhavn office were down to greet us upon our arrival and went out of their way to make sure that our stay was as pleasant as possible. In fact, Don Kohlmann, the president of Nordhavn Seattle, took us to the car rental agency and then loaned us his car's Garmin GPS for our stay so we could navigate the city safely and efficiently. Other boat companies could learn a lot about customer service from these fine people!

Tomorrow we are going to the Seattle Boat Show, and NH may bring a few serious prospects by to see our boat since they don't have a 55 for the show. The 55 has become the all-time fastest seller for NH, with over fifty now sold and the delivery date for the next available one now well into 2010. It is quite a boat, and we could not be happier with ours.

Next Monday, we will begin our trip to the Panama Canal. It is too early to predict a transit day for the canal, but it looks like an October/November occurrence. Between now and then, we anticipate some beautiful days at sea, interesting ports, and excellent fishing. In contrast to our run up the coast last spring, we do not plan to run day and night. We will pick our travel days with an eye to the weather and sit out uncomfortable weather rather than bust through it.

We plan to spend tomorrow with Rod and Nancy Hochman, who recently moved here from our Virginia hometown. Rod took over as CEO of Swedish Medical Center, the premier medical center in the Seattle area. We had the pleasure of working together for years when he was the VP of our medical center in Norfolk, Virginia, and it will be great to see them again. We ate together in Virginia Beach on the night before he left for his new job, and now we will be together again after they drove to Seattle and we floated here. Small world.

As we got closer to Seattle, the NH community funneled together into a very enjoyable group. We have enjoyed the company of Roberta and Ken Williams on *Sans Souci*, Debbie and John Marshall on *Serendipity*, Pat and Paul Upchurch on *Gray Pearl*, and Lilly and Don Weipert on *Lilly Pad* over the last week as we all converged on the Anacortes/Seattle area. Today we met Michelle and Mark Doppe, who are here to commission their new NH 55 as well. So far, we have not met a Nordhavn owner whose company we did not instantly enjoy.

Kathy is finally in her element as she shops herself silly at Nordstrom's and the many other shopping areas that pervade the city. I'm going to the boat show tomorrow, then to the Boeing Plant on Thursday for a tour of the home of those beautiful planes.

In the five months since we started our website *Always Friday's Journal*, the webmaster tells me that it has been bouncing between number one and number two in popularity of the almost 200 sites they run! We have over 400 registered users and many more regular visitors that have not registered. They estimate that we have had over a third of a million page views since beginning our journal.

I frankly never anticipated anyone looking at it other than our friends and family, but I now get dozens of emails daily, from all over the world, reflecting a real interest in what we have done this summer and what we have planned for the fall. We have been contacted about writing an article for a magazine, and even a book, but the last thing I want in my life at this point is a deadline. I began my writings for me and genuinely enjoyed every minute of it; if others found them interesting, that was just a bonus. It has truly been a trip of a lifetime, with new friends and great memories that will enrich every day of the rest of my life. I only wish it could have been an endless summer.

Next stop: Pacific Ocean and points south! We will be trading whales for marlin, and salmon for tuna. It should be fun—but my heart will *always* be in Alaska.

9/19/2007

Seattle was an excellent stop for multiple reasons. First, the city itself is beautiful, vibrant, entertaining, and interesting, in sharp contrast to Vancouver, which was none of those things. There is much to do in the city, and shopping for Kathy was great. Elliott Harbor Marina was excellent, and Emerald Harbor Marine, who did our short list of warranty work, was the best marine business we have seen since we left Virginia. Larry and Rod were totally dedicated professionals who met our every request with proficiency and professionalism.

Don Kohlmann of Nordhavn Seattle could not have been more cordial. From treating us to a seafood dinner to loaning us his

Garmin for use in our rental car, he bent over backwards to make our stay a very pleasant one. The Kohlmann brothers (Don in Seattle and Gene in Dana Point) are the best things that ever happened to Nordhavn. If we were to do it again, we would commission our boat in Seattle and save ourselves the hardships of Southern California and the challenging trip up the coast—as long as we had the opportunity to again enjoy the friendship and expertise of Jeff Merrill of the Nordhavn Sales Division.

Perhaps the high point of the trip was our opportunity to spend a day and several nights with Rod and Nancy Hochman. Both his and the hospital's futures look very bright under his direction. I still wish they were back in Virginia with us.

Jeff Hawkins, whom we met in Dana Point when he came as a prospective buyer to look at Nordhavns, joined us for several days on the boat to see how they performed at sea. The last person to do that (Don and Lilly) are now 55 owners! Jeff was a real pleasure to have on board, and he has a standing reservation to return to *Always Friday* at some point south. I think he will have his own NH when the stars align in his favor.

Again, our Nordhavn friends that were in Seattle with us were a pleasure. Ken and Roberta Williams of *Sans Souci* invited us to their Seattle waterfront home for a most enjoyable evening, with plans to repeat the occasion in Cabo San Lucas in November on the way home. John and Debbie Marshall of *Serendipity* joined us for dinner almost nightly, then accompanied us yesterday to Sequim Harbor to show us their new home with fantastic views of the water and mountains. Their early retirement is going very well. Again, we were unsuccessful in talking them into going south with us to the Caribbean, but hopefully we will get together again somewhere with our sister boats.

Today, Kathy, the dogs, and I are moving west through the Strait of Juan De Fuca, which separates Canada from the US. The weather is beautiful, but there are six-to-eight-foot swells coming in from the west because of a storm in the Pacific or Aleutians. The boat couldn't care less—just an occasional moderate pitch of the bow, but no roll at all.

We will spend the night in Neah Bay before turning south at Cape Flattery to begin the trek down the West Coast. All is going very well on *Always Friday*. Not the action-packed days of Alaska . . . more of a relaxed journey through the natural beauty of the Northwest. Relaxing has never been my strong point.

9/20/2007

Neah Bay, at the juncture of the Strait of Juan de Fuca and the Pacific Ocean, was the most accessible and easiest anchorage we have seen in our travels. The entrance was wide and without currents, and the area available for anchoring quite large. The depth was consistently about five fathoms (thirty feet) with a sandy bottom that held well with a 3:1 scope. We shared it with five other boats (three sail and two power), and there was room for many more. There is not much reason to be there other than transiting to and from the ocean, but if your needs ever include an anchorage in this area, Neah Bay is a winner.

This morning (Thursday), we were underway prior to 7 AM since the next reasonable stop for the night for a boat of *Always Friday*'s draft is a little over 100 nm away. That stop is Grays Harbor in southern Washington. The day has been classic for the Northwest: rainy and overcast with visibility of about one mile. Another big day for radar, AIS, and electronic charts! The winds aren't much—about ten knots—but the widely spaced swells of about eight feet confirmed that we were back in the open ocean.

Our first turn to the south at Cape Flattery took us east of Tatoosh Island through what the Douglass books call the Fair-Weather Route. It is a beautiful and exhilarating short trip through a narrow, shallow, thirty-five-foot channel constricted on both sides by rocks awash at mid tide. In fact, it reminded me of the approach to Elfin Cove in Alaska. In today's conditions, it was a reasonable and safe approach; however, in significant weather the longer, outside route would be a more prudent decision.

Grays Harbor is one of those NW harbors protected by bars that can be deadly in severe weather and opposing currents. To hit the entrance of the bar near slack high tide, we had to invest an extra three gallons of diesel fuel per hour to maintain an average speed of 8.5 knots for the duration of the trip. We are now on schedule, turning 2,000 rpm at a fuel burn of 7.9 gph, averaging our needed 8.5 knots. The efficiency of these boats continues to amaze me. The large cruising boats we were with in Alaska often passed us at twenty knots or more; however, to do so, they were burning up to 200 gallons per hour. That makes me feel a lot better about pushing the throttle up to 7.9 gph today.

Kathy has gotten very proficient at watching the helm while I shower or nap briefly. We are now about eight miles off the Washington coast, with the autopilot keeping the boat "on the green line" of the electronic chart plotter, which represents the course I entered last night. At present, it reports that we are three *feet* right of the course of 110 nautical miles. The radar is set to warn us of any target that shows up within six miles of the boat, and if one does appear, it automatically tracks its course, alerting us if it represents a collision threat.

Along this desolate coast, the AIS confirms that there are no large ships within fifty miles of us. That is in sharp contrast to Vancouver where we had 151 contacts on the screen at one time. The depth sounder alarms if the depth falls below 100 feet. The depths in the Pacific are very different from Alaska. In Alaska, the water was often 500 to 1,000 feet deep fifty yards offshore. Right now, we are 8 nm offshore, and the water is 139.8 feet deep. The responsibility of the person in the helm chair is simply to monitor the electronics for any deviation from the expected while watching for logs, crab traps, little boats, or any other unexpected obstruction in our path. A task made even easier by the nonstop music of your choice from the XM satellite. Columbus might not have even stopped in America if cruising had been this comfortable in 1492.

Our weather information is from the XM weather satellite, which has been very accurate and useful since its resurrection at latitude fifty-five degrees north after sleeping through our summer in Alaska, which is out of its range of service.

We will see how we like Grays Harbor and recheck the weather before deciding on our next stop. Astoria, OR, has been recommended as a good time. However, it is inside the infamous Columbia River bar where the Coast Guard does their heavy-weather training by rolling their forty-five-foot boats. So, if we do go there, you can be assured that it won't be on a rapidly ebbing tide! This NW cruising is *very* different and far more challenging than the East Coast variety.

Always Friday's GPS odometer just tuned past 5,000 nm of travel since we left Dana Point last May. We are a little over halfway through our journey. Somehow, with Alaska almost 1,000 miles behind us, it feels like 90 percent of the excitement is lost in our wake, but maybe Baja and the Caribbean will temper the absence of my favorite place on earth.

I hope so, and I am going to give it a chance.

Fat chance it will equal Alaska!

9/22/2007

Well, it happened again! We are here in Grays Harbor, WA, at Westport Marina. This is one marina that you *don't* want to come into for your first time after dark. After arriving at the entrance buoy last night at sunset, we made our way into the marina with the necessary help of every toy on board. The chart plotter and radar were indispensable, but for the first time, the FLIR really earned its stripes. There is shallow water everywhere, and the maze of red and green lights looks more like Christmas decorations than aids to navigation. But we made it in safely and without incident, tying up among the hundreds of fishing boats in search of salmon and tuna here at the largest commercial fishing center in Washington.

Our original plans were to leave early Friday for Astoria, but the place looked so interesting that we decided to explore the town and stay for a second night. Today we did just that and found the harbor to be quite interesting and the food very good.

But that's not what I meant by "It happened again!" Here is the story:

I was on the bridge of our boat late this afternoon, putting Rain-X on the windows, when the captain of a large fishing vessel moored at our bow came out of his boat. I seized the opportunity to talk to him, and soon we were discussing his recent adventures as well as ours. He was Captain Carl Nish, the owner of the F/V *Lydorein*, a seventy-two-foot tuna boat that has been in his family since its construction in 1965. His father commissioned her, and Carl had been on board for the last forty years. He caught his first tuna at age seven! Four generations of their family had fished the boat, and Carl's grandson seems set to continue the family tradition for years to come.

After talking for a while, Carl accepted my invitation to come see *Always Friday* but asked that even before his visit, we join him and his crew on board *Lydorein* for dinner! You know my response, so Kathy and I stepped off *Always Friday* and onto *Lydorein* for yet another adventure into the world of commercial fishing and the men who earn their livelihoods at sea.

Carl and his family are among the small group of tuna fishermen that still catch their fish one at a time, by a pole and lure. You may have seen the technique on TV (and you may see more of that soon).

The technique is simple and effective. You simply find the fish by circling birds, depth sounder, or forward-looking sonar. Then the fun begins! They take live anchovies, previously caught by net from their tender, and throw them to the fish to lure them into a feeding frenzy behind the boat. Then they take fiberglass poles about fifteen feet long with twenty feet of heavy line attached to a single barbless hook behind an artificial swimming bait and toss the lure into the mass of frenzied tuna behind the boat. When one takes the bait, a strong-backed crewmen muscles the fifteen-to-thirty-pound albacore out of the water and over his shoulder, then onto the deck. The barbless hook falls out, the lure is swung right back into the water for another tuna, and another crewman puts the fish onto the conveyer belt that dumps the fish into zero-degree brine in the hold. That's tuna fishing the old way! Far different than the long liners who string out miles of baited hooks, returning to winch in the hooked tuna from the depths.

Carl took me over every inch of the boat, explaining every aspect of the profession that his family has embraced for four generations. In fact, I found the brine in the hold to be a fascinating example of applied physical chemistry. I was a chemistry major in college but thought that I would *never* use anything I was taught in Physical Chemistry 390. I was right for thirty-nine years, but at the fourth decade of non-use, I have now been proven wrong!

I noticed fifty-pound bags of salt stacked on the deck but was not aware of its use until Carl explained to me how they fill the fish hold with seawater, and then add salt to increase the salinity dramatically. The purpose of the salt is to lower the freezing point of the water. I distinctly remember that there is an equation for computing the degree of the freezing point lowering based on the amount of solute (salt) added to the water by volume. But I sure don't remember the equation from forty years ago.

After adding enough salt to lower the freezing point of water from thirty-two degrees to zero degrees, the freshly caught tuna are put into the tank directly from the sea. Within a few minutes, the fish are frozen solid while still suspended in liquid water that is thirty-two degrees colder than ice. Carl explained that the fish are frozen whole rather than gutted because if gutted, the brine solution would permeate the fish. If left completely intact, the fishes skin blocks the absorption of the salt solution, and the meat remains fresh and salt-free! Amazing technology that allows them to stay at sea for as long as six months before delivering the flash-frozen tuna to market.

Although the boat is nearing a half century of fishing all over the world, it looks almost like new. The boat represents Carl's family's heritage, and its condition reflects the fact that nothing will ever replace personal and family pride. After enjoying a world-class meal of steak and tuna cooked on the deck of *Lydorein*, Carl then offered to give me his "secret" tuna spots in Southern Californian and Mexican waters that he and his family have fished for years. It seemed to me that they were very close to giving us a copy of his family Bible, but I was very happy to leave armed with such valuable information, garnered from four decades of tuna fishing in the waters we will enter later this fall.

So, yet again, we have had the good fortune of making a good friend in the fishing industry. Carl and the F/V *Lydorein* have been added to the ever-growing list of wonderfully friendly people we have met on our trip, and I am now a self-professed expert on pole-caught albacore tuna fishing.

To see Carl and the tuna fishermen in action, you may go to http://www.americantuna.com/ to watch the video of their techniques. If you miss that opportunity, you may get another chance to see the *Lydorein* in action on TV! The producers of *The Deadliest Catch* have made a test segment starring their boat with a strong probability that the pole fishermen may soon be the stars of their own TV series.

So, maybe I was wrong. There may still be life after Alaska. There sure was last night!

9/24/2007

We are now safely moored in Astoria, OR, after a nine-hour trip today through some of the most challenging cruising areas of the Northwest. In sharp contrast to most East Coast cruising, here it takes significant planning and preparation to safely traverse the bars that guard the few havens from the Pacific's potential fury. In fact, the first decision is the classic one of go or no-go. That one kept us in Grays Harbor for the past three days as NW winds beat the entrance bar into a ten-foot frenzy. But last night's review of XM Weather and buoyweather.com suggested that today would be a "go" day.

A call to the Grays Harbor Coast Guard station both last night and again this morning confirmed that the bar was now open to vessels over thirty feet long. The current tables dictated that we leave about 7 AM to avoid the dreaded ebb tides at the bar. When the ebbing tides meet the incoming ocean swells, confused and violent seas of more than forty feet can develop in minutes during storms. Even when conditions appear favorable, such tidal conditions can spawn seas more than ten feet, although surrounded by calm seas both in front of and behind the violence at the bar. All good reasons to carefully time your exit from these NW ports.

In 1933, a sudden storm on the Grays Harbor bar sank fifteen fishing vessels and killed eighteen crewmen. The memorials are there to read at the docks . . . and there is room for still more names. Once you clear the bar on the outbound leg, your challenges have just begun. You must compute your time/distance equation to arrive at the Columbia River bar at a point when passage is associated with a high probability of survival. This bar is considered the most dangerous one in North America, having swallowed up over 2,000 ships and drowned over 700 seamen since those records were first kept.

If that were not enough to get your attention, the turning point is near Cape Disappointment. If that sounds familiar, it may be because the Coast Guard school for rough-weather boat handling is there. They routinely and intentionally roll their forty-five-foot rescue boats 360 degrees while training in these deadly waters! As we approached Cape Disappointment, I called the Astoria CG station on the VHF for a bar report and heard that the bar was open until 4 PM with waves of "only" six to eight feet at present (building quickly to about ten feet at 4 PM when the ebb tide built to near maximum flow). It gets your attention when the CG suggests that you wear life jackets when crossing the bar.

We hit the entrance buoy just right and lined up the visual range to ensure the correct course into the Columbia. Because the seas would be rolling in from behind us, we had closed the storm locks on the rear salon door and lazarette door and fired up the wing engine to ensure its availability should we either lose the main engine or need more power in the currents. Neither of these precautions had ever crossed my mind in Alaska, and you are more likely to be struck by lightning than for the John Deere engine to quit, but this Columbia River bar is in a class by itself, and certainly more challenging than any entry I had ever attempted.

As we entered the bar, Kathy was in the salon with her Nikon in hand to record for posterity the monstrous swells that were supposed to chase us into either Davey Jones locker or Astoria. But alas! A combination of good fortune, good planning, and a good boat carried us through the burial grounds of 2,000 ships with nothing more than a few insignificant deviations from our plotted course.

An hour later, we were tied up in the West Mooring Basin under the bridge in downtown Astoria. A quick walk through town supported our decision to leave early tomorrow morning for Tillamook Bay, another challenging entry over a bar that again justifies the constant presence of the Coast Guard. So, tonight, it will be several hours bent over the XM Weather, the Douglass cruising guide, tide and current tables, and the Nobeltec chart plotter in preparation for an exit over the Columbia River bar at about 6 AM, a 40 nm run down the coast, and yet another date with a bar strewn with the wrecks of boats that took the entry for granted.

It sounds scary, but with a boat like *Always Friday*, equipped as she is, it can be made very safe and almost routine *if* you recognize the potential dangers and mitigate them with acquired knowledge, careful planning, and reasonable execution. There is a certain beauty in the turmoil of turbulent seas. Some might not, but I really enjoy the challenge!

9/25/2007

We are safely moored in Tillamook Bay Marina after leaving Astoria ninety minutes before daybreak to hit the Columbia River bar at slack water. The computations worked well, and after a routine radar run through the bar, we were in the open Pacific and on our way south! Outside the bar, the seas were calm except for slow, rhythmic swells reflecting oceanic violence of some many miles to the west. I frequently adjusted the throttle as the computer gave us our ETA to Tillamook Bay, changing as boat speeds varied with the current. The goal was to hit the entrance buoy at 12:36 PM, and we marked our arrival at 12:34 PM. Nobletec is amazing!

With a reputation almost as notorious as the Columbia River, Tillamook's bar represents a formidable challenge on good days and a deadly threat on bad days. Just last year, eleven lives were lost at the bar when a charter boat rolled in heavy seas that the crew had been advised not to challenge. As if Mother Nature had not made the test difficult enough, with waves breaking on the rock jetties on either side, there must have been a hundred boats filling the area in response to the presence of king salmon. It was if we had been asked to walk through an anthill without stepping on an ant. After blowing several boats out of the water with the Kahlenberg air horn, we successfully navigated the inlet and proceeded uneventfully to the harbor.

Tillamook is a quaint little fishing town, internationally known for its cheese and now alive with salmon fever! The season that has been over in Alaska since late June is just getting started here. The salmon will be center stage for the next several months, and the fishermen are awaiting them in earnest.

As *Always Friday* came to the dock, the "big yellow boat" again caught the attention of most everyone there. Apparently, such boats don't come here often, in no small part because of the bar. As we tied the lines, I asked a fisherman just returning to our dock about the local fishing scene. We struck up a conversation, and I learned that Bruce had recently retired here from the lumber adhesive industry to fish to his heart's content. He was very interested in *Always Friday*, and of course I invited him on board. He was so impressed with the boat that he later brought his wife Toni by to see it . . . *and* invited us to join them for dinner at their favorite restaurant. *Always Friday* had done it again!

Strangers in Oregon no more, we now had friends to show us the sights. Although salmon and halibut were heavily represented on the menu, I took the opportunity to try, for the first time in my life, broiled sturgeon. They are caught right here in this freshwater river, occasionally growing more than a thousand pounds.

The meal was great, and the company even better. By the end of the night, *Always Friday* had been discussed so thoroughly and received so well that there was only one more thing to do: invite Bruce to join us for tomorrow's trip to Newport! So, we are off to Newport early tomorrow morning with the privilege of Bruce's company on *Always Friday*'s bridge. It never ceases to amaze me how few of the nice people on this earth I had gotten to know in my life until this trip. With *Always Friday*'s help, we have made quite a dent in that list of missed opportunities this year.

9/27/2007

We arrived last night in Newport at precisely the correct time for a safe crossing of the bar. Newport has the well-deserved reputation as the easiest bar to cross in this area of the Washington-Oregon coast. It is a great combination of long jetties and a wide entrance, and it is the only bar I have seen up here that I would cross at night. A call to the Coast Guard on the VHF confirmed that the bar was unrestricted (their word for open to all comers), and we cruised in at slack tide with no trouble.

We moored at the marina just under a beautiful bridge, and Bruce's wife, Toni, was there to meet us all, ostensibly to take Bruce back to Tillamook after his short adventure with us. However, we had other plans! We had enjoyed Bruce's company so much, and he was so impressed with the boat, that it seemed only right for both Toni and Bruce to accompany us on the 80 nm leg to Coos Bay so she could see how much fun cruising could be. Every excuse for their not going evaporated under the pressure of our logic, and Toni agreed to become a cruiser for a day. But the night was young, and they took us for dinner (again!) at a local seafood shack that epitomized the term *local seafood*. It was excellent, as was the company.

This morning the currents again dictated our departure time, and the news was cruel! We were underway over an hour before daybreak at 5:45 AM to hit the Coos Bay bar at slack tide. Kathy, Raleigh, Binky, and Toni appeared from below around 9 AM. The sunrise was beautiful, and the ride was smooth except for slow, rolling swells from the NW again. A surprise was the fog that engulfed us throughout the latter part of the trip, restricting the visibility to approximately a quarter mile. But no problem! With all the electronics on board *Always Friday*, you could put blankets over her windows and not slow her down. Our goal was to hit the entrance bar at 3:30 PM, and we turned in at . . . 3:30 PM! The bar was wide but still challenging in the thick fog, but the radar confirmed the channel defined by buoys, and we arrived safely—to a full marina.

As had been the case so often this summer, potentially adequate room for us was wasted by boats moored without regard to optimizing the available space. From the bridge, we asked a commercial fishing captain if he might pull his boat forward, and he said, "Happy to!" A nice surprise. Another private boat owner had already offered to move his boat back, so adequate space materialized from the willingness of the two captains to let us in at the transient dock. We are now safely moored, possibly for three to four days if the gale from the NW makes its presence known tonight. If the weather holds for another day, we may make the short run to Bandon, OR, (the home of the famous golf courses at Bandon Dunes) tomorrow, and then stay there for the weekend as the storm blows by. The XM Weather equipment has served us very well in this area where bad weather can quickly threaten your life.

Bruce and Toni have left us for Tillamook, hopefully with an enjoyable experience under their belts after their short time on *Always Friday*. Since Bruce has recently retired, his schedule is dictated only by king salmon and Toni, so it may well be that we will see them again. They are building a home in Cabo San Lucas and might be there when we pass through that area later this year. *Always Friday* is an attraction at every port, and new friends like Toni and Bruce continue to be unexpected bonuses that have sprung from our new home on the water.

9/29/2007

Hello from Coos Bay! That salutation may be appropriate for most of the next week.

A major weather system is moving this way, and buoyweather.

com says that the Pacific is not going to live up to its name for the next week. In fact, I got a call this afternoon from Carl Nish, our new friend and commercial tuna fishing captain on board F/V *Lydorein* whom we met and enjoyed company with in Grays Harbor last week. Carl called from offshore to tell us that they were running back into the harbor to avoid the storm that has us tied up in Coos Bay.

When Carl goes out, he stays out for months at a time. For him to come in with only twenty-five tons of newly caught albacore on board confirms that he thinks that a heck of a storm is on the way. His call was to invite us on board *Lydorein* if we were still in Westport Marina. I quickly suggested that he turn south and join *Always Friday* in Oregon, but he was already within 12 nm of Grays Harbor, killing time until the ebb tide subsided so he could cross the bar there. So, if a boat more than twice the displacement of *Always Friday*, run by longtime, very knowledgeable professional fishermen, is running before this storm for port, you can bet that *Always Friday* is here for the duration.

Last night, while others were closed in their boats, I wandered the docks, talking to the fishermen here with their classic NW fishing boats docked in Coos Bay. The captain of the *Glass Slipper* was very interested in our boat and could not have been nicer to talk to. When I told him that we were considering a run to Bandon today, he listened to my logic and then suggested that if I followed that path, it would be a safe run, but I might be stuck behind that bar for days longer than if we stayed in Coos Bay. So, with that observation from an old man of the sea who has fished out of this harbor for forty years, our plans changed to "Stay put in Coos Bay." You will never find anyone more receptive to local knowledge than I am! There is no place for ego or poor judgment on the coast of the NW Pacific. This is one unforgiving place.

We have discovered one diversion that has us occupied to some degree: this place appears to be the crabbing center of the world. The dock is lined with people in lawn chairs pulling Dungeness and red crabs out of the water by the dozens. It seems so easy that Kathy and I thought we might join the crabbing crowd. We had our trap, but no bait. So off we went to the tackle shop.

You will never guess what they use for bait around here! I'll give you a hint: there is a big market in furs here, and mink farms abound. You guessed it! When the mink is sent for the big sleep so that women can go to the opera in style, their worldly bodies are saved from the fires of the city dump to be sold for crab bait. So, we bought one, or at least half of one; that's the way they are sold: cut in half. I requested the front half for our purchase. If there was an afterlife for mink, ours would have his eyes available so he could duck when a crab came after him.

So far, we have caught several dozen crabs, and our bait looks none the worse for wear. I think that he is probably putting that ducking option to good use. If the bait holds up overnight, I may go buy the back half of the mink so if a sea lion goes after him, he will have all four legs to run away. I am trying to be sensitive to his needs since they do not seem to have been a priority to anyone else in his previous life.

That's it from Coos Bay. Not much going on (as you can see from the mink story).

10/01/2007

A stormy and lazy but interesting day in Coos Bay harbor. The gale flag is flying, and the rough-bar warning is flashing rhythmically from the shore adjacent to the harbor's exit and our berth at the pier. The harbor is now filled with commercial fishing boats that would not be here if they had a rational choice, for now is a prime fishing time for salmon and albacore. We have watched four tuna boats, gill netters, and power trollers, all greater than seventy feet in length and twice the displacement of *Always Friday*, return from the sea today after finding the ocean too dangerous for anything but running for the safety of shore. One of the boats tried to get into a slip for over an hour before giving up to the wind and resigning itself to circling the harbor until the wind abates.

Even though it is raining heavily and blowing enough to make the antennas sing, we can still hear the surf from the bar as it pounds the rocks of the jetty. This is the NW coast that has earned its reputation as a burial ground for boats and their crews, and these are the kind of days that spawned that fear and respect among mariners.

As on all the bars we have passed through since leaving the Strait of Juan de Fuca, the Coast Guard has a station here with a forty-five-foot patrol boat on constant duty in anticipation of trouble on the bar or at sea. These are the boats designed to roll 360 degrees in rough water and continue their mission. We have watched them pass *Always Friday* several times per day as they head into weather that others are warned to avoid. I continue to be amazed at their willingness to put their lives on the line for others.

Of all days, STARZ was playing *The Guardian* on satellite TV, and we watched it while moored within a few hundred yards of Coos Bay Coast Guard Station with the real men (not actors) waiting there for a call from the sea! After watching the movie, Kathy decided to make them some hot chocolate and cookies in hopes that they might recognize how much they are appreciated by those who they watch over at sea. In my opinion, they are dramatically underappreciated by the citizens of our country.

Yesterday, we watched the tuna boats unload their catch of albacore and talked at length with a retired fisher who now spends his days filleting fish for the markets. He is a magician with his knife, leaving almost no meat on the skeleton after completing his work. As he cleaned the fish, five or six harbor seals and two gigantic sea lions (over a half ton each) circled below his cleaning station, awaiting the scraps. The sea lions had no interest in the boney skeletons but would not let an ounce of boneless meat get by them when tossed into the harbor.

As he worked, he made us aware of a startling bit of news we had not heard before. When we walk Raleigh and Binky down the dock, we are essentially trolling for sea lions with them as bait! More than once here at this harbor, barking dogs have attracted the attention of hungry sea lions and precipitated an aggressive attack; the massive creatures leaped from the water onto the dock, grabbed the hapless dogs, and slid back into the water to enjoy their snack.

Having spent the summer protecting our dogs from Alaskan eagles, bears, and wolves, we thought that we had returned to the safety of the lower forty-eight, but *nooo*. Raleigh and Binky are still on the menu at the NW Coast Diner. So, we will remain diligent in our protection of our little family members—and take a few mink bodies with us to divert the attention of any hungry sea lion that might look their way. One thing is for sure: this isn't Virginia Beach!

It is obvious that we will not be leaving here tomorrow, as the bar report reflects ten-foot, steep breaking seas over the bar. Again, it is closed to all vessels less than forty-five feet, and all others are required to wear life vests if they choose to challenge the seas (we won't). And that's just the bar!

Offshore, the seas are ten to fifteen feet. We can do that. We have done that. But we won't do that when we have a choice not to. My goal is to keep the sea lions as the most dangerous threat that we face.

10/04/2007

Always Friday is in California! We crossed the line just south of Brookings, OR, and are now moored in Crescent City, CA. It is a sleepy little fishing and crabbing center with almost no pleasure boats to be seen. However, it has one very important point in its favor: obvious personal pride in their fishing fleet. Ninety percent of the commercial boats look like they were just painted, and almost all are beautifully maintained. There is no reason to take such care of working boats other than personal pride, since a clean boat shouldn't catch any more fish than a rusty one. I, for one, really admire that in an owner. And not just in boats. I must admit that I have an admiration for the eighteen-wheel-truck driver when I see his rig all bright and shiny by his own hand. But the rarity of private boats here has not stopped the crowds that have come down to the dock to see the "big yellow boat from Virginia"! We are now the stars of multiple cell phone photographs, and certainly the topic of conversation among the locals.

The weather looks favorable for at least another day of running in small-craft warnings before the gale catches us from the NW. If it does, you can be assured that we will be safely moored somewhere out of harm's way. But all is not dull here in the NW.

There is going to be a personal celebration on the Pacific sometime next week. It won't make the newspapers or evening news. In fact, no more than a half dozen people will see or feel the significance of the occasion that represents a milestone of this summer. What is that event? The *Lilly Pad* and *Always Friday* will pass on reciprocal headings somewhere off the Pacific Coast as we both head home for the winter. See, I told you it wouldn't stir fiery emotions among the public.

It all goes back to Dana Point where Kathy, Raleigh, Binky, and I took delivery of *Always Friday* last spring. In what turned out to be the first of many close friendships our boat has given us, John and Debbie Marshall were commissioning their NH 55, *Serendipity*, alongside our boat. John had been in contact with a prospective NH 55 buyer who expressed an interest in riding up the coast in one of the boats before committing to a purchase so he could "see how it handles rough weather." I distinctly remember those words, and we laugh about them every time we talk or get together. Well, John had committed to a professional delivery crew for his ride to Victoria, so he gave the buyer my name as a prospective ride up the coast.

I remember our first phone call as one in which he related the fact that he had been a military pilot and had cruised the Seattle area extensively. So far, very good! When his personality shined through over the phone, and he confirmed that he was a nonsmoker and didn't drink at sea, I had me a bridge partner for the first 1,100 miles of our adventure to Alaska.

Don Weipert turned out to be a perfect partner for the trip. He was knowledgeable, capable, and full of stories of his piloting days that made those long hours of a nonstop run to Victoria not only tolerable but even very enjoyable.

The northbound trip to Canada in the spring is well known as the near-ultimate challenge of cruising boats. You can be sure that you will have the wind, the waves, the swells, and the currents directly in your face every foot to the way, and the winds always rise to twenty-plus knots or more in the afternoon as the inland deserts heat up for the summer, drawing the wind from the sea. If you have an interest, you may go back to the updates of late May to see the details of what we experienced. The weather was horrible, even worse than usual for that time of year. The insurance company had "suggested" that we take a delivery captain for the first 1,000 miles of the trip to further familiarize us with the new boat. Well, we did, and he lay incapacitated by seasickness on the floor of the boat for several days, unable to move from his position locked around the pedestal of the salon table. If he had charged by his value to us, he would have owed us change from a nickel.

So, Don and I drove the boat twenty-four hours per day while Kathy kept us fed and happy through one of the great adventures of the summer. Every day, the forecast was for improving weather, and every day, it seemed to get worse. The standard winds were twenty-plus knots directly on the bow, and then came the gale off Cape Mendocino! One night (it couldn't have happened in daylight and given the same effect), the winds began to howl so loudly through the antennas that it was difficult to talk over the noise as we sat side by side on the bridge! The Airmar weather machine registered forty-five-plus knots (about 50 mph), and Don got his wish to see how the boat handled rough weather... in trumps! We both sat in amazement as the boat pitched into the seas but, essentially, did not roll, thanks to the stabilizers' almost magical contribution to the adventure.

If you go back to the photo gallery of the trip, you will see pictures of both of us at the helm during the storm. At the time of the pictures, the seas were reported at fifteen feet with frequent twenty-footers, and we watched many breaks over the bridge windows as swells went by well above our heads, more than twenty feet above the waterline. Don's comfort level was strained at best since his previous boating experiences would have led to a mayday call for Coast Guard rescue under such circumstances. But that night, we remained comfortable, cozy, and safe on *Always Friday*'s bridge.

The night was punctuated by multiple calls and emails from Lilly, his wife and expectant widow, who was following the weather on the internet, informing Don that he was obviously in a life-threatening situation with a small probability of survival. I of course tried to make her feel better by informing her that if we went down, it would be quick, and they would never find a trace of the boat in this longtime burial ground for ships.

Neither Don nor Lilly was amused by my lighthearted assessment. But *Always Friday* trudged on, generating growing confidence in all of us (except the incapacitated delivery captain) that this boat was *amazing* in heavy seas. A few days later, we arrived safely in Victoria, BC, none the worse for wear. Lilly was ecstatic to see Don in one piece, having given up on any chance for his survival at sea under conditions the boat had taken in stride. The delivery captain was gone even before the boat was securely tied, never (hopefully) to be seen again.

Remember that Don's motivation for joining us at sea was to

"see how it handles rough weather"? His assessment will come motoring by us sometime next week as he pilots his own Nordhavn 55, *Lilly Pad*, up the coast to his home port in Seattle.

So, we will be watching the AIS monitors and radars for confirmation that these two boats will cross paths in the mighty Pacific Ocean. If weather and circumstances allow, we hope to rendezvous at sea for a brief celebration of the friendships and adventures that lie behind us... and hopefully ahead, thanks to our Nordhavn 55s.

10/05/2007

We left Crescent City yesterday (Thursday) morning in small-craft warnings that did not faze *Always Friday*. The outbound bar was easily passable, and the seas were unsettled with the wind from the south. The goal was to get to Eureka, CA, at slack high tide to avoid the wrath of one of the most infamous bars on the NW coast. Since our departure time from Crescent City and arrival time in Eureka were nonnegotiable for safety's sake, the only variable under our control was our speed over ground (a simple time/distance equation: 60 nm in eight hours required an average SOG of 7.5 knots). So, we chugged along at 7.5 knots, with Nobeltec confirming our ETA at near slack flood tide.

As we came closer to the Humboldt bar guarding the entry into Eureka, the VHF came alive every quarter hour or so with notices from the Coast Guard station at Humboldt Bay, warning all interested mariners (us!) that the bar was presently closed secondary to breaking waves of over ten feet between the narrow jetties. The fact that those conditions were occurring at maximum ebbing tide suggested that things should be much more acceptable when we arrived about four hours later at a flood tide. When the tide is going out, the fresh water rushing out of the rivers meets head-on the ocean swells coming into the inlet. The result is the same as if a 255-pound linebacker had collided at the line with a 240-pound fullback—they both are pushed into an upright position, and neither moves forward or backward. Over the bar, that same collision generates a standing wave, sometimes measuring up to forty feet in height! Those are why the ships and crews lost on these bars over the last several centuries number well into the thousands.

Over the next few hours, multiple calls from *Always Friday* to the Coast Guard confirmed that conditions were improving with the onset of the flood tide. For the last hour of our trip, we slowed to 4.8 knots (900 rpm and 2.3 gph) to hit the tide just right. The CG confirmed that the bar had been declared safely passable by a boat of our size, and we began the complicated approach to the bar only after we had complied with the CG's "request" that we don life jackets for the brief run over the bar. Kathy disappeared for a few minutes, returning with Raleigh and Binky all decked out in their own West Marine doggy life jackets!

For those of you who are pilots, the approach to the bar is very much like a complicated non-precision approach to minimums in a crosswind. It begins with a 110-degree turn eastward from a southerly heading after having crossed the apparent entry vector into the inlet if you used only visual cues. That leaves you angling into the inlet with the swells trying to push you toward the jetties. Once you hit the head of the inlet, a starboard turn of about thirty degrees rescues you from a heading that would otherwise violently introduce you to the rocks. With Kathy constantly suggesting that we prematurely "turn right," we followed the published approach . . . and much to Kathy's surprise, cruised in uneventfully.

It was, I am glad to say, an anticlimactic end to a harrowing crossing of the Humboldt bar. We have traversed nine of them here in the NW for a total of seventeen passages to date (we still must leave Humboldt to complete our bar experiences). Of all the things we have done this spring, summer, and fall, the experiences on the bars are the ones that I would least like to repeat. There has never been a passage that I felt was unsafe, but neither has there been one that I enjoyed. For any who might follow our path in the future, it is my strong opinion that they should always be avoided during ebbing tides or at night. These things are challenging enough when everything is in your favor. Tilt the odds towards the bars, and they will, sooner or later, *win*. You can make a strong argument that the most prudent decision would be to run straight through from San Francisco to Victoria and avoid the bars all together.

So, we are safely in Eureka for the night—and probably several more, in view of thirty-five-knot winds moving this way and seas that make travel not unsafe but clearly uncomfortable.

10/07/2007

If you were to dock in Eureka, CA, for the night, and find yourself there for yet another day before departing for Bodega Bay, your memories, if any, would be of a boring, sleepy little town with one mediocre restaurant within walking distance of the docks, unless you met Tony Carter! Good fortune put us on the same dock Tony has lived on since returning from Mexico last year. I caught him on the deck of his old wooden boat and complimented him on the beauty of M/V *Coast Pilot*, with "1944" neatly painted on the stack.

From our first conversation, it was obvious that Tony is a special kind of man. As we talked, his past came alive in fascinating conversation that riveted us for two days and nights in Eureka. Tony is a retired long-haul tugboat owner-operator with about five decades of experience at sea. His profession took him all over the world to every continent multiple times, encompassing millions of miles and over *eighty trips* through the Panama Canal.

But Tony is not what you would expect—he is much more!

He struck me as a highly intelligent, witty, true gentleman, self-educated in maritime history, as well as a connoisseur of the performing arts. He went to the Eureka Symphony the only night of the three that we did not capture his attention. He has been an advisor to many of the West Coast maritime museums and can keep you enthralled with discussions of the "old days at sea" for hours. And his boat! You would have to see it to appropriately appreciate it. The M/V *Coast Pilot* began its life in 1944 as a military utility tug of sixty-four feet with an eighteen-foot beam and a seven-foot draft, constructed of wood. Upon his retirement, Tony bought the boat (one of two known survivors of the fourteen originally built for the government) and rebuilt her completely into a cruising yacht capable of worldwide travel. He has just returned from a year or so in Mexico and is contemplating a trip to Maine before long.

As he showed us every foot of the boat, his pride in her shown through brightly and contagiously. Not only was the little ship beautifully designed and reconstructed into yacht status, but even more impressively, the interior was accentuated with historically significant marine artifacts and artwork, as well as personal mementoes of his decades at sea. It is a beautiful little floating marine museum that would hold anyone interested in the sea spellbound for hours.

But *Coast Pilot*, as impressive as she is, played second fiddle to Tony. Within ten minutes of meeting him, we had invited him to join us at the local seafood restaurant for our first night in Eureka. When he learned that thirty-plus-knot winds were going to keep us in the harbor for at least another day, he suggested that we join him on a tour of the area in his twenty-three-year-old Mercedes diesel sedan that has been kept just as well as his boat. So, the next morning, Raleigh and Binky were left in charge of *Always Friday* while Kathy and I joined Tony for an enlightening tour of the local area, unavailable to the average tourist or transient boater.

The first day, we went through the town of Eureka, with beautiful

Victorian homes that reflect the days in which logging was the gold of this area. The homes are beautifully maintained, freshly painted, big-scale dollhouses with all the decorations usually found only on gingerbread houses at Christmas time. These people obviously lived very well when timber was king. On the Eureka waterfront was moored the M/V *Mataket*, the oldest licensed tour boat in the country. She has been immaculately maintained (and/or restored) for the past century, and still takes passengers down the Humboldt River daily. In fact, Tony occasionally serves as her captain when the regular crew is unavailable for any reason.

So, Eureka is a little town that time has passed by as logging fell into disfavor for economic and environmental reasons, but its citizens continue to pump life into the town as their labors of love allow the beauty to persist without an economic base to replace the logging industry that went the way of the lumberjacks. With Tony, we saw it all: the   of the river deltas (that spawn the terrible bars of the NW) and the magnificent Pacific Ocean vistas visible from Highway 101. Kathy was in heaven as we stopped in the little shops that dotted the towns along the way. Perhaps the highpoint of her two days on the road with Tony was a visit to the town square of Acadia, CA, for the weekly open market. The town has become a favorite haunt of those who have made California famous. "Unusual" people were there in profusion, and tomatoes and celery were probably not the only plants you could buy if you knew the "right" people and looked appropriate for the purchase.

As a sixty-one-year-old, gray-haired guy in khaki pants and an *Always Friday* embossed shirt, I was not deemed a probable purchaser and was approached only by those offering eternal salvation. I turned that opportunity down; if I go to heaven, I want it to be in Alaska! To top it all off, on the afternoon before we left, Tony sat down with me for over an hour and reviewed the nautical charts from Eureka to the Panama Canal, offering many bits of valuable information known only to those who have traveled that coast many times over many years. At least 75 percent of his enlightenment is not even mentioned in the cruising guides I have used heavily over the past months and will use constantly until we return home.

On the night before our departure, we invited Tony on board *Always Friday* for a halibut dinner from our Glacier Bay freezer stock. After a most enjoyable evening, Tony presented us with a travel DVD of Mexico and Central America that he had found informative and valuable for review before visiting there.

So, another serendipitous friendship has added immensely to the enjoyment of our cruising experience. When Tony arose early just to say goodbye and throw us the dock lines from *Always Friday* as we left Eureka, our last words to him expressed our sincere hope that we cross paths again in some ocean sometime soon. Tony Carter and *Coast Pilot*—more gifts to us from *Always Friday* during the trip of a lifetime.

10/13/2007

We left Eureka, CA, at midmorning on Sunday the seventh to catch the slack tide for our eighteenth and last trip over the treacherous bars of the NW. Again, with appropriate planning and acceptable weather, the bar passage was easy and anticlimactic. Three hours later, on an ebbing tide, it could be the trip from hell. Such are the bar experiences on the coasts of Washington, Oregon, and California—very good reasons to run nonstop along this thousand-mile coastline! The trip from Eureka to Bodega Bay was to be our first overnight trip with just the two of us on board. We had carefully chosen a weather window that would give us an excellent chance for a smooth passage, and we got just that.

The degree of automation in *Always Friday*'s navigational equipment allows us to set a guard perimeter on radar that alerts us to the entry of any radar target into an area six miles in diameter. The ARPA (automatic radar plotting assistance) plots the expected course of any target that shows up on the screen, while AIS (automatic identification of ships) identifies and plots the position and course of all similarly equipped vessels within approximately twenty-five miles of us. The Nobeltec chart plotter is set for our course to our destination, and a quick look at the chart display should confirm that *Always Friday* is on the expected course line. So, Kathy's responsibilities are condensed to awakening me if anything on the screens or instruments concerns her at all. It has worked very well, and we are very comfortable with traveling under such circumstances.

We timed our overnight run to arrive just after daybreak in Bodega Bay, and our plans worked to perfection. Approximately fifteen minutes after daylight, we were off Bodega Head for the entry into the narrow run into the harbor . . . in fog so thick that you could not see more than fifty yards. I had run that channel twice before on our way north and knew it to be a relatively easy radar run, so we proceeded inbound with the foghorn announcing our presence, much to Binky's dismay. A half hour later, we were safely moored at Spud Point Marina. Don Weipert's NH 55, *Lilly Pad*, was still well south of us but destined to join us in Bodega Bay about twenty hours later.

Before we had even completed the tie-down process, I looked up to see a friendly-looking guy with a Nikon around his neck who offered to assist us with the tie-up of *Always Friday*. He was Chris Lauritzen, a weekend resident of the town with a beautiful home on the waterfront. He later told us that he had looked up from his porch to see the boat of his dreams coming into the harbor and had hurried down to the docks to get some pictures!

Chris is not your usual dock wanderer. His family has been in the California towboat industry for a century, and he has been an integral part (now the owner and harbormaster) of his family's marina in Oakley, CA, for almost fifty years.

In no time, Chris had accepted our invitation to come aboard for the full tour. To reciprocate, after securing *Always Friday*, he took us on a tour of the town and surrounding area. A ride to the cliffs overlooking the shoreline yielded not only breathtaking views of the Pacific crashing onto the California coast but also the chance to see three trophy deer, wild turkeys, and a covey of California quail. Unseen but present were the mountain lions that we were once again told represent real threats to Raleigh and Binky if we walk them in the area. A tour of Chris's home fronting on Bodega Bay was followed by his joining us for a seafood meal at his favorite local restaurant, all of which would have gone undiscovered without Chris's hospitality.

When he asked of our plans for the southbound trip after Bodega Bay, I told him of our lack of success in getting a slip in Sausalito or San Francisco within the next few days. One phone call to a friend in San Francisco had us a slip at Pier 38 adjacent to Market Street in the heart of downtown! He then accepted our offer to join us a few days later for the 60 nm trip under the Golden Gate into San Francisco. But before that experience, we had another highlight of our trip when Kim and Steve Sanford, friends for decades before their move to Atlanta, joined us for a few days into wine country.

Using *Always Friday* as our home base, we took daily trips into Napa, Sonoma, and San Francisco, enjoying the beauty of the vineyards and visiting the wineries of some of the most famous names of the valley. Kim and Steve are very knowledgeable wine connoisseurs and members of several of the finest wine clubs. Their company added immeasurably to our enjoyment of the area. Kathy and Kim's afternoon of shopping allowed Steve and I to enjoy three or four hours of quiet time together, sitting in Border's Book Store, while the women turned Nordstrom's upside down.

For our last night in Bodega Bay, Don and his crew of Paul and Mark from *Lilly Pad* joined the four of us for a great seafood dinner in one of Bodega Bay's best restaurants. The following morning, *Lilly Pad* was northbound for Seattle while Kim and

Steve said goodbye for Atlanta before *Always Friday* left with our new friend Chris on board, bound for the Golden Gate Bridge and San Francisco. The weather forecast was for nothing more than small-craft warnings; however, the seas from Bodega Head to San Francisco Bay were much worse, with twelve-foot, confused seas from both the northwest and south and winds of about thirty knots.

Chris was amazed at how well the boat and autopilot handled such weather and seemed to enjoy a practical demonstration of *Always Friday*'s nav systems under conditions that would keep others in port without contribution to the trip. Upon our arrival at Pier 38, Chris treated us to dinner at his favorite San Francisco restaurant, the Slanted Door, an Asian bistro with a well-deserved local reputation as one of the best in the city, before returning home to prepare for a hunting trip to Utah. His company was a real pleasure and another example of new friends brought to us by *Always Friday*!

Today (Saturday) is a beautiful day in the city, with bright-blue skies and a temperature approaching seventy degrees. We spent the morning at a farmers market near the ferry terminal where the California myth of organic food's superiority pervaded almost every stall. I realize that some strongly believe in the organic craze, but I'm not changing my mind.

This afternoon, we are off to Union Square, then a San Francisco seafood dinner before turning southward again tomorrow for San Diego within the next week. There are many attractive ports between here and there, but the weather will continue to dictate our schedule.

10/14/2007

Saturday afternoon in San Francisco was again dedicated to Kathy's enjoyment of shopping, culminating in her purchase of a purse that defied all economic reason. After consummating that purchase, we caught the Muni to Chinatown at the recommendation of the concierge at Nordstrom's for a world-class Chinese dinner at the R&G Lounge on Kearny Street. It was a place you would not notice in passing unless you saw that the clientele largely comprised affluent Chinese. The food was great and reasonably priced. By 9 PM, we were back on *Always Friday* for the night.

After sleeping relatively late (7:30 AM), we arose to a foggy San Francisco morning with all the must-see sites obscured by the weather. Since we had only a short run to Half Moon Bay, we decided to have breakfast in the harbor and leave about 11 AM. A small restaurant on the harbor, the Java Spot, was a very nice experience with an excellent omelet, made even better by the fact that Paul, the owner, sat with us at our table as he heard of our summer experiences. Paul came to America over fifty years ago from Greece and retired as a traffic engineer some years ago. To keep sane, he opened his harbor-side restaurant about thirty years ago and has been going strong ever since. When he heard of our adventure, he dedicated our breakfast to his efforts to convince us that we should next take *Always Friday* to the Greek Isles! He was an excellent host and an enjoyable guest at our breakfast table.

At 11 AM we were off for the Pacific. The fog only partially obscured the landmarks of San Francisco. In fact, the Golden Gate Bridge was there for our enjoyment, partially cloaked in fog to the degree that the tops of both towers were obscured by the fog, while the roadway of the bridge was clearly visible. Quite a sight!

As we passed under the bridge, I happened to be on the phone in conversation with Jim Hart, one of my best friends in Virginia Beach. He had heard of a continuous minicam that broadcasts on the net everything that happened at the Golden Gate Bridge. As he pulled up the site, we were passing directly under the center of the bridge in view of the camera! What a bonus. Live coverage of our passing under one of the landmarks of the world. Act II will occur when the same opportunity for webcam coverage occurs at the Panama Canal.

Shortly after our arrival in Half Moon Bay, we had the pleasure of meeting Alan and Kristen Spence on board their Amel 53, *Charisma*, moored here next to *Always Friday*. They began their two-year odyssey to New Zealand *today* with an appropriate send-off by friends from the St. Francis Yacht Club in San Francisco. Their homeport is Napa, CA, so you can only imagine how well stocked their wine locker is for the long journey. After a very pleasant visit on board *Charisma*, they agreed to meet us on board *Always Friday* tomorrow night in Monterey Bay where we both anticipate a several-day layover as a storm with seventeen-foot seas blows by.

Tonight, Kathy is grilling a marinated pork tenderloin for our culinary pleasure. She is a truly amazing chef! Raleigh and Binky have an inexhaustible supply of chewies and couldn't be happier. I have never had as much fun in my life.

All is well on *Always Friday as* our adventure continues to flow southward with Mexico in our sights. Life is tough out here on the high seas, but somehow, I will hang in there!

10/16/2007

With a weather forecast predicting one of our nicest days yet on the Pacific, we left Half Moon Bay at 8 AM for the 62 nm trip to Monterey, staying within five miles of the coast all the way. The weatherman was right this time, and the seas were essentially flat for almost the entire trip. As we crossed Monterey Bay, I noticed that the depth sounder was not registering a meaningful number, although at its settings of LF (low frequency) and 75 percent gain, it should have been capable of confirming depths of several thousand feet.

The answer became obvious when I checked Nobletec to find that we were over Monterey Canyon, and the depth was 8,240 feet! I think that was the deepest water we have seen on our trip. The sea life in this area is amazing. Along the way to Monterey, we were frequently entertained by dolphins, seals, and whales, with the number of seals exceeding any we have seen before. I suppose that may be the reason we are in the heart of great white shark country. From Bodega Bay southward to Monterey, the area is frequently closed to surfing or swimming because of the frequency of shark sightings. In fact, it is closed right now after confirmation that the great whites are presently here in large numbers! Other than salmon sharks (a cousin of the great white and just as mean looking) in Icy Strait, Alaska, we haven't seen a shark on our trip.

As we entered Monterey Harbor, we were met with the barking sea lions that at times are difficult to talk over. They are there by the hundreds, frequently lounging on the rocks, buoys, or *boats*. The mooring buoys in the harbor, some measuring six feet across, often are decorated by sea lions sitting on their apex with their heads held high in the air, yielding a mirror image of the classic seal with a ball on his nose. The sea lions have few friends in the harbors of the NW. The creatures, often weighing over a thousand pounds, are infamous for taking over docks, or even sinking boats as they clamber onto the vessels in numbers that exceed the buoyancy of the boat. Their territorial nature justifies in their minds their right to claim your dock, your vessel, or your pet if they so desire (and the state of California is on their side)!

Monterey Harbor is a large marina dominated by the unusual combination of sailboats and commercial fishing vessels. The entry is amazingly tight, something like driving the boat into a tight one-car garage. Our entry was further complicated by the concurrent exit of a children's sailing club, with little twelve-foot boats darting in every direction. Under those circumstances, the right-of-way usually given to sailing vessels gave way to the international rule of Big Boat Goes First, and we safely entered without incident.

Alan and Kristen on their boat S/V *Charisma* arrived just before us after getting an early start at daybreak that morning. As planned, they joined us on *Always Friday*, then for dinner at the Sandbar & Grill, a restaurant so close to the harbor that our window seats looked directly into our boat. Apparently, it is quite unusual for boats of our stature to be in the harbor, for *Always Friday* was the topic of conversation among the restaurant staff and patrons.

The food was excellent and the company even better. Alan and Kristen related the fascinating story of their preparations over the past several years for their trip to New Zealand, including the purchase and rerigging of their fifty-three-foot Amel for the trip. Alan is an industrial engineer in Napa, CA, whose client list has included some of the most famous vineyards in the world. He has been responsible for the infrastructure design and construction of some of the most successful wineries of the area. You can imagine how fascinating our dinner conversation with them was (at least for us). It looks like we will all be here for at least several days as the Pacific storm, now carrying thirty-foot seas, passes through. Monterey is not a bad place to be stuck. We plan to see the world-famous aquarium and visit the many shops and restaurants the town is known for.

And better news—two of our best friends from Virginia, Hank and Dixie Wolf, are in Pasadena and called yesterday to say that they were flying down to join us! Their visit here will dilute our depression over the fact that they could not join us this past summer in Alaska. There is no way to overstate how much the presence of our friends on *Always Friday* has added to our enjoyment of the adventure of a lifetime.

Today we will wander the streets of Monterey, serenaded by the songs of the sea lions. One thing's for sure . . . we aren't in Virginia!

10/19/2007

Monterey is a choice place to be stuck by bad weather, and we are just that. Tonight is our fourth night here, and it looks like we will have two more Monterey nights in our future before the weather breaks for a Monday departure for San Diego. The storm has already hit the ports north of us with a vengeance. I heard from Rod at Emerald Harbor in Seattle that they had winds of over 50 mph in the harbor last night, and Bruce Brevard emailed me today to say that Tillamook, OR, was hit by 70 mph winds today. I can only imagine what that bar must look like now!

The seas are over thirty-five feet high NW of here and are rising to fifteen-plus feet offshore here tomorrow. The surf is beautiful, but even the surfer dudes are on shore right now. The decision to stay in port is an easy one for us and almost everyone else here. I say *almost* everyone else because two guys left here this afternoon in a thirty-five-foot sailboat that the sailors here say was ill equipped for rough weather. While at the fuel docks, we heard them pondering how to make their handheld GPS work. When warned of the coming weather, their response was "You can't sail without wind!" The Coast Guard may need to sleep with one eye open tonight.

The day after our arrival, we spent almost the entire day at the Monterey Aquarium. It is an unbelievable experience and well worth the $50 for two tickets. We wandered the streets of Monterey and enjoyed what we thought were the highlights of the area . . . until Hank and Dixie arrived from Pasadena. They are both avid golfers and frequently play the greatest courses in the world. Within a half hour of their arrival, we were sitting on the veranda of the Lodge at Pebble Beach, overlooking the eighteenth green of one of the most beautiful golf courses in the world.

The bay was amazingly beautiful under blue skies and a bright sun, and my lunch of an open-faced lobster sandwich was almost as memorable as the view. Hank and Dixie then took us through all the shops of Carmel, toured the fantastic residential areas of Pebble Beach and the surrounding courses, and topped it off with a ride down the seventeen miles along the rocky coast, made even more beautiful by the power of the storm that has been pounding the Pacific for days. A great Italian dinner in downtown Carmel was a fitting culmination to a great day with two of our very closest friends.

Before Hank and Dixie had to return to Pasadena, the four of us arose early today to a breakfast of crab omelet, followed by a few more visits to the shops and galleries of Carmel. Our best buys were four Tilley hats, which made us look very much like accomplished mariners.

Tonight, Alan and Kristin from S/V *Charisma* are joining us for dinner at a local Chinese restaurant. Tomorrow, Kathy and I will go exploring in our little Mercedes-Benz rental car that we got on a special offer for $19.99 per day for the weekend (the best deal we have seen in CA).

The weather looks good for our departure for San Diego on Monday. There are at least a half dozen boats here waiting for the weather to break before going south for multiple destinations, including Mexico, the Marquesas, Australia, New Zealand, and (in our case) the Panama Canal. Frank Wilson, my offshore fishing partner for twenty years, will join us Monday for the trip south, ensuring that the freezers will soon again be filled, with salmon and halibut being replaced by tuna and snapper.

Remember Doug and Jeane McPherson from Ketchikan? Doug was the pilot on board the *Noordham* at Marjorie Glacier in Glacier Bay, AK, when the giant iceberg fell from the glacier right in front of us. It looks like he and Jeane may well join us for the trek down the Mexican coast. Their presence will confirm the fact that Alaska is the gift that keeps on giving.

10/22/2007

After a solid week in Monterey, the weather has given us the opportunity to resume our southbound journey. Monterey has been a great place to be "stuck," and we have had some very enjoyable days here. Alan and Kristen Spence of S/V *Charisma* joined us for a day on the coast with lunch in Carmel-by-the-Sea, a beautiful little town that has as its motto "Come for a weekend; stay for a lifetime!" When you see the beauty of the place, such a scenario becomes totally understandable. Kathy found a beautiful oil painting of a maritime scene which we now own as an indelible memory of our trip.

We have seen the Pacific Coast at its best as the fury of the storm presented the rocky shoreline in its most impressive state. Although the East Coast is very impressive during big storms, we don't have the rocky shorelines of the West Coast to accentuate the massive power of the sea.

Frank's arrival here this morning has been unavoidably delayed until the afternoon, so we now plan to be on the open Pacific by 5 PM. The seas are relatively calm at six feet, which *Always Friday* hardly notices, and the forecasts for the waters south of here is very good. However, Mother Nature continues to raise her hand in warning as we move into the Santa Ana winds, which are blowing at hurricane force around Los Angeles, not to mention that our destination city, San Diego, is now on fire!

The usual story of an easy fall passage down the West Coast has not been the case this year. Our schedule is in shambles, but thankfully, it was only written in chalk anyway. Rather than predicting arrival times for any point in our odyssey, our rule is now "We will get there when we get there!" Safety remains our primary concern, and on this coast, Neptune tries to pull you into the depths of his domain a thousand different ways every day.

10/23/2007

Fifteen minutes after Frank's arrival from Virginia, we were on our way out of Monterey Harbor. As Tatem, our favorite server at the Sandbar

& Grill, waved a big goodbye from the window of the restaurant overlooking our berth, we wound through the narrow channel leading to the open ocean. As if Tatem's goodbye had not been enough, the sea lions acknowledged our departure with deafening barking, answered in kind by Binky and Raleigh. By no means an understated exit from one of our favorite California ports so far!

We hit the open ocean just at sunset for a beautiful scene as we turned south for Southern California. Alan and Kristin on S/V *Charisma,* about 65 nm in front of us, reported acceptable seas of about five feet, and a good ride under power. After dinner, Frank and I spent several hours going over the electronic systems on board *Always Friday* in anticipation of his taking a watch on the upcoming all-night runs. He and I have been fishing together for twenty-five years, and he is a very experienced boatman, but the systems of *Always Friday* can be intimidating at first look. Frank's profession is CAD/CAM computer work, so he caught on very quickly.

The Pacific from Monterey Bay to Point Conception was essentially devoid of commercial traffic, with no big ships within twenty-five miles of us all night. In fact, our only traffic contacts were slow-moving, southbound sailboats that we overtook and left in our wake. The three-quarter moon was bright and the ocean calm, making for a beautiful passage. The moon set about 4 AM, leaving a crystal-clear sky illuminated by billions of stars that humans are only privileged to experience in areas totally devoid of light pollution. The only times I remember enjoying such beautiful stellar shows were the nights on the Colorado River while rafting through the Grand Canyon fifteen years ago with our close friends Bill and Mindy Young. I wish they had been with us last night to compare notes on the brilliance of the stars. It is sad that when many think of light shows, they think of Las Vegas or New York. In my opinion, the incomparable beauty of nature easily trumps any man-made spectacle.

During the night, I noted that our speed dropped from 8.5 knots to less than 6.5 knots for no apparent reason. All gauges looked good, and engine room checks were all okay. I even checked our wake to be sure that we weren't dragging a crab pot or other impediment to our progress. A call to Alan in front of us confirmed that he too had noted a slowing of his speed over ground (SOG), so even though the currents are supposed to be favorable on the southbound leg, I attributed the drop in speed to an adverse natural force.

However, at daybreak, the real culprit could be seen following in our wake! A veritable crop of bull kelp entangled in our starboard stabilizer. The stalks are as large as your wrist and about twenty-five feet long. Again, it was obvious that Neptune had not given up on keeping us in his Pacific domain for as long as possible. So, twenty-five miles off the coast, we stopped the boat, cut away what we could reach, and then reversed the boat to essentially back out of the trap the kelp had laid for us. When we resumed our course on the same engine settings, our speed increased from 6.4 to 8.7 knots, and fuel consumption dropped to 6.1 gph, almost a gallon-per-hour improvement.

Today has been one of those magnificent days at sea that convinces you that cruising the world would be a great choice for a rewarding life. Now 25 nm offshore and nearing Point Conception, one of the most infamous death traps for sailors of old, we are surrounded by seals, whales, albacore, dolphin, and seabirds of many varieties. And apparently we are in a nursery of the sunfish—the 1,000-to-1,500-pound ocean oddities that are shaped like a spade and lay flat on the surface with no apparent worries in life. We saw not only several adults of massive size but also four or five groups of baby sunfish, no more than a foot across, lying in groups of five to ten as if in marine kindergarten recess! Memorable sights never seen by any of us on board, although we have seen many adults offshore in the Atlantic. This ocean is literally alive with never-ending surprises.

When we left Monterey, our destination was San Diego.

However, several factors have led to a change in plans. The Baja Ha-Ha, a sailboat race from San Diego to somewhere in Mexico, will start from San Diego this weekend, and there is no dock space suitable for *Always Friday*. Our eighteen-foot beam (width) makes slips hard to find and, in this case, essentially impossible on the weekend of a big sailing event. So, a call to Dave Harlow in Dana Point, the home of NH, yielded the favor of one of their slips, and the bonus possibility of knocking off the last few points on our punch list before heading into the wilds of Mexico next week. Doug and Jeane from Ketchikan are going to be able to join us next week for the border crossing and foray into the unknown (to us at least) waters of Mexico and Central America.

Tonight, we will traverse the Santa Barbara Channel, cruise by the lights of Los Angeles, and arrive in Dana Point sometime Wednesday morning.

Life on the open ocean is addicting. If the Betty Ford Institute had a marine division, we would probably be potential inpatients.

10/24/2007

We are now safely moored in Dana Point, the home of Nordhavn, after a 320 nm, forty-hour, nonstop run from Monterey. The weather was perfect, which is hard to believe so soon after a period of such violent storms. The ride was so comfortable that you could have left a Coke on the table in Monterey and finished it in Dana Point, and the seas so flat that you could have paddled a kayak here (if you were considerably younger than I am). But for once, the trip and the boat are not the story of this trip.

Southern California is ON FIRE! The TV newscasters suggest that the devastation is confined to San Diego, and indeed the fact that the city is severely threatened is the primary reason we are in Dana Point rather than San Diego as planned. However, as we passed Los Angeles about 3:30 AM, the hills to the south were aglow with fire, and the sky was totally obscured by smoke. From Santa Barbara to Dana Point, the hills were in flames, and the skies filled with planes flying in echelon in groups of four as they dropped fire-retarding chemicals onto the flaming hillsides. For the next sixty miles, the clouds of smoke hid the sun, and ashes fell from the sky as if a snowstorm were blanketing the area.

As we sit here in Dana Point Harbor, all the vents, doors, and windows are closed tightly to diminish the accumulation of the "snow" inside the boat. The sky is dark gray, and the midday sun is represented by a dimly glowing ball, even though the weather is perfect. There is a surreal feeling to the smoky day, and there is talk of little more than the fires. At least in Southern California, a very scary Halloween has come a week early.

Upon our arrival in Dana Point, we were met at the docks by Gene Kohlmann and Tommy Haner, executives of Nordhavn, who took our lines and welcomed us back from Alaska. Within a few minutes, the phone rang with a call from the Fort Lauderdale Boat Show. It was Jeff Merrill, our California Nordhavn sales rep who was such a positive force in our prior Dana Point commissioning experience for *Always Friday*, checking on us to make sure that our arrival had gone smoothly. It is amazing what a little personal attention, offered when it is not necessary, can do to make you feel welcome after being gone from the home of Nordhavn for six months.

We will spend a few days here completing our pre-Mexico checklist before leaving for our first stop in Ensenada on Sunday. Raleigh and Binky must get their Mexico physicals for entry, and Kathy has an appointment for a root job and manicure! I, on the other hand, will dedicate my time to useful endeavors, such as changing the engine oil and restocking the spares kit. So, practicality and frivolity are forced to coexist—a necessity in the cruising world. (I hope she doesn't read this!)

10/27/2007

We are in Dana Point with the excitement building over our departure tomorrow for Mexico and points south! The boat is in perfect condition after NH corrected an intermittent electrical gremlin that was rebooting all the computers, AV equipment, and clocks when the generator was turned on. It appears to have been a fault within the inverter, so NH pulled it and replaced it with a new one. No problems since! The Kaleidoscope is loaded with DVDs, so Kathy's future looks bright. Frank has more fishing equipment on board than some commercial boats, so he is happy as a clam. In fact, we are ready for anything from dorado to marlin, and the freezer will soon be loaded again, sharing space with the remaining halibut and salmon from Alaska.

Early tomorrow afternoon, Doug, pilot of the *Noordham*, and Jeane McPherson will land at John Wayne International from Ketchikan, AK, to join us for part of the remaining trip. He and Jeane showed us their town and entertained us in their home before we left their beautiful state in August, so now we will reciprocate by having them in our "home" as we travel some of the most beautiful country in the world. The weather is good, and Baja is alive with fish now, so it should be quite an experience for all.

Tonight, we are invited to a cookout on San Clemente beach with Mike Cook and his family. Mike's mother had introduced us to Bill and Mary Pfiefer of Ketchikan, which began the series of great experiences with new friends in Alaska. Alaska continues to play a key role in our lives 2,000 miles south of her borders!

We left Dana Point last spring and since that time have covered 6,136 nm in 926.9 engine hours, burning 5,175.5 of diesel fuel. The generator has been utilized for 425 hours, many of which were attributed to the scarcity of fifty-amp shore power in the NW ports where the weather frequently trapped us as we moved down the coast. Everything about the boat has met or exceeded our expectations. We depart tomorrow with our ultimate southern target the Panama Canal.

Internet and cell coverage will be spotty for this segment of the trip. We have satellite phone and SSB capability (as well as Central American cellular internet access) on board; however, I anticipate that our updates will be significantly less frequent than before. We will make notes and update the site with our experiences as technology allows.

Our trip of a lifetime is at its halfway point. If the second half is as good as the first, it will be a wonderful trip through Mexico, Central America, the Caribbean, and ultimately home to Virginia!

SOUTH OF THE BORDER

10/30/2007, Tuesday

THE RUN FROM Dana Point to Ensenada was very pleasant in seas of about three feet and light NW winds. Doug and I spent several hours familiarizing him with the navigational and power systems on board *Always Friday*. Although Doug, as an Alaskan ship's pilot, is very familiar with the operation of such systems, the buttons and commands require considerable hands-on experience before anyone would be comfortable standing night watch alone. It was very interesting to learn that the pilots universally operate in north-up mode on both the chart plotters and radars, with all predictors set at six minutes and all vectors reported in true, rather than relative, formats. It is somewhat counterintuitive (especially since we are heading south), but I can see that it will have some advantages once the mental adjustments are made. Once we leave the Panama Canal, it will become an almost moot point, as the rest of the trip will have a heading of predominantly north.

We timed our Ensenada arrival for the early morning and hit it on the nose. It is an impressive port with large cranes for cargo ships and a significant presence of sail and power yachts . . . but no fuel docks! Diesel is sold only by the fifty-five-gallon drum, rolled to the boat, and pumped a barrel at a time into the tanks. We tied up at the Baja Naval Boatyard with plans to top off *Always Friday* with about 600 gallons; however, they could not get more than nine barrels (495 gallons), and we had to wait for its arrival by pickup truck at 2 PM. That was somewhat of a blessing, as we had to sign into Mexico at the local CIS office (I don't know what it stands for, but I am sure that it is *not* the Spanish word for efficiency).

For a country that condones by silence the travel of 20,000,000 of its citizens into our country, they certainly don't make our entry into their country very easy or pleasant. An officially condoned arrival requires the participation of five different government agencies. We are now the proud owners of tourist cards, an import license for the boat (for ten years) and its three diesel engines, and one vessel and five individual fishing licenses. After all was done, we were able to get into Mexico for only $1,000. But it's not over—you *must* pay to get out of here too! Maybe our immigration service could learn something from these people and retire our national date with pesos.

On the recommendation of Roger, the harbormaster, we ate at Alfonso's Restaurant and had an excellent Mexican lunch. By 4 PM, we had loaded the fuel and were on our way south again. Frank disappeared onto the aft deck and submersed himself into rigging the *thirteen* rods and reels with every kind of bait for every kind and size of fish that swims the Pacific. He takes fishing to an art form that would impress even the non-enthusiast.

During the first night out of Ensenada, the seas built to about six feet, adding a gentle motion to *Always Friday*'s progress down the coast. Kathy, Jeane, and Frank cooked a beautiful steak dinner. The meat would have been the envy of any restaurant, and the view out the window was as beautiful as any in the country.

The three men are standing three-hour shifts during the night (11–2 AM, 2–5 AM, 5–8 AM), freeing Frank for the early-morning bite we anticipate for every morning at daybreak. The nights remain spectacular with more stars overhead than you could ever imagine. As city dwellers, you have no idea what light pollution does to your view of the heavens until you experience the same view from far at sea or deep in the wilderness.

This morning was our first one with lines in the water with the rising sun, and after five minutes of fishing, we had our first fish on board. It was a Pacific bonito, and five more followed it into the box over the next hour. The water temperature is still too low for the tuna and billfish we will be seeking further south, but the bonito will serve as excellent bait for those fish when we get into their territory in several days. We are fully prepared to do battle with fish of several hundred pounds and hope to do so! The answer to your next question is "Eat a few, and throw the rest back!"

At present we are 130 nm south of Ensenada and 98 nm north of Cedros Island, running about 15 nm offshore on a heading of 165 degrees. We can make it to the Panama Canal nonstop from here, but we plan at least two intermediate stoops—one in Cabo San Lucas to see Ken and Roberta, and the second for fuel in Zihuantanejo about 1,000 nm to the south of here. The plan for the night is to adjust our speed to hit the fishing grounds at Cedros Island at daybreak. We did the same thing last night and ran at 1,250 rpm, yielding five knots at 2.4 gph. The boat is amazingly efficient, especially if you don't have a deadline to meet.

10/31/2007, Wednesday, Halloween!

The weather last night was not as predicted. The winds rose to over twenty knots in the evening and stayed there all night. That was not the problem—the problem was that the winds were directly out of the north, and we were going south. For non-boaters: that produces a following sea, and autopilots have more trouble with that most any other sea state. We had eight-to-ten-foot swells breaking on all sides, and the boat spent much of its time wallowing through the seas with its speed compromised by the induced inefficiency of our course through the water.

The blessings of dry exhaust (where the exhaust is delivered twenty-seven feet above the boat rather than at the stern as with wet exhaust) were very apparent, as we have not had even a whiff of diesel exhaust fumes in the boat. With a boat with stern exhausts going eight knots and the wind from directly astern blowing at twenty knots, the boat would quickly fill with exhaust fumes unless every window, porthole, and door was tightly secured.

Our watch schedule worked well, and I woke Frank from deep sleep about an hour before sunrise to prepare for our first day of serious fishing in blue water of at least seventy degrees. The lines went into the water just NW of Turtle Bay, and in no time the game fish were all over Frank's smorgasbord of piscatorial enticement presented from five Penn International reels (50s and 30s; wide spools and two speeds, for you fishermen). His impressive assortment of softheads, Kona heads, cedar plugs, feathers, and multiple others, rigged impeccably, make it almost unfair to the fish.

Within several hours, *Always Friday* had been visited by skipjack tuna, yellowfin tuna, beautiful dolphin (the fish, not Flipper), Pacific bonito, a striped marlin, and probably a wahoo that made a strong run and then departed the scene. The freezer is now well stocked with yellowfin tuna and dolphin. Two of the skipjacks were kept for bait, and all the rest went back into the Pacific. Dinner tonight will be compliments of residents that woke up this morning in the ocean but will sleep tonight in our tummies. Some may think we need a bigger freezer—I think we just need to eat faster!

The flying fish are also frequent visitors, and always signify the presence of blue-water game fish in the area. We were also treated to a sight so rare that Doug, who has spent his life on the open ocean, had never seen it before! Frank was the first to spot the dark shadows inside an eight-to-ten-foot swell. We weren't sure what this Halloween day was presenting to us... until another swell lifted four of them partially out of the water. We were being treated to the rare sight of four manta rays swimming on the surface in unison through the open Pacific.

Their bodies were twenty feet across, and almost as deep. On both sides of their mouths were meaty projections shaped like candy canes but more than a foot in length. So, one day we see a group of baby sunfish with their half-ton mother, and the next we are visited by manta rays. But even that was not the last notable event of the day. As we were cruising along about 5 nm offshore, we noticed a gigantic commotion just east of us. We turned the boat towards the action and were amazed to see a school of *big* yellowfin tuna leaping completely out of the water onto their hapless prey.

The biggest I ever caught was 150 pounds, and the biggest I have seen was 200 pounds. These were considerably larger than any that I have ever seen. Frank, who has the most experience of any of us with big fish, estimated them to be over 300 pounds! We fished towards them, but they had sounded before we got into their area. Had we hooked one (or four, which frequently happens in tuna schools), we would have been there for several hours—if we were able to turn them at all. This place is just alive with marine life, and we have 2,000 miles of bountiful ocean in front of us. I told you this was going to be exciting!

Right now, it is 2:30 PM and siesta time on board *Always Friday* before the afternoon bite gets us back to serious fishing. Everyone but me is asleep. I don't understand that. We are going to be dead for billions and billions of years. We can sleep then! I'd rather spend the hours looking in wonder at the wasteland of the Baja Peninsular surrounded by the bountiful and beautiful Pacific. If you haven't done something like this in your life, change your plans to include such an adventure. If you don't, you will croak without knowing what you have missed. Believe me, after what we have seen for the past 7,000 miles, you will have missed a lot!

11/01/2007, Thursday

The weatherman was wrong again last night. He promised us calm seas, but nature delivered twenty-knot winds that put us in the troughs of sizeable swells throughout the night. In fact, it became so uncomfortable that we changed course about 2 AM, successfully seeking a more acceptable ride. The beam and following seas continue to make life tough for the autopilot, but overall, the ride is not bad.

Frank had our baits in the water about 5:30 AM, and shortly thereafter, the first dorado (dolphin) was in the box! They are among the most beautiful fish in the sea, with their vivid fluorescent colors that quickly fade when taken from the water. The first dorado weighed over twenty pounds, which was fortunate for those caught later in the day. That fish filled our needs for dorado fillets, so all others we caught today went back in the ocean, probably to enroll in seminary school. Not many dolphins get a second chance when Frank catches them!

The most exciting event of the day was a strike that essentially emptied our 50 Wide Penn reel of 600 yards of fifty-pound test line! He hit the lure, took off for California, and never looked back. Before we could turn the boat to follow him, 1,800 feet, or six football fields of line, were in the water. He threw the hook, and we spent the next fifteen minutes reclaiming the line from behind the boat.

The fish most likely responsible for the show would be a large tuna of at least several hundred pounds, or a marlin. We know both are in the area because we have seen them. In fact, this afternoon, I looked out to see a marlin swimming beside the boat no more than fifteen yards away. We dragged the lures over him, but he showed no interest in our efforts. We have fished all day with a custom sport fisherman approximately seventy-five feet from the Gulf Coast of the US and a long-range party boat out of San Diego that stays in Mexican waters with its fishermen for two weeks at a time. This is serious fishing out here in some of the most productive waters in the world.

Kathy and Jeane hit the home run of the day when they put together for our lunch appetizers of ahi (yellowfin tuna) sashimi followed by seared ahi fillets. We had to keep four lines in the water all afternoon to replenish our stocks after Frank, Doug, and

I imitated great white sharks at the dinner table. Tonight, we have on the menu fish tacos starring freshly caught dorado from the refrigerator of *Always Friday*!

We have now run nonstop for over 500 nm from Ensenada over the past seventy-four hours. For the first time in memory, we may be a little ahead of our frequently altered "schedule." We will probably be in Cabo San Lucas in several days, although we could get there in one day if we ran all night tonight and didn't fish aggressively tomorrow. However, tomorrow's path takes us directly over one of the best marlin/wahoo areas along the Baja Peninsula. To be ready to give it our best effort, we have decided to anchor in Bahia Santa Maria adjacent to Bahia Magdalena, get a good night's sleep, and be on the marlin grounds at daybreak tomorrow.

Frank, a fourth-generation Hokie, is now deeply involved in the Virginia Tech football game, coming to us via satellite. If Tech wins, he will be good company tomorrow. If not (as we noted after the Boston College debacle), he may well be bait for tomorrow's shark fishing on board *Always Friday*!

The boat continues to be all we could hope for. The food is excellent (as always), and the company great.

11/02/2007, Friday

Today was an amazing day on *Always Friday*! To give you a feel for the excitement, Frank, an avid fisherman with worlds of big game fishing experience in many oceans, said that if he had only one more day to live, he would want it to be like today was for us.

We awoke about 4:30 AM as the sun was beginning to light up the eastern sky, and left Santa Maria Bay for the open ocean shortly thereafter. This area adjacent to Magdalena Bay is one of the most famous fishing spots in the world. We put the lines overboard before we were clear of the bay, our anchorage for last night. Within minutes we had a Pacific yellowtail in the box. We have nothing like it in our part of the Atlantic, and it is one of the most sought-after game fish on this coast. It is considered one of the best eating fish on the planet, and one that frequently headlines the sushi restaurants. We cleaned him and put him in the refrigerator with plans to introduce him to soy sauce, wasabi, and ginger for his last meal as our lunch.

As we headed offshore, all the signs for marlin were there. The water was eighty-two degrees and a beautiful royal blue. The sky was filled with frigate birds, gulls, and pelicans circling and diving into concentrations of unseen fish . . . presumably either yellowfin tuna or striped marlin. Hemingway would have been in heaven, and so were we!

Frank had his unbelievable assortment of highly specialized and beautifully rigged lures ready to go as soon as we hit the fifty-fathom (300-foot) curve just a few miles offshore. Once they were in the water, the fun began. The next six hours were proof positive that Nordhavn could, without embarrassment, advertise any of their boats as long-range offshore sports fishermen. We have four rod holders mounted in the transom, as well as a custom rod rack for the boat deck for spare rods and spin casting rigs. Frank had rigged outrigger clips to the SS railings to mimic a drop back when the fish hit, and a teaser rig (lures with no hook, used to draw fish into the baits) was run from the centerline cleat to trail directly behind the boat. It was a very impressive presentation of world-class lures, but they had never been fished behind anything like *Always Friday*.

As we rolled along in beautiful weather at about eight knots, we sighted our first group of diving birds with fish tearing up the surface underneath them. We turned *Always Friday* into the melee, and in no time, we had three striped marlins in the baits. Of the three, we hooked one, but he threw the hook quickly. Frank then pulled out one of the heavy spinning reels and threw him a chance at immortality, the title of "first marlin caught on board *Always Friday*"! With his stripes glowing brightly, he took the lure and proceeded to run like a greyhound and jump like a gazelle for over an hour. Finally, he tired to the point that we could bring him alongside for pictures before releasing him to fight another day. We estimated his weight to be around 150 to 200 pounds, but his beauty was more in his heart than his size. You wouldn't believe how hard he fought.

So, now *Always Friday* was a Baja big game fishing boat! The biggest fish award temporarily passed from Hugo's 135-pound halibut in Alaska to Frank's 200-pound striped marlin off Baja. But, just like in Alaska, this was no one-fish day. Over the next six hours, we had striped marlin attacking the baits, often in groups of two or three at a time. Everyone on board that wished to do so brought a trophy marlin to the swim platform for pictures, followed by their return unharmed to the ocean. We had several double hook-ups, and Frank and I, with Doug driving the boat, teamed up to land a double header of striped marlin—quite an accomplishment in the fishing world.

I enjoy driving the boat at least as much as fishing, and we were amazed at how agilely we could maneuver *Always Friday* in her new role as a sports fisherman. Who would ever expect to see a fifty-five-foot Nordhavn backing down on a marlin? Well, it happened multiple times today, and very successfully. Not only did we back down on fish, but we also turned in the length of the boat to chase greyhounding billfish before they could spool us and spun the boat on its long axis to bring the fish closer to the boat for release. I would never have believed we could make this boat dance to the marlin tunes, but it never missed a step.

One of the secrets to our success was Doug's suggestion that we use the handheld VHF radios to effectively tie the cockpit to the bridge. That idea, when coupled with the aft camera allowing the bridge to see the fisherman, made *Always Friday* almost the equal of sport fishermen in terms of effectively fighting fish behind the boat.

So, what was the final count? In six hours, we raised twenty-four striped marlins into the baits, hooked fourteen of them, and brought seven to the transom for release. Even more amazingly, we spent the last few hours not trying to hook the fish but trying to take the lures *away* from the marlin before they were hooked! Lastly, we took the hooks off the lures so we could enjoy their aggressive antics without a chance of hooking them (we used only artificial lures today). Frank and I agreed that if we had fished all day and tried to catch as many marlins as possible, we could have brought at least twenty-five to the boat.

All of this went on all day in an arena which included beautiful blue water, moonscape-type mountainous Baja terrain, whales, porpoises, giant sea turtles, as well as some of the most beautiful game fish in the world. We released the largest dorado we have caught so far—about thirty-five pounds. Kathy vetoed our keeping him since we don't have another inch of freezer space available.

Midafternoon lunch consisted of the yellowtail sashimi we caught earlier this morning. Talk about fresh fish! Dinner tonight will be marinated flank steak cooked on the grill as we cruise all night to Cabo San Lucas, with arrival there about midday tomorrow. We had hoped to see Ken and Roberta Williams of *Sans Souci* (their NH 68) at their home there, but Ken is at sea behind us, participating in a Southern California rally. We will see what Cabo has to offer, and then possibly take a short foray into the Sea of Cortez before resuming our southward journey.

Always Friday is rolling victoriously through some of the greatest sport fishing waters in the world, and no Viking, Hatteras, Rybovich, or Merritt is laughing at the yellow boat with full freezers flying *seven* marlin release flags.

We can't wait until ma*ñ*ana!

11/03/2007, Saturday

We are about to enter the harbor at Cabo San Lucas. The weather is beautiful, the scenery fantastic, and our plans flexible.

We will decide on the next step after anchoring in the harbor and taking our tender *Friday Nite!* into town to see what's there. I think we will find a tourist mecca like Skagway, AK. If so, we will be on the ocean by the afternoon.

11/04/2007, Sunday

After having seen enough of the tourist's view of Cabo San Lucas in one afternoon, we got a good night's sleep anchored in front of some of the many condos and weighed anchor at 5:30 AM with the sun already well up into the sky. The weather was beautiful and the forecast excellent, so we chose a route towards Cabo Corrientes on the Mexican mainland. That entails an open ocean run of about 275 nm, with an anticipated arrival at that waypoint about 2:30 tomorrow afternoon. There we will proceed down the coast to Zihuantanejo, arriving there Wednesday morning.

It is supposed to be the antithesis of Cabo San Lucas, and a popular stopping point for boats on the way to the canal. We plan to stay there at least one night before starting again for Panama. We are now about 850 nm from Dana Point and 2,100 nm from Panama. If clear weather continues to allow us to make close to 200 nm per day, we will be able to make up some of the time we lost on the NW USA coast. The ocean today is almost flat and the winds a refreshing ten knots. The air temperature is about eighty-four degrees, and the water temperature eighty-three. XM Radio WxWorx, our satellite weather source, and buoyweather.com both predict smooth waters for the next several days. The ride over the open ocean surrounded by beautiful blue water, dragging four lines for whatever might want to see the inside of our refrigerator, with no sign of life within fifty miles is very relaxing—almost addicting!

The outcome is fine, but we had our first medical challenge

this afternoon when a thirty-pound dorado just gaffed by Frank managed to throw the hook into Frank's forearm. He and I have fished together for twenty-five years or more and gaffed many hundreds of fish between us with no prior accidents with hooks or gaffs, but this one got lucky.

If you are squeamish, don't read this, but remember the outcome is all good. The fish took an artificial bait rigged in tandem with a pair of 10/0 hooks about the size of the "hook" made by your thumb and index finger when you extend your finger. After placing the gaff exactly where you should, Frank was lifting the fish into the boat when it kicked wildly, throwing the hook into his mid forearm. The entire hook of about four inches went into his arm, arced, and the point with a razor-sharp barb exited the surface of his arm, leaving him deeply "hooked" with the entry and exit holes about three inches apart, both now filled with a steel hook.

It was extremely fortunate that the fish came off the front hook, because had it remained on the first hook, with Frank deeply hooked with the second hook, the tissue damage in his arm would have been significant. He was moving his fingers normally, and sensation was intact. There was no evidence of significant vascular injury, and the wound was relatively clean. The problem was that we had nothing on board that would cut a hook designed to bring a 500-plus-pound marlin to his knees. So, the decision was made to file the barb flat, then reverse its entry path out of his arm.

In our medical kit, I had everything we needed to cleanse the injury and deaden the pain by infiltration of a local anesthetic before pulling out the hook that looked more like a small anchor. While I held the protruding hook, Doug filed away the barb; then I removed it with a quick, semicircular move. Bleeding was minimal, and the fingers moved normally after removal. The fifth finger and inside half of the fourth were numb, but that was compatible with the local anesthetic's effect on the ulnar nerve, confirmed by the fact that normal sensation returned several hours later. After aggressively cleaning the area with Betadine, applying a pressure dressing to minimize bleeding, loading him up with ibuprofen, in conjunction with elevation and local ice packs for about six hours, Frank was well on his way to recovery. The antibiotics we hoped we would never need will be put to good use, as fish-related injuries can be a source of serious infections.

The strongest lesson learned from this experience is to always have available a bolt cutter capable of cutting through the largest hook on board. As Doug said, Frank became our largest "catch and release" trophy of the trip! By dinnertime, he not only was back at full speed but also insisted on cooking the yellowfin tuna dinner we had planned.

Now back to more pleasant things! Have you ever heard of the "green flash" phenomenon? It occurs only rarely, but when it does, it is dramatic. Just as the top of the sun disappears beneath the horizon at sunset, certain atmospheric conditions combine to yield a green flash. I have looked for it many times but seen it only once before, from our beach cottage in Cape Hatteras about twenty-five years ago . . . until today! The skies were clear, and we had a perfect view of the sunset off the starboard side of *Always Friday*. As we watched with low expectations of a return on our effort, the sun dipped below the horizon, and we all said at once, "The green flash!" It happened, it was clear, and all three of us saw it without a doubt. I may never see it again, *but* I have now seen it twice, with the experiences separated by over twenty-five years. It's real—don't let anyone tell you differently!

Our little city with a population of five continues to chug along over the Middle America Trench (almost three miles deep), self-sufficient and safe on board *Always Friday* in what would otherwise be an environment so hostile as to make survival almost impossible. Our engine and navigational equipment push us straight down the line towards the canal at about 200 miles per day, while the generator powers the air conditioners that change the eighty-five-degree, high-humidity air into a pleasant sixty-eight degrees!

When the hot showers and washing machine almost consume our freshwater supply, the magic switch on the water maker allows us to turn sea water to fresh at the rate of 600 gallons per day. When boredom threatens, satellite radio serenades us with myriad choices of tunes, news, or sporting events, while the Kaleidoscope offers a choice of 250 movies stored for our enjoyment many miles away from any movie theater. When room in the freezer allows, Frank turns multicolored plastic lures into fillets that sell for $12 per pound in the grocery store, while Kathy and Jeane turn those fillets into dinners that would make any New York restaurant proud. Such is the burden of long-distance cruising on board *Always Friday*.

Soon it will be tomorrow, and that is particularly good news.

11/05/2007 Monday

A lazy day today, made rewarding by the fact that Frank's injury is healing nicely with no signs of infection. The entry and exit sites are clean, and there is no unexpected redness or heat over the area. All that coupled with the fact that he has had no chills or other evidence of fever suggests that we have dodged a potentially big bullet.

After I took the elastic bandage off today, I saw no benefit in replacing it. But nooo! Frank wanted it back on for the pictures that will follow his next prize catch. So, if you see Frank next January after his return home, and the bandage is still on, please ask him to tell you about his horrific injury. He *will* have pictures!

At present we are making good progress towards Zihuantanejo. In fact, we are exactly halfway there, averaging 8.4 knots at 5.8 gph since our departure from Cabo San Lucas. The open water passage of 270 nm is now behind us, and the rest of the trip to Zihuantanejo will be within 20 nm of the shore. Unless something slows our progress, we will have to slow down tomorrow to avoid entering the harbor at night. Who says Nordhavns are slow? We are having to hold this racehorse back.

The most impressive visitor to Frank's set of lures today was a blue marlin of about 300 pounds. He crashed the baits, came completely out of the water to pounce on one of the colorful rigs . . . but missed every hook and was gone. If Frank had hooked the marlin only half as well as the dorado hooked Frank, we would have had quite a show on our hands. As a consolation prize, we will be eating fresh dorado for dinner tonight.

My efforts to become proficient in celestial navigation using a sextant continue. Today we took sun shots, and since my 5 AM watch encompasses sunrise, I'll be trying some star shots in the morning. Nobletec, our navigational software, has the star positions and appropriate tables included for our use. All these efforts are undertaken only as a reflection of respect for the mariners that preceded us by hundreds of years. *Always Friday* has multiple GPS units on board which give us our position within feet with no effort at all, but the aura associated with mimicking the brave sailors of centuries ago is one I find very attractive.

So, as we prepare for another night at sea, all is well on *Always Friday*. Alaska is one and a half times the breadth of the continental US behind us, and the Panama Canal gets closer every minute.

11/06/2007, Early Tuesday Morning (5 AM)

With unexpected internet access off Manzanillo, Mexico, I am adding this quick Tuesday update to reassure all that Frank is now back at full strength. In fact, as the sun is rising, he is sitting in the aft cockpit with four lines out.

If you see him later, be sure and ask to see his scars. He loves them!

My sextant star shots went well this morning, and I was able to confirm that we are somewhere near Mexico. I'll leave the picky stuff to the GPS for now.

As an aside, the Verizon AirCard for internet access, AT&T Blackberry for email in and out when there is no internet, and Verizon Central America cellular plans are now performing well for us.

11/07/2006, Tuesday

After the short, unexpected period of internet access this morning when the brief update was sent, we have spent an uneventful day on smooth seas, moving towards Zihuantanejo. The fishing remained highly productive, and three beautiful dorado of about twenty pounds each fell to the trick of slowly trolling by a source of shade. In today's case, the shade was generated by two sources: a board and a big sea turtle lying quietly beside the board!

As the boat passed the board and turtle, we saw the shimmering images of several brightly colored fish beneath the water — dorado. As the lures passed the turtle, one of the fish struck the bait, and the fight was on. In a few minutes, we had him beside the boat, but instead of gaffing it, we left it in the water to take advantage of a genetic trait well known in these fish. As the hooked fish swam behind the boat, two others joined it right before our eyes. We threw chunks of bonito to them to get them into a feeding frenzy and then tossed them a hook baited with more bonito on spinning rigs. After a few minutes, we had all three resting comfortably, asleep in the cooler. Don't know why they do that, but they do.

So, the refrigerator is again brimming with one of the tastiest fish in the sea, and we had lots of fun to boot. No marlin or wahoo today, but we missed several violent strikes that could have been those or ahi (yellowfin tuna).

Since we dropped below the 20th northern parallel, it has become so hot and humid that we have chosen to run the air-conditioning constantly. It's almost ninety degrees outside, but inside it is almost chilly.

The boat's Spanish lessons continue by virtue of the Rosetta Stone computer program (my username is *el Buddyo*), and my sextant abilities are now consistently allowing me to identify my nearest continent of residence. Dinner tonight was very fresh dorado over angel hair pasta with broccoli and parmesan cheese served in air-conditioned comfort with mood lighting, music, and wine (except for the bridge team) in the salon of *Always Friday*.

As we have followed the coastline of Mexico, our course has changed from south to almost due east. In fact, our present course into Ixtapa is ninety-four degrees. With that change in course, the meridians of longitude are falling towards that of Virginia (seventy-six degrees)! We have gone from our maximum westerly meridian of 137 degrees to our present one of 101 degrees, so we are more than halfway home by the East-West parameter. For those of you less geographically inclined, we are due south of Texas. With that eastward movement, the time change between us and home is rapidly evaporating. We are now GMT -6 hours, which makes us only one hour behind Virginia time, down from a four-hour difference in Alaska. This migration of numbers towards Virginia Beach's baseline forces the reality that this adventure will end before long, but I don't want to think more about that now. Home may be a future waypoint, but there are many fascinating ones between here and there to enjoy. There, I'm thinking straight again!

The resorts of Ixtapa and Zihuantanejo are off the bow, and we arrive there in the morning after our third day at sea from Cabo San Lucas.

We have been trying, without success so far, to contact Tina McBride by email. She is a Panama Canal transit agent recommended to us for assistance in arranging for our passage later this month. As you might expect, it requires a ton of paperwork to get through, and an agent's help is said to be almost essential. Tony Carter of the M/V *Coast Pilot* in Eureka, CA, briefed me on what to expect, and since he has made the trip over eighty times, I thought it wise to listen carefully to his thoughts. I found his observation that the canal is much better run since we gave it away to be quite interesting, as well as surprising.

The trip from the Pacific to the Atlantic, now about 1,500 nm away, will be a yet another high point of the trip. When we reach the internet camera running twenty-four hours per day that sends real-time images of the vessels as they pass through the canal, we will be easy to spot: the *very* small, yellow boat with the waving fools on the bow!

11/09/2007, Friday

Zihuantanejo turned out to be a very pleasant experience. It is a 500-plus-year-old port that has maintained its identity in the face of increasing popularity as a tourist destination. The people are extremely polite and accommodating, with far less of the in-your-face sales tactic noted in Cabo San Lucas and other tourist meccas. We anchored *Always Friday* in the main harbor and caught one of the ever-present pangas to the city dock. Pangas are small (eighteen to twenty-three feet), locally built, essentially open outboard boats they use for every purpose imaginable, including fishing all night fifty or more miles offshore with no lights or radio.

Victor, the local port captain and immigration official, was friendly, very helpful, and wanted nothing more than a cap from *Always Friday* for his efforts. We made it a point to eat in the restaurants recommended by Victor and frequented by the locals. The food was truly Mexican, very good, and no one got sick. Kathy and Jean reprovisioned *Always Friday* effectively at the local market, and we are well stocked for the next leg to Guatemala. The shopping was as good (or as bad) as all the other Mexican ports I have seen. The major difference was the general attitude of the people—low key, polite, and very friendly. It almost made me want to by a sombrero measuring three feet across . . . but I resisted.

Kathy of course found the bracelet she has been looking for all her life, and no doubt will again in the next port. Frank and I went roosterfish fishing in a panga with two very enjoyable native Mexicans. One spoke excellent English, the other essentially none. To catch roosterfish, the guides would take the boat almost into the breaking waves from the offshore side; then we would cast into the breaking waves. Not something you would think to do on your own. Roosterfish are very elusive and tough to land. We raised four, hooked two, but did not get either one into the boat. However, we got good looks at these strange-looking fish before they broke free. Between roosterfish, we caught jacks and bonito in numbers that ensured the perpetual absence of boredom. Very entertaining fishing.

The mate that spoke no English was an experienced commercial offshore tuna fisherman, with many trips to Panama under his belt. He was fascinated with our summer's trip and offered us sage advice on the waters ahead. Again we heard the emphatic advice first offered by my friend Carl Nish of the F/V *Lydorein* in Oregon, then reinforced by Tony Carter of the M/V *Coast Pilot*: "Don't mess with the Gulf of Tehuantepec!" The gulf, now about a day in front of us, is infamous as a place in which the winds whip over the water from shore, frequently increasing from near nothing to sustained blows of over eighty knots in minutes. The anecdote for this potentially deadly place is simple: stay within a few miles of shore and the winds blow over you, rather than through you. So that is exactly what we will do.

This morning at first light (about 6:30 AM), we weighed anchor and set our course for Guatemala. Frank has a friend there that wants to show us how good the fishing is there, but he will have a challenge beating what we have seen on *Always Friday*. In fact, my writing of this update was interrupted by a sailfish toying with Frank, who has again taken his place behind the four big Penn Internationals.

During the afternoon, a sailboat approached us from the south, motoring in the absence of favorable winds. As we passed, the VHF radio came alive with a beautiful British accent, calling the motor vessel off his starboard bow. That was us—*Always Friday*! We answered and began a very pleasant conversation of about fifteen minutes in which we learned that he was on board the S/V *Mr. John*, bound for the Baja peninsula with plans to spend several years there. Amazingly, he had departed from the Chesapeake Bay area, passing within ten miles of our home before heading south to the Panama Canal. We are essentially following the same route on reciprocal headings!

We exchanged our weather observations of the past several days, including the sad news (for sailors) that there was not much wind behind us. He confirmed that the Gulf of Tehuantepec had been its usual self with winds of forty knots in the heart of the 200-mile-wide waters, but with light winds within a mile of shore. After exchanging pleasantries, he was off to the north and we to the south. The cruising community is a very pleasant crowd. I would have enjoyed the opportunity to spend more time in conversation with our friend on *Mr. John*. I guess there can be no more fleeting an association than two ships passing on the high seas, never to cross paths again. Sad in a way—I think I would have liked him.

Now the night is here. Acapulco is ablaze with lights off our port side, and the sky is filled with millions of stars. The seas are calm except for the occasional slap as dolphins leap through the wake off the bow of *Always Friday*.

Good sleeping tonight. And tomorrow is my sixty-second birthday!

11/10/2007, Saturday

Now into our second day out of Zihuantanejo, we are 240 nm closer to Guatemala in smooth seas, beautiful blue water of eighty-six degrees, and clear skies. As we passed Acapulco last night, we were treated to the beautiful sight of a seaside city lit by thousands of lights on a clear, star-filled night, yielding a scene that will become deeply embedded in the memories of this trip of a lifetime through Mexico and Central America.

After arising at 4:30 AM for my bridge watch, I found that Kathy had prepared for me (not unlike cookies for Santa Claus) my favorite breakfast of croissants and jelly in recognition of my sixty-second birthday. That, in conjunction with the fact that I got calls from both of our children last night as we passed Acapulco, kicked my maritime birthday party off to a great start. After taking the helm from Doug, I checked the Blackberry and found that somewhere during the night, it had somehow connected and picked up thirty-one messages in this isolated ocean. All were birthday wishes from either old friends or followers of our trip I have never personally met. All of them made my day even better!

The warm, deep-blue water has brought with it the fish that we came here to pursue. We still have several fishing hours to go in this day, and we have been inundated all day with some of the most powerful and beautiful fish in any ocean. It began when something big spooled our Penn International 30W without our even seeing the responsible party. The odds are that somewhere out there is a very big blue or black marlin with over 600 yards of forty-pound test dental floss hanging from his (or her) bill (the big Marlin are always females).

During the morning, Pacific sailfish were frequent visitors to the lures behind *Always Friday*, entertaining all with their acrobatic antics before being released unharmed into the blue. We have some beautiful pictures of sails jumping behind the boat, as well as close-ups before their release. The sea is filled with turtles. You wouldn't believe how plentiful they are. At any given moment, you can usually find three in the waters immediately surrounding the boat.

Frank's high point of the day came when XM Radio was blasting the VA Tech–FSU game into the cockpit from Blacksburg. At the very moment his beloved team scored a touchdown, a beautiful blue marlin of about 300 pounds crashed the bait, hooked itself, and began a run of 300 to 400 yards that put the greyhounding fish ahead of the boat. Greyhounding is when they are running at full speed after first feeling the hook, jumping repetitively as they go—one of the most exciting scenes in sport fishing. We fought him with the boat backing down and turning in concert with his attempts at escape until, after about twenty minutes, we finally had him right behind the boat. As we prepared to pull him to the transom for release, the hook pulled and he returned to the Pacific, tired but uninjured.

But the afternoon was young. Before the sun set, we had a spearfish in the baits, trying to take a lure that was too big for his small bill, four sailfish at once hitting every bait we had, and an unusual situation of a hooked striped marlin that actually broke the line at the Bimini twist knot but didn't know that he was free since the hook was still in his bill. We watched him jumping five or six times as he headed into the sunset with our lure now his own personal property, unattached to its previous owners. He will have quite a story to tell at his next club meeting, and something for show-and-tell as well.

At the end of the day, Frank's fishing log reflected over twenty billfish, including both blue and striped marlin, sailfish, and a spearfish. We were privileged to witness these champion athletes of the sea as they cavorted time after time behind *Always Friday* in Olympic form. None of the fish were injured, and all those brought to the boat were returned to the sea with nothing more than sore muscles and a bruised bill. You will be relieved to know that Frank survived the day uninjured as well.

Tonight, my birthday dinner will consist of rack of lamb with all the trimmings. After that, it is back to business, as we are about to enter the notorious Gulf of Tehuantepec. We will be plastered within a mile of the shoreline for the next 225 nm to avoid the potentially catastrophic winds that have given the gulf its reputation. The Gulf of Mexico is only 117 overland miles from here, and the winds accelerate across that land mass to incredible speeds, often near 100 mph. We have a safe course plotted on Nobeltec, but the tolerance for error will be very small until the gulf is behind us. We won't take it lightly, but such challenges are part of the enchantment of the sea.

11/11/2007, Sunday

It is sunrise, Sunday morning, and at this very moment, the bright-orange, medium-sized star that lights our world is presenting itself for another day. We are now in the dreaded Gulf of Tehuantepec, and so far, so good. Even though the winds are negligible at present, we are prepared for their eminent arrival should they decide to show up unannounced. As I write this, we have a 600-foot container ship passing a mile off our starboard bow as it follows the safety of the shoreline with us. The shoreline passage is such an accepted pathway that the points along that course are well delineated by lighted navigational markers on shore.

Since entering the gulf about 10 PM last night, the climate appears to have changed significantly. The air temperature has dropped from eighty-six to seventy-three degrees, and the water has cooled by almost thirteen degrees to seventy-five. The deep-blue colors of the warm waters have given way to the dark-green hues of colder water, and there is little doubt that the marlin and sailfish chose not to follow us into these waters that billfish consider frigid. That's no real concern, as we will meet them again tomorrow in the warm waters when we leave the gulf en route to Guatemala.

Since I have internet access from somewhere at present, I will make this morning's update brief to get it online. (See addendum below)

So far, the Verizon AirCard has exceeded expectations in terms of broadband access down here. We have apparently moved out of range of XM WxWorx and XM Radio, as they are no longer available. I can tell you from experience that XM WxWorx has a range from latitude fifty-five degrees north to sixteen degrees north. XM radio was still working at the northern extreme of our trip (latitude fifty-nine degrees north) and just went quiet this morning. The Sea Tel satellite TV system went dead after Ensenada. I am told that the signal is still there, but Mexico requires another antenna. We were not told that by ALCOM until we found ourselves without TV. Thanks goodness our AV system did not skip a beat secondary to Kaleidoscope and iPod compatibility.

Bouyweather.com has been an excellent source of offshore weather forecasts for us throughout the cruise. It was less important when we had NOAA weather on a constant basis, but down here, it has been invaluable, especially since WxWorx went out of range.

Addendum: Too late! By the time I got our position and "Where are they now?" pages updated, we had lost our internet connection. Now we are up to noon Sunday, and do I have news for you. TEHUANTAPEC IS FOR REAL! When around 7 AM, I last described surrounding conditions as "so far, so good," the wind was about ten knots and the seas an insignificant three to four feet. *However*, now (around noon) we are seeing the conditions that made this gulf infamous.

The winds intermittently gust to thirty knots by our wind gauge, even though we have done as suggested and have "one foot on the beach," a quarter mile offshore in fifty feet of water. All the hatches are tightly closed, but the sound of the wind still forces you to raise your voice when speaking. The seas this close to shore are reasonable, but as the distance from shore increases, the effect of the wind on the seas is multiplied dramatically. Had we not followed the advice of so many who have preceded us through these waters and taken the straight path across this gulf, we would be in the midst of angry waters that would have made the folly of our navigational decision clear. And these winds get five times higher than the show we are witnessing now!

When we were in Cabo San Lucas, we spoke to the captain of an eighty-foot sport fisherman from the States that had taken the straight path and gotten away with it. His feelings were that since he could run twenty knots, he could get out of trouble if it came up. After seeing this today, I seriously doubt his logic, and would not want to ride home with him. So, I will now join those who admonished me not to challenge the Gulf of Tehuantepec. No matter how pretty the weather looks, *avoid* the temptation to run across this gulf. Keep one foot on the beach and enjoy this show of nature, the likes of which I have never seen before.

11/15/2007, Thursday

We arrived at Marina Pez Vela in Puerto Quetzal, Guatemala, to a warm welcome from the marina staff, immigration officials, and a dozen boaters who had never seen anything like *Always Friday*. It was obvious that someone influential had told them we were coming, and we knew who that was. Frank had arranged weeks in advance for us to stay here for a few days at the marina developed by his good friend from the fishing world, Fernando Aguilar.

Fernando is a native-born Guatemalan educated as a chemical

engineer in the US and now a very influential and successful citizen of his native country. He is an international leader in billfish conservation and well known throughout the International Game Fish Association as a champion of fair-catch rules and the release of these beautiful fish when caught. But even more impressive than his credentials are his personality. He is the quintessential Latin gentleman, and he made our visit one of the more memorable ones of the trip. He developed this marina in response to the world-class marlin fishing that surrounds this area, and the fishermen of the world are flocking to it. At present, the record for most billfish releases from this marina in one day by a single boat is 120 fish! Many offshore fishermen go a lifetime and don't see that many fish, much less catch them in a day.

There is an air of excitement here as some of the best-known boats in the sports fishing world are gathered in this marina for two tournaments scheduled for the next week. But not only is the fishing phenomenal, the area is fascinating as well. A restaurant at the end of the that serves excellent local cuisine, making it unnecessary to go into the third-world town for anything other than curiosity. But Fernando introduced us to the real pearl of Guatemala—Antigua!

We had been told by many of the North Americans (the locals are quick to remind you that they too are Americans here!) that you must not leave Guatemala without seeing Antigua, and they are *right*. Fernando came to the boat about 9 AM, treated us to breakfast at the marina restaurant, and then took us to Antigua in his big Suburban, about an hour's drive from Puerto Quetzal. The ride through the countryside was fascinating as the fields of sugar cane in the lowlands gave way to the coffee plantations among the slopes of the volcanoes as we climbed the 6,000-foot elevation to the ancient city of Antigua.

It is a bustling center of the new and old, with the old dating back to the 1500s. The architecture is beautiful and the city very clean. The local artisans are very talented, and their expertise ranges from beautiful artwork to metalwork to furniture making. There you will find many items that would be at home in the houses of the rich and famous. But Fernando had the crown jewel reserved for us for lunch: the Casa Santo Domingo Hotel! It is the only five-star hotel in Central America, and it deserves six stars if there were such a thing. The food was phenomenal, the surroundings just as good, and Fernando's hospitality even better. After touring all the high points of the city, we were back at the boat by sundown, having seen the best of Guatemala with the nicest of gentlemen. If you are passing through Central America, retrace our steps. You will not regret it.

Today we are off to Panama, about 900 nm from here. If the weather holds, we should be approaching the canal in four to five days, but if necessary, we will anchor in one of the many oceanside bays and wait for smoother seas.

All is going well here on *Always Friday*, and one of the most memorable events is about to occur—the transit of the Panama Canal!

11/16/2007, Friday

Our morning departure from Guatemala was delayed until 6 PM while a local electronics technician finally repaired our SSB radio. Reception has been intermittently blocked by interference that ALCOM, the installers, could not rectify. Now that we are out of range of the internet, cell phones, satellite TV, and XM (both radio and WxWorx), the SSB is our most effective communications tool for weather, news, personal communications, and emergencies. David, the technician, and two of his assistants finally isolated the problem to a connector that had been improperly wired. With that repair, we were back in action on the airwaves and back at sea about sundown. Frank was forced to leave us for business commitments, leaving us with freezers filled with tuna, wahoo, and dolphin, and memories of over forty billfish raised behind *Always Friday* over some of the most productive fishing areas in the world.

The eastern sky is beginning to glow a faint orange as the sun prepares to pop over the horizon in about an hour, but for now, the coastline remains bright with the lights of El Salvador. As we move through Central America, I have been surprised by the density of the populations along the coasts of Mexico, Guatemala, and El Salvador. I had expected long stretches of barren land, but that has been the exception rather than the rule. Right now, the Salvadorian coast is lit up not unlike that of South Florida.

We have no plans to visit all these port cities along the way to Panama, primarily because of the hassle and expense of entering these little countries. The immigration procedures are more designed to generate unjustifiable income than to control the influx of undesirables. We have spent almost a thousand dollars just to enter Mexico and Guatemala, and Panama awaits us with her hand outstretched as well. But of course, I now possess a Mexican import license for the boat, which is good for ten years, and a *Zarpe* from Guatemala proving to Panama that we legally left Guatemala—how useful!

If you are a foreign national traveling into the United States, there is no charge for your entry. But if you are expecting a break on fuel prices, think again. We just paid $3.75 a gallon for diesel fuel in Guatemala—a dollar per gallon higher than Alaskan or Californian prices, and a $1.25 more than our lowest costs on the NW coast this year. Down here, they know what we pay for fuel in the States, and they know that we need it to get home, so apparently, they feel comfortable in socking it to us. Once again, the nice guys of the United States finish last!

My personal assessment is that this ride through Central America is a great trip once. Others come here and never leave—just personal preferences, I guess.

11/17/2007, Saturday

It is 3 AM and many would shudder at the thought of being up at such an hour, but you may not realize what you are missing. The moon has set, leaving a beautiful, pure darkness pierced only by millions of stars and several planets. Saturn is brightly beautiful off the port bow, forty-three degrees above the horizon, while Venus is about to make its first appearance under Saturn from below the horizon. The dominant star off the starboard bow is Sirius at an azimuth (compass reading) of 200 degrees and an altitude (elevation off the horizon) of sixty degrees. By the time your alarm clock goes off, this magnificent celestial show will have folded its tent and disappeared into the sunshine. Just as sad is the news that if you chose to attend this show at home, the light pollution of the cities would most likely preclude your full enjoyment of the celestial spectacle. You simply must be someplace people rarely go to see what nature has to offer. The open ocean on a clear night is one of Mother Nature's venues of choice, and the show is great.

The last twenty-four hours has taken us by El Salvador and Honduras, and we are now approaching the ports near Managua, Nicaragua, with its brightly lit coastline. Costa Rica is about a day away, and Panama the next country after that. We anticipate arriving in the staging area for our canal passage on Wednesday the twenty-first. From that point on, our schedule is pretty much at the mercy of the Canal Authority. All the available information emphasizes the obvious fact that the canal does not exist for the convenience of the pleasure-boating community. The degree of a welcome extended to us remains to be seen, but the experience hopefully will be in the "priceless" category.

The boat continues to perform flawlessly. At present, we appear to have escaped the adverse current of about a knot that has characterized most of the SE headings this passage demands.

We are now making 8.9 knots (over 10 mph) at 1,750 rpm, burning 5.8 gph. We have slowed our speed to time our arrival at the canal staging area in the early-morning hours rather than in darkness.

Our trip log shows that we have covered almost 8,600 nm in about 1,250 engine hours since we left Dana Point, CA, last spring! You may be surprised to learn that our return trip to Virginia has already taken us most of the way across the US. In fact, we are now directly south of Pensacola, Florida (although we are 1,100 nm south of there). For you pilots, we are on the Virginia Beach 202 radial at 1,596 nm on a heading of 148.3 degrees. At present, we are heading away from home to get to the canal, and then, after our passage, we will make the big swing toward the NE to our homebound course.

The challenge of the next twenty-four hours will be the Gulf of Papagayo off Costa Rico. It is the little brother of Mexico's Gulf of Tehuantepec with dangerous winds from the Gulf of Mexico multiplied by the short, flat mainland separating that gulf from the Pacific Ocean. Again, we will be in an area infamous for generating winds approaching 100 mph that can come up in minutes from essentially flat seas. We will be taking the same approach as we traverse Papagayo, turning towards the shore just as we pass south of the rock used a waypoint for this passage.

The weather remains beautiful and the forecasts very good. SSB radios really come into their element down here. I never turned it on in Alaska, but south of latitude sixteen degrees north, it has been our sole source of communication. Every day we check in with the Maritime Net on twenty meters where current weather is available on request. They also keep track of our current position, forward any messages, and relay information from other boats even when thousands of miles away. It is quite a service and would justify expending the effort to get an amateur radio operator's license from the FCC. Also, it is no small comfort to know that the US Coast Guard can be reached anytime via the SSB. I don't think that a mayday call out here would receive the same attention from the Nicaraguan

Navy that it would from our CG. As a bonus, the BBC and the Voice of America are there for news that is otherwise unavailable, and daily conversations with my father-in-law (WA4JIM) in Florida are routinely available via the SSB.

Much of what you use the SSB for is available to you without an amateur license, as you can listen to others talk without restrictions. However, the full benefits of the radio nets that operate throughout the world are restricted to those with an FCC license. Get one if you are coming down here. The first level of licensure is very easy and can be easily done in a weekend. The higher license levels allow more liberal use of the frequencies available to amateur operators and require a little more effort to qualify, but none are hard, and there is no longer a morse code requirement for licensure. It adds a significant level of comfort while in the stark, foreign, and somewhat threatening environment of the Central American Pacific Ocean.

So, we chug along in air-conditioned comfort, eating like royalty and enjoying an experience few are privileged to witness. If you have ever contemplated doing something like this, do it. And soon! Your remaining lifetime is a day less than it was yesterday, and the clock is ticking.

11/18/2007, Sunday

It is 4 AM, and we are now all firm believers in the Tehuantepec-Papagayo wind phenomena. The Gulf of Papagayo in Costa Rico is only a fraction of the size of its Mexican big brother, Tehuantepec, but its ferocity exceeded our Mexican experience. As soon as we made the turn at Cape Santa Elena, the northerly winds greeted us with force-5 seas on the Beaufort scale even though we were only a mile offshore. If you have an interest, Google "Beaufort scale"—it's a classic in the mariner's world. The highest seas we have experienced were force 8 off California's Point Mendocino last May.

The ride went from smooth to uncomfortable almost instantly as the winds were coming directly on our port beam, and the seas beat unrelentingly at our most vulnerable point. So, we heeded the advice given to us by Carl Nish and Tony Carter with more than a century of offshore experience between them. We took *Always Friday* to within a quarter mile of shore. Dual depth sounders and redundant charts assured us that the water was no less than fifty feet, and the results were almost magical. The winds continued to howl over our heads, but the short distance from land denied Neptune the opportunity to boil the seas that *Always Friday* now traveled in smooth comfort.

This was truly the cruising with "one foot on shore" we had heard so much about as the anecdote to these funneling winds of Tehuantepec and Papagayo, and it really works. In fact, if you don't take this approach, you are playing into the hands of these tempestuous seas. If you pass through this area and good weather tempts you to "go straight across," you would be well served by hearing the experienced voices of Carl and Tony whispering, "Don't do it!" in your ear. My advice means nothing in comparison to those men of the sea, but I assure you that if I ever come this way again, one foot will be on the shore.

One advantage of passing so close to shore is that you visit the seaside towns of Costa Rica without the hassle of the immigration process. We passed several towns so closely that you could read the names on the sterns of the fishing boats moored there but never saw anything that would draw us further into the harbors. One particularly memorable event occurred as we passed a small village during the blackness of night. As we stood on the forward deck behind the Portuguese bridge, a fireworks display sprang from the center of town! I have no idea how they knew that we were coming, or who told them that it was my birthday month, but I certainly appreciated their efforts on our behalf.

We are now approaching Guiones Point, Costa Rica, and the chart reflects an adverse current in the area. Our speed has slowed to one of the slowest of the trip—6.2 knots! Our next waypoint will take us 30 nm offshore, so we should be out of its effects soon. From Cabo San Lucas south, the predominant current has been against us at a rate of about one knot. In fact, we repeatedly saw our speed change from 7.5 to 9.5 knots each time we reversed course to chase fish earlier this week.

We have just passed another milestone; we are into single-digit latitudes, now at latitude nine degrees north. That is in comparison to our northernmost point in our trip, latitude fifty-nine degrees north at Skagway, Alaska. Since each degree of latitude reflects 60 nm, we are now 3,000 nm south of Skagway. Since we have also traveled so far east, Skagway is almost 4,000 nm from us at present. Our southernmost waypoint will be latitude seven degrees, twenty minutes north—about 175 nm south of our present position, and about 425 nm above the equator. At that point, we will turn northeast to approach the Panama Canal staging area.

Nordhavns may be slow, but they are relentless. The maritime equivalent of "The Tortoise and the Hare!"

The seas are smooth (force 1 if you looked up the Beaufort scale), the winds calm, and the temperature a balmy eight degrees even before sunrise. We have the ocean to ourselves; nothing on the radar, nothing on the AIS. Beautiful isolation in a potentially hostile environment made into a five-star resort by *Always Friday*.

11/19/2007, Monday

It is 3:45 AM, and again the seas and winds are calm, and the sky is clear. The stars are so bright as to almost light up the world without any effort from the sun at all. Occasional strokes of lightning, something I have not seen since last spring, light up the Costa Rican sky above the mountains, although no clouds, and certainly no rain, accompany it. In fact, we have not seen a drop of rain since Monterey, CA.

After spending the night 30 nm offshore as we run from point to point, we are now less than 2 nm from the Costa Rican coast, abeam of Punta Salsipuedes, the last prominent point of Costa Rica before we cross into the country of Panama. Although we are only 235 nm from the canal as the gull flies, our obligatory path around the southern tip of Panama will add almost 100 nm to the trip before we arrive at the staging area for the passage. The AIS and radar are beginning to reflect the funneling of the world's maritime traffic into the Panama Canal that takes thousands of miles off the trip to Africa and Europe (and Virginia). After going days at a time without seeing any sign of commercial sea traffic at all, the Gulf of Panama is beginning to light up with 700- to 1,000-foot ships moving like moths to a light towards one of the great engineering feats in the history of man.

Our forward progress continues to be compromised by a significant current. For the past two days, we have been averaging about 6.8 knots in flat seas. Again yesterday, to confirm that we weren't dragging some long-liner's baggage, we reversed our course and saw our speed instantly increase to 9.4 knots, confirming an adverse current of approximately 1.3 knots to be the culprit responsible for our slower-than-expected progress. In fact, our book *Ocean Passages of the World* reflects the presence of this current all along the Central American coast. It's there, so if you plan to come this way, count on its presence. On an optimistic note, we anticipate picking up helpful currents on the Atlantic side, culminating in an almost four-knot boost from the Gulf Stream when we hit it.

We have a new passenger on board! Yesterday, when about 30 to 40 nm offshore, we were visited by a beautiful little multicolored swallow that seemed to have lost its way to shore. He circled the boat several times, and then flew in and out of the bridge house twice before lighting on my arm! Although I am not much at reading the expressions of birds, he seemed exhausted and relieved to find a haven from the seas. So, we made him a home safe from Binky and the sharks and fed him a first-class dinner of water and breadcrumbs. I would love to tell you that he gulped them down with deep appreciation . . . but he didn't. He looked at our offerings like we would pig's feet in a Chinese market. But at least he has stayed with us for the last fifteen hours as we shuttle him closer to shore, and a new home in Panama.

At present, we are exactly 1,500 nm due south of Atlanta, GA, 50 nm from the Panama border. Since leaving Puerto Quetzal, Guatemala, we have covered about 600 nm in eighty nonstop hours. Our plan to arrive at the Panama Canal with about 700 gallons of diesel fuel on board is right on track. It looks like we will arrive at the canal Wednesday morning. When we go through is dependent upon the considerable governmental bureaucracy associated with the Panama Canal Authority, but it should be soon!

11/20/2007, Tuesday

Monday was a lazy, beautiful day with the weather just as good as it has been—excellent!

In the morning, shortly after the sun came up, the little bird that dropped by the night before looked around, saw that he was very close to land again, and left. I'm probably making too much of it, but he didn't just leave. He rose into the air, took a lap around the bridge house right in front of me, and rolled right towards the Panamanian mainland. It was a scene reminiscent of *Top Gun* when Tom Cruise buzzed the tower—little bird saying thanks for the ride as he flew into the sunrise.

As we crossed into Panama this morning, our course took us very close to land, and the scenery was beautiful. It is not uncommon to see what appear to be thatched-roof resorts, but we never saw a single person on the beach. In fact, they appeared to be abandoned.

We had an interesting encounter in the afternoon that really struck home with Kathy. About twenty years ago, we were trolling for sailfish off the Zane Gray Reef in Panama when several sea snakes came by the boat. Kathy has been petrified of them ever since. Maybe because I told her they could climb on board over the railings. Well, yesterday I saw one on the surface right by the boat. I didn't tell Kathy, but over the next half hour, three more passed right by us, no more than ten feet from the hull . . . and Kathy saw one! She was very rational about it, but a swim while we are at anchor is out of the question for her. Although quite venomous, they are harmless unless severely provoked. Almost all bites occur when fishermen stick their hands into piles of netted fish, unaware of their presence. Kathy remains convinced that they are a real threat to Raleigh, Binky, and us. Our swim later in the afternoon in eighty-six-degree water at Isla Parida was uneventful, with Kathy watching from the "back porch."

The currents slowed our progress to the degree that our anticipated Tuesday arrival would not occur until midnight, so back to the charts for an alternative plan. Having spent the last four nights at sea with watch schedules playing havoc with sleep, we decided to take a night off and anchor in a beautiful little cove on Isla Parida. The cruising community's website had given it rave reviews for beauty, safety, and ease of entry, so we plotted a new course for a night on the hook there. We arrived about 3:30 PM and dropped the anchor in about fifteen feet of water with good holding on the first try.

The beach had beautiful white sand with a backdrop of palm trees and blue sky. A sailboat was leaving as we arrived, and another by the name of *Plan B* from Washington state was now sharing the anchorage with us. I called him on the VHF radio and learned that he was waiting for a Panamanian visa for his wife before they could continue their odyssey to the South Pacific. We exchanged pleasantries about each other's recent experiences, including my strongest admonition that they be sure and see Alaska before they croak. Then he hit me with the big one! A native was selling lobsters for next to nothing one cove away: only a short ride in the tender. Shortly thereafter, we were the happy owners of seven beautiful lobsters for $20.

Tonight's dinner of grilled lobsters served under the star-filled Panamanian sky with the beach and palm trees forming the backdrop for the feast is exactly what makes this life on the sea so gratifying, attractive, and addictive.

It is now about 5 AM, and we left Isla Parida in the dark about an hour ago, now on our way to the Panama Canal. The navigational equipment on *Always Friday* makes things possible that simply would not be without them, like winding our way through these small islands surrounded by shallow reefs an hour before sunrise in total darkness! With the radar, sounder, plotter, and FLIR, you can do so with confidence and safety, but without them, you would not want to be here.

I have no idea where the signal came from, but while anchored, the Blackberry picked up 156 emails for me. Concurrently we had good cell contact for the few hours we were at Isla Parida anchorage, which disappeared this morning when we were only five miles away. I answered as many as I could and will get the rest at the next opportunity. There is still no sign of internet connectivity here.

In one of the Blackberry emails today, our agent directed us to check in with the Canal Authority upon arrival in the bay, then head for the Flamenco Yacht Center where she has us a slip. We will then begin the administrative process that must precede the transit, refuel, buy groceries, and prepare for the ride across Panama. Once on the Atlantic side, we plan to spend a few days in the San Blas Islands of Panama before striking out for Cancun. The boat can easily make the trip nonstop from Panama to Miami, but we may make a stop in Belize, or run nonstop to Cancun. Of course, as always, all plans are contingent upon the weather.

I talked to Bill Calliott by satellite phone in Virginia Beach today and heard that it was forty degrees, cloudy, and cold. Not down here! A breezy eighty-five degrees. This is close to paradise, and *Always Friday* brought us here in comfort.

Next stop—the canal!

11/21/2007, Wednesday

Another lazy, enjoyable day at sea most notable for its geographic milestones. Late in the afternoon yesterday, we passed the southernmost point of our trip at latitude seven degrees, eleven minutes north. Now for the first time, rather than heading south toward the canal, we are beginning to move towards home on a northeasterly course. We have completed our trip across the US, as Charleston, SC, is directly north of us at present, although it is more than 1,500 nm away. Our northernmost point in the trip was Marjorie Glacier in Glacier Bay (latitude fifty-nine-plus degrees north), now 4,200 nm to the NW.

Since last spring, *Always Friday* has taken us 9,200 nm, the equivalent of four times across the US, with another northbound transcontinental-lap equivalent to go before we are home. If we had left Virginia on an easterly heading, the distance covered on our trip to date would have taken us to Greece and back home again! Nordhavns are indeed the Energizer bunnies of the boating world, and we are chugging happily along.

We have seen our first raindrop since San Francisco, with heavy rain showers during the afternoon and night reflecting our arrival in this tropical area. The humidity is extremely high, and it would be quite uncomfortable (close to unbearable) without the air conditioners.

As we passed an oceangoing sailboat yesterday during the late afternoon, I called the skipper on the VHF just to see what he was up to. With a strong but friendly French accent, he answered with the news that he was on his way to Mexico for a year. We told him what to expect on the seas we just left behind and he briefed us on his recent canal passage, which had been uneventful. As he sailed by us with a big wave from the cockpit, he expressed his appreciation for the call, with the comment that no one else had ever called just to talk. I don't understand why everyone wouldn't do so. World-class adventures and adventurers surround us—why not grab every interesting story you can?

It is now 3:25 AM and we are about sixty-five miles from the canal staging area. At present, it is very dark, and the Gulf of Panama is alive with canal traffic from all over the world. The closest ship to us is the *Maerk Dieppe*, a monster of almost 1,000 feet in length and a beam of nearly 100 feet. It just passed within a mile of us, seen only on radar and the AIS in the rainy dark. Ship traffic is heavy, compounded by the fact that everyone is on the same track, either inbound or outbound from the canal. At present, we are being overtaken by three ships and meeting two others, all on a maritime pathway no more than three miles wide through the 125-mile-wide Gulf of Panama. The radar is compromised by the heavy rain, but the FLIR, AIS, and plotters keep us well informed of our surroundings. We are indeed "playing with the big boys" out here, but *Always Friday* is well prepared for it.

Blackberry just came alive, but still no sign of the internet. Hopefully, it will raise its head as we approach Isla Flamenco and Balboa where we will spend tonight and maybe another before transiting to the Atlantic side.

One of the high points of the trip is about to unfold (but my heart is still in Glacier Bay).

11/22/2007, Thursday, Thanksgiving Day!

Today's update will be quite long for several reasons. First, there is a lot to tell you about this fascinating but frequently frustrating place. Secondly, I have plenty of time to write as I wait for the next in the unending stream of Clouseau-type inspectors to arrive for completion of the paperwork required to transit the canal.

Yesterday, as we came within 15 nm of the staging area for passage, we contacted the Flamenco Signal Station with our agent's name and position to initiate the process of checking in for passage. They were expecting us and checked off our timely arrival. We then proceeded towards Flamenco Yacht Marina where we had a slip reservation for the next two to three days, again arranged by our agent. As instructed, we called ahead to the harbormaster to announce our impending arrival . . . to no answer.

Finally, as we rounded the breakwater to enter the harbor, they called us. After hovering in the harbor for about ten minutes, they had our slip ready, a starboard-side tie with fifty-amp power, exactly as requested. So far, so good! Tina McBride, our agent, was on our good list (and still is).

In no time, the harbor's line handlers had us secured and the boat's 240V electrical system powered from shore for the first time since Dana Point. We had emailed and left voicemails on Tina's cell phone, but somehow that did not serve to let her know of our arrival. Two hours of quarantine later, she arrived to begin the reams of paperwork required for passage. Most of it was like the charade of immigration clearances required in all the Central American countries we have visited, but then came the "special" requirements! Our first visitor was to be the garbage and refrigerator inspector. His job was to reassure the canal administration that we had no rats on board. Now, this marina is filled with North American luxury yachts that would not allow a fly on board, much less a *rat*! One might argue that that is proof that the inspector is doing a great job—or you might rationally conclude that a rat has never seen the inside of one of these boats since time began.

Well, the able inspector arrived in has baseball cap turned sideways, sporting a T-shirt (we had dressed Raleigh and Binky in their best collars to insure against any chance of confusion of their genus and species by the inspector). Ten minutes later, his job was done; no rats, and we owed him $15 for his efforts and our essential clearance paper. But not really! Since it was now after four o'clock, there was a $150 overtime fee. So now we have the rat inspector whom fate had obviously delivered into a profession commensurate with his abilities at a prorated charge of almost $100 per hour *before* overtime at ten times his usual fee. More money down the drain . . . or rat hole. Welcome to Panama, gringo! A quick discussion with our agent led to her commitment to pay the overtime fee from her fee, which of course means that she told him, "No way!"

As Tina briefed us on the anticipated events of the next few days, we learned that we are in a drug-run, crime-ridden city that is unsafe for unattended North Americans if you leave secure areas such as our marina. Kathy was devastated by the suggestion that no one wear any jewelry or fine watches at all. For a woman who feels vulnerable to charges of indecent exposure if she has on less than $10,000 worth of jewelry, it was quite an adjustment to make! Her initial response was to exchange gold trinkets for sterling silver, but when that too was deemed too provocative, she finally gave in and wore only her Breitling watch into the jungle of the city. Tina warned us that a foray into town alone was not advisable. No problem—we now have a guard-driver for the day at $12 an hour to ensure our safe return to the boat.

Tina had answers for all our needs associated with the passage. I will be in command of the boat and responsible for all aspects of *Always Friday*'s operation—the canal is responsible for virtually nothing. Our PC advisor, a pilot-in-training not yet qualified to take the monster boats through, will be with me every foot of the way, *but* I was warned that if he appeared to be making an error that might jeopardize our boat, it was my responsibility to correct his error. So much for the usual maritime rule that a pilot is responsible for a boat under his command! We will have two Panamanian line handlers on board to manage the four 150-foot lines that will control our position in the three locks. You might think that the handlers are included in the toll, but no—they are $130 per day more. And the lines? Not included—you rent them for $100! And fenders? We have great inflatable ones but were advised that they might not prevent the destruction wrought by the walls of the canal. No problem; we can rent old tires in a bag for $100. We did.

We have been assured of a center-chamber, tug-side tie for the passage. That means that we will go through with a very big ship occupying almost the entire lock. One of the tugs responsible for the big ship will be secured in the destructive position next to the wall of the lock, and we will be tied to the side of that tug adjacent to mid chamber. Tina has assured us that that is the preferred arrangement for boats that consider cosmetics to be important. Any other arrangement is often associated with multiple, deep reminders of contact with the walls.

Next came Jorge, the admeasure for the Canal Authority. He was a very friendly, capable, and knowledgeable representative of the CA of whom they should be quite proud. He knew and did his job well. There was a very long list of required equipment that had to be shown present and in good working order. All were very reasonable... like a horn, knot meter, compass, rudder angle indicator, radio, etc. The only catch was that any yacht over sixty-five feet must have a "pilot's plug" as part of the boat's AIS for the pilot to plug his computer into for the full capability of AIS to be realized. If you don't have one, you are required to rent a portable AIS from them for another $150. It became a moot point for us when the boat was shown to be less than sixty-five feet long, otherwise it would have been yet another unexpected charge. We showed Jorge our AIS integrated into the plotter and radar, and he agreed that our system was superior to that of the canal, but rules are rules, and we would have been forced to rent an inferior AIS to supplement our better one.

Then came a basic question: how long is a Nordhavn 55? Not so fast; it's not fifty-five feet long. In fact, they pull out their tapes and measure it. The length for their planning includes the bow pulpit and swim platform, not included in the NH specs. So here is the answer: a Nordhavn 55 is sixty-two feet, eleven inches. You can't argue with a tape measure!

I hope he doesn't tell the harbormaster, who is charging us $1.65 per foot per night as a fifty-five-footer.

Several things now confirm that we have essentially completed our west-to-east journey across the United States. First, we are now directly south of Charleston, SC, therefore now only about 150 nm west of Virginia Beach's longitude. Secondly, we have now returned to the same time zone as Virginia's EST. Even before we had confirmation of Panama's time zone, our longitudinal position told us that we were about to gain another hour. So, if you are easily bored by fascinating mathematical computations, you really should skip the rest of this paragraph. Excuse me while I add a personal message here that will mean something only to my good friends, who will recognize the significance. Tom, Jack, Hank, and Bill—skip this! Frank, Jim, Wick, and Steve—read on; it's interesting! But you probably know it anyway.

What relationship does longitude have to time zones? It is the whole story! The computations are predicated upon several facts. First, the earth is round (I have personally confirmed that this summer!), making the equator a 360-degree circle. If you take 360 strings and tie them equidistantly to the North and South Pole, you have the meridians of longitude defined on the globe. By convention, the first, or prime, meridian passes through Greenwich, England. When the sun is directly overhead Greenwich, it is 12 noon GMT

(Greenwich Mean Time or Zulu time). Since the sun moves around the world 360 degrees in twenty-four hours, it is moving at a rate of 15 degrees of longitude per hour (360/24=15). How did we know that we were in for a time change? We knew what time it was when we left Guatemala, and we knew that we had traveled 13 degrees of latitude against the path of the sun upon arrival in Panama, so it should be an hour later by the clock . . . and it was. So, if Virginia Beach is near longitude 76 degrees and Southern California can be found at about 120 degrees of longitude, what is the time difference? Forty-four divided by fifteen per hour makes it three hours earlier. I find it interesting to understand how those things work out. Kathy says I am a nerd.

Anyone want to know how the pirates cleaned out the gold-bearing galleons in olden days? It is the story of latitude, but I won't bore you with that one now.

Tonight, Thanksgiving dinner will be at a great restaurant that we enjoyed last night. The seafood was unique and excellent, dictating a return tonight.

Tomorrow we will fill the fuel tanks of *Always Friday* in anticipation of long runs to Belize, Cancun, and then Key West, but first we are going to spend a few days in the San Blas Islands on the Atlantic Panamanian coast. The adventure continues!

11/24/2007, Saturday, Canal Transit

With today's long anticipated passage through one of the engineering wonders of the world eminent, I arose at 4 AM to be certain that our 6:45 departure from Flamenco Yacht Marina would go off without a hitch. Although the boat's propulsion and steering systems have been flawless, the Panama Canal was no place for the first mechanical glitch of *Always Friday*'s life. So hydraulic fluid levels, system pressures, fuel manifold selectors, oil levels, stuffing box drip levels, etc., were checked for the last time before committing to the transit. The Canal Authority does not tolerate delays from anyone, and if they occur, there are dire financial consequences. With any concern for a vessel's ability to maintain the pace of canal traffic, a tug is called to stand by for assistance, and you have instantly spent $2,500 in tug fees and sacrificed your buffer fee of $600! Of the thirty-eight vessels transiting the canal today, only two are private boats: *Always Friday* and a forty-five-foot sailboat (more about that boat later!). It is obvious that this is very big business, and we are inconsequential in the big picture unless we stop the flow of traffic.

How big a business? The big boys pay six-figure fees per day for the privilege of taking thousands of miles off their trip and many thousands of dollars off their fuel bills while traveling among the continents. In fact, a cruise ship paid over $300,000 last month to do just what we are doing today for less than 1 percent of that! As directed, we and our two line handlers, Roberto and Winston, were alongside channel buoy 4 at 7 AM to pick up our transit advisor, who functions as a pilot for boats under sixty-five feet.

The transit advisors are in the process of becoming pilots, but the time frame is as long as four years before they take the big ships through. We had the good fortune to draw Frank Samundio, a native Panamanian who could not have been more able, helpful, or informative. Rubin, a tugboat master, was along today as a part of Frank's training, and between them, we learned more in a day about the history and function of the canal than you could glean from books in a month. Since only a small percentage of the 40 nm trip through the canal involves the locks, we had ample opportunity to avail ourselves of their considerable canal knowledge and experience.

But nothing tops taking your own boat through the Panama Canal! With Frank's advice always at hand, we drove *Always Friday* every foot of the way, not willing to miss any experience this opportunity might present. The first set of locks from the Pacific side are the Miraflores

Locks that lift you eighty-four feet from Pacific level to the level of Gatun Lake. The next phase of the trip is the 35-plus nm ride down the man-made wonders of Gaillard Cut leading to Gatun Lake, one of the largest man-made lakes in the world, covering over 400 square miles. Upon arrival at Gatun Locks, approximately twelve hours after beginning the journey, you are lowered the eighty-four feet to the level of the Atlantic Ocean to renew your journey. But that simplistic explanation fails to convey the enormity of the accomplishments of the engineers who "did the impossible."

The lock system was necessary not because there is an appreciable difference in the levels of the Atlantic and Pacific Oceans—the difference is less than a foot—but because there is a major difference in the tide swings of the two oceans. The Pacific high and low tides differ by approximately seventeen feet (we saw just that in Flamenco Yacht Marina), while those on the Atlantic side swing no more than a foot or two. If you were to dig a sea-level canal between the two oceans, the radical difference in tides would make the tidal flow incompatible with shipping—so the lock system was devised to solve that dilemma. It has worked beautifully for almost 100 years, and a new canal, set to open in 2014, is now under construction parallel to the original one, using the same basic plan as the first. That is quite a compliment to the original design!

To lift or drop these massive ships the eighty-four-foot difference in the levels of the Oceans and Gatun Lake, forty-four to fifty-six million gallons of fresh water from Gatun Lake are used to flood each chamber of the lock. The filling or draining process takes about ten minutes, and you can easily see the changing water levels along the walls of the lock. Not just see them—you can feel them! The turbulence is dramatic. In fact, we were in the first Miraflores Lock with the only other small boat of the Canal's Day, the forty-five-foot sailboat. As the water rose with dramatic force, we saw that very light boat tossed around like a feather in the wind to the extent that it appeared to be in serious trouble. The degree of pitching and rolling associated with the influx of water was so violent that the transit advisor on board the sailboat subsequently requested a slower flow rate to minimize the instability of the process (but the sailboat's travails were not yet over).

The trip down the canal took us through the haunts of crocodiles, poisonous snakes, monkeys, peacock bass, and, perhaps the deadliest of all in the old days, insects. Mosquitoes were instrumental in killing many of the 20,000 casualties of the canal's construction, with their weapon being malaria. Crocodiles remain a real threat as evidenced by the loss of a Panamanian man in the waters adjacent to Gatun Lake a few years ago.

But as you approach the third and final chamber of the Gatun or Miraflores Lock, a new potential threat raises its head. It is well known, scientifically understood, and clearly warned of in any publication written for the operator of a vessel passing through those locks. It applies only to the third lock on either end that empties you and its water into the respective oceans. The challenge arises from the fact that the locks fill with fresh water from Gatun Lake, but when the final locks empty into the ocean, the fresh water is almost instantly mixed with salt water from the sea. The sea water is heavier than the fresh water, so it rushes to the bottom of the lock, violently forcing the fresh water and any small boat in the lock out into the pathway to the ocean!

Both Frank and Rubin briefed me on the procedure required to overcome the violent but predictable exit currents. As soon as the gate opens, the response must be full power, with immediate corrective measures for the current pushing you into the starboard wall of the lock, followed by a countercurrent attempting to force you in the opposite direction, before a third current again attempts to slam you into the right wall again. Though warned of the violent nature of the currents generated by the mixing of fresh and salt water, I was still surprised by their strength. We rolled about thirty degrees in opposite directions while accelerating under full power to yield a ride usually reserved for theme parks.

The experience was otherwise just as predicted, and *Always Friday*'s response got us through unscathed. But the sailboat, now in the opposite chamber with a tugboat and considerably lighter than *AF*, did not fare as well. As the crew of *Always Friday* watched in awe, the sailboat was grabbed and tossed by the current in a fashion usually reserved for movies like the *Perfect Storm* before being ejected into the Atlantic on a heading 180 degrees from that planned—in other words, it was spit out backwards. Whether it hit the wall or not, we could not see, and do not know, but Frank said that such gyrations were often associated with wall collisions and significant damage.

After returning Frank and Rubin to the pilot boat and Roberto and Winston to the dock at the local boatyard, *Always Friday* dropped anchor off the city of Colon, Panama, for a night of welcomed rest.

Our four Panamanian guests had contributed greatly to the thrill and enjoyment of our Panama Canal passage, one of the true highlights of our adventure. Frank, Rubin, Roberto, and Winston will always be significant parts of our very pleasant memories of this special day! Although she was not with us for the passage, our canal agent, Tina McBride (tinamc@sinfo.net and www.panamcanaltransits.com), played an essential role in the success of this past week. She arranged for *Always Friday*'s dockage, all preparation and scheduling of the transit, our excellent line handlers, and all the challenges of the immigration process with skill and efficiency. She clearly met or exceeded all our high expectations. There may be other canal agents, but in my opinion, Tina McBride is all you need to know if you follow our path through Panama and its canal.

Always Friday is now in its home ocean, in one piece, without a scratch and with all aboard healthy and happy. Ninety-four hundred nautical miles behind us and about 2,500 more to go before we are home! Next stop: San Blas Islands tomorrow. They are supposed to be a true tropical paradise, inhabited by Indigenous people, and not often frequented by outsiders. We will tell you more about it soon.

11/25/2007, Sunday

We anchored in Foxtrot anchorage just off Colon with about fifteen other private boats, mostly sail powered. At daybreak, we were on our way out of the Cristobal anchorage for the big ships and surrounded by car carriers, bulk carriers, and tankers awaiting their turn through the canal.

The city of Colon is protected by a very impressive seawall necessitated by the large swells that frequent the area. As we came through the entrance to the harbor, the swells were indeed present and impressive—about eight feet and ten seconds apart, yielding a bouncy but tolerable ride for the next ten hours to the San Blas Islands. Upon arrival, it was if we entered a time warp. The tiny islands, no more than a quarter mile wide, had huts with thatched roofs, sometimes only one to an island.

As the big yellow boat inched through the poorly charted waters, the natives began to converge upon us from each island, holding their wares out for our inspection. But this was not junk marketing reminiscent of Skagway. These were true natives with tattooed faces, pierced nasal septums, and ankle beads right out of *National Geographic*. Their dugouts were obviously locally made with the awl marks clearly visible, and the paddles bore more of a resemblance to a limb than a paddle. Their sails were a single triangular piece of fabric run up by hand when the breeze was appropriate, generating a crude but strikingly beautiful image against a backdrop of these tropical islands.

The first two natives to get to us were fisherman selling the octopus strewn on the floor of their dugout. Since Kathy did not know how to cook them, we attempted to ask about "langoustes" or lobsters. They seemed to understand but had none at the time. When Kathy asked by hand signals for permission to photograph them, they quickly stood up in the dugout, held an octopus in each hand, and smiled from ear to ear. So much for the cruise guide's advice that they don't want their picture taken!

To show our appreciation for the pleasure of visiting their home islands, we gave each of them a pair of flip-flops from Old Navy (Kathy had been told that they were highly cherished by the natives, so she bought a dozen pair before we left California) and a handful of cookies and candy. You would think that they had just won the lottery, and maybe they had in their world.

When word of their success spread among their tribe members, *Always Friday* became the center of commerce for everything that comprised their gross national product. Mothers in unstable canoes paddled out with infants held by four-year-olds to peddle bowls made from coconut shells, colorful fabrics, and wood carvings. Kathy bought a bowl for $3 that would probably sell for $20 in the city market but was able to resist the other shopping opportunities. Although fascinating, it did not have the same attraction to her as Nordstrom's, and finally we had to say no to the rest of the crowd gathering in the waters around *Always Friday*. But none paddled away without cookies and candy!

Quite an experience, and none of the manufactured feel of the American Indian villages.

Tonight, we are anchored off Limon Cay with the fires of the natives lighting the beach. Tomorrow we are going to Cayos Coco Bandero for another night on the anchor. The SSB is giving us a weather forecast of smoother seas as the week progresses, so our next long leg to either Belize or Cancun should be more pleasant than the ride from Colon to San Blas. After an excellent shrimp dinner, it will be off to bed with the trade winds rocking us to sleep in this true and unspoiled tropical paradise.

11/26/2007, Monday

This morning we covered the 15 nm to Coco Bandero in several hours, only to find the islands so exposed to the weather than we were uncomfortable in anchoring there. The fact that we could see twelve-foot waves breaking on the shore added to our concerns, but the five-hundred-foot freighter lying forty-five degrees to its port side, locked in death throes on the reef, cemented our decision to seek shelter elsewhere. The ship was a relatively recent victim of the reef; not only were its masts still intact, but the rigging and antennas also looked ready for service... if only the ship could float!

So, back to the charts and Bauhaus's book, *The Panama Cruising Guide*, for another option. We settled on an island named Canirtupo, or Green Island, about 10 nm away. After a very slow and careful approach to the recommended anchorage, we were safely hooked to the sand in about twenty-five feet of water. Once again, the local Indians were around the boat, selling their wares, which include the *molas*—or tapestries—for which they are famous. We made our requests for "langouste grande" and we think we were told, "Tomorrow!" Down came *Friday Nite!*, and off we went to explore the islands and their beaches. Upon our return, a swim in the eighty-five-degree water was a refreshing way to end the afternoon.

Two new friends from a sailboat anchored near us accepted my invitation to join us on board *Always Friday* for a visit. Dennis and Paula have been cruising for four years after their early retirements as an engineer and artist, respectively. They educated us about the local Indian tribe and related some of their fascinating experiences with the natives here over the last several weeks. Paula has become quite knowledgeable on the topic of molas and shared her outstanding collection with us. They gratefully accepted about ten of our old magazines, having been deprived of such pleasures as the price of cruising solitude.

Another neighboring sailboat dedicated to pursuing a circumnavigation caught a twenty-five-pound snapper from the back of their boat this afternoon, so I may have to drop a hook down there tomorrow. However, the only fish I saw today was a small barracuda, which I consider inedible in the Caribbean because of ciguatera poisoning and not really a food fish for anyone other than hungry natives.

Today was truly a quiet day in paradise surrounded by friendly Kuna people. We may stay here for another day or head for another island with a different view and different products for sale. Kathy really loves this place. It's the shopping, I think!

11/27/2007, Tuesday

It rained hard about 3:30 this morning—the beautiful sound of heavy rain hitting the deck magnifying the joy of being in a tropical paradise. Around midmorning, we weighed anchor and set a course for Isla Porvenir, the site of a grass runway where Jeane will catch a small plane to Panama City and ultimately home for long-standing family commitments. Doug is having so much fun that he is going to stay with us until at least Cancun.

A high-pressure system north of us is generating winds from the NE of twenty to thirty knots with fifteen-foot seas that should diminish over the next twenty-four hours. I have been using multiple weather services down here, but perhaps the most impressive one is a free service from the National Hurricane Center in Miami. Billy Smeltzer, a delivery captain that we befriended in Guatemala, told me of their program in which a phone call puts you in touch with an expert meteorologist specializing in the area in question, who then delivers a detailed briefing just like you get from FAA Flight Centers as a pilot! When I did so today, I spoke for about fifteen minutes with a very knowledgeable briefer who went out of his way to answer every question and assist in our plans for the transit from here to the Yucatán Peninsula. If you are an offshore cruiser, you should strongly consider availing yourself of the expert services of that center.

Later that same day:

We are now anchored about 200 yards off the grass runway and town of El Porvenir, with the Kuna Indians surrounding *Always Friday* with shopping opportunities, some of which were too good to pass up. As an example of the work ethic of these people, we asked yesterday at our last anchorage if lobsters were available. Two young men conveyed to us somehow that there were none available that day, but they would have some the next day. We left at midmorning without a sign of the young men or lobsters. About 5 PM today, a dugout pulled in behind *Always Friday* and yelled a greeting. It was the two men from yesterday's anchorage . . . with seven lobsters! They had paddled twenty-plus miles in a dugout canoe through moderately rough seas just to bring us the lobsters they had promised to find. They charged $9 for seven lobsters, and when we gave them $15, they too looked like lottery winners!

We also had the opportunity to witness a true National Geographic moment . . . in fact, a real one! The channel has been running a series called *Taboo*. One of the featured taboos is a tribal ritual of the San Blas Islands Kuna people (who now surround us on *Always Friday* in numbers of about 50,000) in which if a family has a disproportionate number of male children, the next male child is raised as a female and functions as a woman for their entire life. They are trained to take on feminine traits, no matter how masculine in appearance, and wear female clothes and makeup while accepting the tasks usually given to women in their society.

Interestingly, they are accepted into their society without a stigma of homosexuality or transvestitism, and in many cases appear to be highly respected members of the Kuna society. When we finally get our pictures on the website, you will see two of the men that have embraced the female role. One is quite interesting. He sold Kathy a mola he had handstitched with great skill and diligence, and he will be pictured on the site, holding it up on the stern of *Always Friday*. He appeared to be about twenty years old, very athletically built (like a linebacker), but dressed as a woman, with flowing hair and thick makeup. His mannerisms were clearly effeminate, in sharp contrast to his obvious masculinity. We were told that they occasionally revert to the masculine role when an adult but usually spend their entire life in this flip-flopped sexual role. Yet another experience not frequently encountered while cruising the Chesapeake Bay. What an adventure this is!

The degree of convenience offered to us by the capabilities of *Always Friday*'s systems was brought to light again today when Doug and Bill from the S/V *Lastori* came over by tender to ask if we had any extra ice. They had been weeks without a single cube during their travels from Cartagena, Columbia, to the anchorage we now shared. They are now on the return leg to Southern California with plans to be home before Christmas. We filled their cooler from our freezer, and they gratefully headed back to their sailboat for a much-anticipated rum and Coke!

It is interesting to note that although we have seen about two dozen cruising boats here in the San Blas Islands, *Always Friday* has been the *only* power boat. There is a reason for that: we are in the middle of nowhere, and only boats with impressive range can come here (and get back home). Sailboats, with their inexhaustible fuel supply (the wind), can go anywhere if you are not in a hurry. But power boats, with their relatively short range, are tied to the availability of diesel fuel, unless you have the range of a Nordhavn.

When we left Flamenco Yacht Marina in Panama City for the canal passage, we had 2,350 gallons of diesel fuel on board. The full tanks of *Always Friday* will easily allow us to go to Miami nonstop, or even to Virginia Beach if we throttle the engine back a few hundred rpm. So here we are! Surrounded by sailboats with no ice while we enjoy air-conditioned comfort and the option to go straight to any destination without regard to wind direction. Sailors truly seem to love that lifestyle, but I will take the power boat option every time.

Tomorrow, for the very first time, we will take a heading designed to take us directly home to Virginia Beach. If the weather allows us to do so, we will head for Cancun, Mexico, while leaving the options of intermediate stops open if the winds dictate that approach. If things go very favorably, we may deviate towards Cuba, leave that island to starboard, and go directly to Key West (or even Miami). Such are the options in a boat with the capabilities of *Always Friday*.

Safety remains the number one priority and will not be compromised for any reason. Sadly, our adventure is winding down towards the final chapters, but we still have miles to go and more challenges ahead. I like that.

11/28/2007–11/29/2007, Wednesday–Thursday

We were up at 5 AM to take the tender down to run Jeane the 100 yards to the airstrip where she was to catch her Twin Otter aircraft for Panama City and ultimately San Francisco. She has been a real pleasure to have with us, and we will miss her good humor and high spirits.

Her 6:30 plane arrived at 8:30, so our departure time for Cancun was slightly delayed. The weather briefer in Miami had told us to expect high seas initially but rapidly improving conditions as a high-pressure area north of us dissipated. So, we were not surprised or bothered by seas of about eight feet as we began the five day, nonstop journey to Cancun. However, as we moved offshore, the seas became more impressive, and soon we were facing winds out of the north at twenty-five-plus knots and building seas of twelve to fifteen feet. The boat handled it fine, but it was far more uncomfortable than you would want to endure for five days.

We tried various course deviations with no real benefit, so we settled down to a compromised speed of seven knots to await the improved weather promised by the forecaster. Throughout the night, nothing but the salon and (by necessity!) the bridge was habitable secondary to the boat's reaction to the strong seas. When the heavy salon chair that had not been moved by any preceding weather flew across the room and took out the louvered doors of the AV system, it was time for a change. Another plan B situation!

The charts suggested that a change in destination from Cancun to Grand Cayman Island should yield significant relief on several fronts. First, the new heading of almost due north would get us out of the troughs of our present beam seas. Secondly, Georgetown, Grand Cayman, would be reached a day sooner than Cancun simply because it is considerably closer. And finally, it is a British island that Kathy and I know well from our frequent scuba trips there—a much more hospitable experience than more of the Mexican jumping bean immigration procedures. So, we three agreed to turn further north to Georgetown, Grand Cayman Island. Another example of the flexibility of traveling at your own pace, on your own nonexistent schedule.

Since we are now about 200 miles from shore, we have no cell or internet service, so the SSB radio came through again. I called the Maritime Net on 14,300 kHz, informed them of the change in our destination, and asked them to post our position information and destination change on their internet site's "ship tracker" feature. They then tied me in with Kathy's father, an amateur radio operator in Florida, for me to reassure him of our safety and wellbeing. An amazing service to boats at sea with no other reliable means of communication! In fact, on *Always Friday*, we have the option of using the satellite phone, but I reserve that option for circumstances where we have no other good choice—very expensive and not very reliable.

Now we are at latitude thirteen degrees north with expectations of regaining XM Radio and Weather near latitude sixteen degrees north, about 180 nm north of our present position. The weather is clearly improving, but I can still hear the wind as it whistles through the antennas at something over twenty-five knots. The ride is acceptable, and we are moving directly towards Grand Cayman Island at about seven knots. Kathy made BLTs for dinner tonight, the first meal that the weather had allowed us to prepare since leaving the San Blas Islands. Yesterday was a Gatorade and Oreos day.

The SSB was alive today with reports from near St. Johns Island, the scene of an earthquake of 7.3 on the Richter scale. Most of the talk centered on the probabilities of a tsunami from the quake, and most assessments were that one was very unlikely since the epicenter was in only nine feet of water. Other than the fact that we have two very good friends, Skip and Brenda, vacationing in that area, that question is of no practical concern to us, as we are in the safest place you can be for protection from a tsunami: at sea!

11/30/2007, Friday

The weatherman was right, and we did the right thing. We are now just north of the 14th northern parallel, and the weather has improved considerably. The wind is down to ten to fifteen knots, and the seas have fallen to a comfortable (at least in this boat) six feet. The swells remain about ten feet, but the period has lengthened to over ten seconds, taking most of the sting out of them. Our speed has picked up to 8.5 knots now that the head seas are down, yielding an ETA into Grand Cayman, 275 nm due north of here, of early Saturday night.

Doug and I are splitting the bridge watch every three hours during the night. Since there is very little to do other than engine room checks, fuel tank management, and close attention to the navigational instruments, that has worked quite well. Kaleidoscope and the iPod continue to take us through this area of total "entertainment silence" as we await the return of XM Radio and Sea Tel TV. As I picked up the detailed weather forecast from WLO on SSB this morning, the importance of that piece of equipment was again reinforced. It remains my strong advice that if you are ever coming this way, get your amateur radio license and a SSB radio before you come. And know a SSB is not a radio that you take out of the box and start talking to someone thousands of miles away. It requires considerably more homework than a VHF before you can use it effectively.

The boat is performing flawlessly in an environment that would put many boats at risk for their survival. Doug, who has spent all his adult life at sea, said it well last night: "Nordhavns can't make rough seas comfortable—even cruise ships can't do that—but they sure can make you feel safe in any sea that you might find yourself thrown into!" As the ultimate compliment, Doug is now looking at a Nordhavn 47 as his and Jeane's future retirement home.

So, we chug on with enough fuel to reach Virginia, enough food to get to Europe, and enough water to get to the moon. Grand Cayman Island is off the bow; then Key West is around the Cuban corner. Ten thousand nautical miles down; fifteen hundred more to go before Binky and Raleigh are again chasing squirrels in Virginia!

12/01/2007, Saturday

Now four days out of the San Blas Islands, I am of the strong opinion that the Caribbean Sea in late November is no place for a social visit. The usual word is that the trade winds don't begin to be a problem until mid-December, and we had made our plans based on that premise. However, this has been as rough a passage as we have experienced except for the Point Mendocino gale last May . . . and it has been sustained for almost the entire 600 nm trip! At present, we are taking white water over the pilothouse with regularity with twenty-plus-knot winds off the starboard bow generating breaking seas of eight to ten feet with steep swells of twelve feet or more. The boat handles it well, but man cannot build a boat (or ship for that matter!) that the sea can't toss like a cork. Last night was marginal for opening the galley, but Kathy insisted, and we topped off the day with another great wahoo dish. But today is another Gatorade and Oreos day. We are less than 50 nm from Georgetown, Grand Cayman, and should have the anchor down shortly after dark. Since we had no plans to come here, we have no applicable travel guides and must rely on the Nobletec electronic charts. Luckily, they have considerable information on anchorages and depths, so that should suffice until we are able to glean more local information tomorrow. We are hoping to sleep at anchor without levitation tonight. That would be a welcome change!

Later: Upon arrival near Georgetown harbor, a call to port security yielded a very nice, very British lady who was quite helpful in getting us into port. She assigned us a mooring buoy, complete with GPS coordinates, with the admonition that if we chose to drop anchor, we would be subject to substantial fines if we touched a reef with the anchor. We will clear customs in the morning, and Doug will be on his way back to California after riding almost 2,500 miles with us. His admiration for Nordhavns has been reflected by his frequent perusals of the brokerage sections of the yachting magazines on board. Kathy came through as usual with an excellent dinner that would have rivaled any shoreside restaurant had we been allowed by immigration to leave the boat.

So, it's off to bed, made even more comfortable by the stability of *Always Friday*'s sheltered mooring. It's nice to be free of the Pac Man–like gyrations of an angry sea. Quite a change over the last four days.

12/02/2007, Sunday

We awoke to a beautiful eighty-two-degree day with bright sunshine and blue skies and occasional white, puffy clouds. The wind is still blowing, but we are on the leeward side of the island, and in sharp contrast to the last few days, the breezes are our friends. The anchorage is populated by cruising boats from multiple countries, again predominantly sailing vessels . . . with one *big* exception! Paul Allen's (co-founder of Microsoft) boat, M/Y *Octopus*, is here! It is something over 450 feet long, with helicopters on each end, a 56-foot tender, and a submarine large enough for dozens of passengers. It looks more like a cruise ship than a yacht and is too large to moor on anything other than a cruise ship's mooring ball.

I heard the captain talking with port security on the VHF this morning about his inability to find adequate moorage. Apparently, his solution is to drift down the beach all day since dropping his anchor over the reefs might even strain the budget of Paul Allen. So, after sharing Glacier Bay, AK, with M/Y *Laurel*, we now share Grand Cayman with M/Y *Octopus*! These are two of the premier private yachts in the world, and their views have been no better than *Always Friday*'s.

We are about to depart for the immigration docks for clearance into Grand Cayman. Doug will leave from there, and we will await more favorable winds before leaving for Key West or Fort Lauderdale. We have the last laugh on King Neptune. He has blown us into a beautiful place we would not have seen had the seas been more receptive to our presence.

12/03/2007, Monday

Yesterday was one of those really surprising days when things that could have been a hassle turn out to be not only easy but, even more importantly, very enjoyable! The helpful lady from GCI Port Security called us on the radio, directed us to the North Pier, and arranged for the immigration officers to meet us there. To top even that performance, she then offered us the opportunity to stay at that dock all day until the cruise ship next scheduled there arrived in the early morning of the following day, all at no charge. And things continued to get better.

When the officers arrived to complete our entry papers, they were friendly, very professional, and a real pleasure to have on board. This was in sharp contrast to what we had seen in several other countries (including our own). Trevor and Malachi walked us through the necessary steps in no time, and then stayed a while for a visit and a Coke. I showed them all over *Always Friday*, and they were quite surprised by its capabilities. The electronics and the engine room generated prolonged discussions, but the FLIR system (forward-looking infrared or night vision) was the hit of the show.

Trevor was so impressed with the propulsion systems that he went and got the port engineer to look at what the wind had blown into Grand Cayman. In a very brief period, we had two new friends who gave us their home phone numbers in case we needed anything and offered to pick us up later that evening and deliver us to any restaurant we chose for dinner. Talk about a royal welcome! The lady at port security, Trevor, and Malachi could function as the Department of State for Grand Cayman and immediately be a respected country on the international scene. The expected one hour of drudgery associated with immigration check-in turned into a six-hour visit with some of the nicest, most capable people you could ever hope to meet.

Just as we were about to leave the boat for lunch, two clean-cut American men showed up on the dock with questions about *Always Friday*. You guessed it again . . . we invited them aboard for a tour! We didn't know it at the time, but they were two officers from the USCG Cutter *Thetis*, moored not far from our buoy. In fact, Tom was the captain of the ship, and Brian his legal officer.

This tour of the boat took considerably longer than usual since our audience was, on this occasion, truly professional mariners. Before we had finished, we had not only looked at all the toys on board but also turned them on and played with them. As it turned out in this small world, both men were from Virginia Beach, and the list of common friends was impressive. Of particular interest was the fact that Tom's dad, Ed Crabbs, had relieved my skipper, Al Fancher, in Fighter Squadron 32 in the mid-seventies when I had the privilege of serving as a flight surgeon with Carrier Air Wing One on board the aircraft carrier USS *Kennedy* (CVA-67)! Tom, through his dad, knew of all my old shipmates from those days when he, as a teenager, idolized the fighter pilots I flew with daily during three of the best years of my life.

At least an hour was consumed with stories about Al Fancher, Zeke Burns, Ed Andrews, Don McCrory, Andy Damlekan, John Allen, Fred Lewis, and Rick Parlett. As the years accumulate, memories such as those and the ones of this trip become more important. But the book on *New Friends of the Day* was not yet closed! As I checked my Blackberry for new emails, there was a message that I had not expected.

Under the title "Welcome to Grand Cayman," it read:

> Hello Buddy and Kathy,
>
> My name is Lee Arie. While taking my Sunday walk today through town today, I noticed *Always Friday* clearing customs. What a beautiful boat. I have admired the Nordhavns since first setting sights on one about 5 years ago.
>
> When I returned home, I Googled your boat's name and have been reading up on your adventures. Your "vacation" is my goal. Thank you for sharing through your website.
>
> Anyway, I just wanted to send you a quick note to welcome you to Cayman. If there is any local knowledge

needed, please do not hesitate to ask via e-mail or my cell. Safe travels, Lee Arie

Surprise! I immediately called and invited him to come see us. Since he lives only a few blocks from the harbor, he was on board in no time. Once again, *Always Friday* had been the difference in being just another tourist or a welcomed guest of the country. So, in four hours, our boat introduced us to Malachi, Trevor, Tom, Brian, and now Lee while Paul Allen sat on his rich fanny on board *Octopus*, a yacht too big to come into port. I may take our tender over to *Octopus* today and offer to introduce him around the town.

Lee turned out to be a real pleasure to meet. He came here about ten years ago from Orlando and never went back. He is now the general manager of a large car dealership here, and happy with the casual lifestyle. When I mentioned our frustration over the lack of internet access, he went back to his apartment and retrieved his wireless receiver for our use. That is why we now have about ten days of new updates and almost a hundred new pictures on the web page today. This evening, we are going ashore to meet Lee for dinner, as good things continue to flow from *Always Friday*'s impressive appearance in the harbors we visit.

Tomorrow Jeff Hawkins is going to join us from Texas for the trip around Cuba and into South Florida. We met Jeff in Dana Point, CA, last spring when he was there looking at a Nordhavn as a prospective buyer. He has since become a good friend and will be a welcomed addition to the crew on the three-day passage into the States.

We are spending the day in Georgetown today, with the boat guarded by Raleigh and Binky. They are not allowed ashore since they have not been inspected by the Cayman Department of Agriculture. Apparently, they have our two little dogs confused with heads of lettuce! But that is no problem; they haven't touched ground since the Republic of Panama. Two more weeks at sea, and they will be candidates for scurvy. I'll get them an orange when we go ashore.

12/04/2007, Tuesday

Jeff arrived on time from Texas, and a trip to immigration had him added to the crew list for tomorrow's departure to Key West and points north. Kathy loaded the tender with groceries, and we were off to *Always Friday* with plans to join Lee and his girlfriend, Michelle, for dinner at their favorite local restaurant, the Calypso Grill at Morgan's Harbor on the North Sound.

Before dinner, we picked up Lee and Michelle on *Friday Nite!* for a glass of wine before leaving for the restaurant. Then, with five of us in the tender, we were off to the harbor for a twenty-minute car ride to one of the nicest restaurants you could imagine. It is so far out of the way that you would never stumble upon it without local guidance, which we had in style with Lee and Michele. It was a great combination of location (outside on the water), ambiance, and excellent food. If you are ever in Grand Cayman, find the Calypso Grill; your efforts will be well rewarded!

Kathy and I were last here in Grand Cayman about fifteen years ago, and the place is now unrecognizable from what we saw then. Lee explained that part of the reason for the dramatic building boom is Hurricane Ivan, which devastated the island four years ago. From the rubble of the storm has risen a first-class, first-world resort city anchored by nothing less than a Ritz-Carlton Resort.

Even though it does not seem appropriate in eighty-five-degree weather, the Christmas season is upon us here, and Grand Cayman takes its holiday decorations very seriously. Tastefully done lights were everywhere, attempting to do the impossible—bring an aura of what we have always thought of as Christmas to a tropical island basking in eighty-five-degree sunshine! "I'm Dreaming of a White Christmas" done by a calypso band is an unusual touch. The news from home of truly winter weather there makes the Christmas spirit even harder to summon up on this tropical island.

Lee's obvious interest in Nordhavns and *Always Friday* led to an invitation to join us for the ride to Key West . . . and he accepted! So, our crew list has another addition for tomorrow's departure.

12/05/2007, Wednesday

I was up early (5 AM) to launch the tender to accompany Lee to immigration for the exit paperwork for *Always Friday*'s departure. In no time, we were back on board and ready to go. By 7:30 AM we were underway, passing within a few hundred yards of Paul Allen's boat M/Y *Octopus*, with its tender *Man O' War* tied alongside. The tender is bigger than *Always Friday*!

With just a few degrees of deviation from the most direct path to the western end of Cuba, our path took us over Pickle Banks, a famous fishing spot for blue-water billfish, tuna, dolphin, and wahoo.

We soon had four lines in the water, ready for any denizen of the deep that might drop by. The chart plotter projected our arrival over Pickle Banks about 2:30 PM, but an hour before that, a viscous strike violently took both starboard lines down with the reels screaming that beautiful sound of Penn International clickers going full tilt. About a hundred yards behind the boat, a beautiful blue marlin began a series of greyhounding leaps behind us that snapped the line from the 50W reel, leaving it tied to the back of *Always Friday* with the smaller 30W rig! But she (marlins as big as this one are always females) was well hooked, and the fight was on. Jeff was on the reel for the continuous give-and-take between the fish and *Always Friday*, as she sounded repeatedly, with the boat almost constantly in reverse in an attempt to regain line. On multiple occasions, the fish had almost all our line in the sea, but she was never able to get it all. After two hours, the biggest fish we have had behind *Always Friday* was lying on the surface, as exhausted as Jeff!

It was considerably larger than the blue we caught off the Mexican Pacific coast a few weeks ago, and we estimated that one to have been about 300 pounds. We had all seen big marlin before, and the consensus was that this one was something over 400 pounds! She is back in the Caribbean tonight, tired, with a sore bill but otherwise none the worse for wear. Jeff feels far worse! We will be back on the reels early tomorrow as we pass through some truly great fishing waters just south of western Cuba; in fact, some of Hemmingway's favorite spots were in this area.

We will be out of touch until we hit Florida but will update our position on ShipTrak.org daily by SSB. In sharp contrast to last week, the seas are almost flat, and XM Weather says that they will stay that way all the way to the Keys. It is truly beautiful out here, and we are having the most unique Christmas season of our lives—trading reindeer for blue marlin, and the possibility of snow for the certainty of the blue Caribbean Sea in beautiful eighty-two-degree weather. Not bad at all!

12/06/2007, Thursday

Last night was the kind of night that would turn anyone to the cruising lifestyle. The weather is stone-cold perfect. The seas are barely rippled, the wind less than five knots, the temperature in the high seventies, and the stars brighter than city dwellers will ever see them. Kathy threw together a dinner of crab cakes that would make *Bon Appetite* magazine's cover, served on real china with tunes from XM Radio again permeating the euphoric scene. Life is *incredibly good* on *Always Friday*.

The best seat in the house after dinner was the Portuguese bridge where the celestial Super Bowl was in full swing. Billions of stars were twinkling like diamonds from horizon to horizon, many of them concentrated in as dramatic a demonstration of the Milky Way as you could ever hope to see. Every few minutes, a shooting star would bisect the heavens with its path clearly visible for several seconds. Even that description fails to convey the beauty of the scene magnified a thousand times by the clarity of the Caribbean sky and the brightness of the stars when seen in the absence of the light and air pollution of man. Just when you think the scene can't be improved upon, your eyes are drawn from the skies to the sea where the bioluminescence emanating from the bow leads you to expect Tinkerbell's presence with her magic wand, sprinkling light in the path of *Always Friday*! Kathy and I stood there for half an hour, captivated by the opportunities *Always Friday* has given us to see a world that so few even know exists.

Jeff, Lee, and I split the watch into four-hour segments, with the AIS, radar, and plotter reflecting the concentration of ship traffic as everyone funnels into the NW passage around the western tip of Cuba. It would be hard to sleep much better than we did last night.

The morning began with a long, steamy, hot shower (try that on a sailboat), followed by one of Kathy's breakfasts that jump-starts the day in style. But this breakfast was interrupted by the riveting but welcome scream of a Penn International reel as another from Neptune's realm fell for the colorful enticements we are dragging from *Always Friday*'s stern. After about ten minutes, the evening's dinner menu was finalized, with the presentation to Kathy of a thirty-five-pound dolphin, a blank easel for her to work her culinary magic on our behalf. Her position as MVP on the cruise is not at all in question.

It is only 10 AM, and we have already hooked and lost another big dolphin and had another marlin whacking the baits without a hookup. Frankly, we have had all the billfish action any of us really want. Several hours of manual labor for the blue marlin and half that for the others is quite a commitment for fish that you release after bringing them to the boat, especially when we have released close to a dozen so far. Personally, I am standing by with my soy sauce, ginger, and wasabi as the ultimate nightmare for any yellowfin tuna that might pay us a visit.

And remember, we are not fishing; we are traveling! All this action is taking place at cruising speed as we pass through fishing grounds made famous by Hemmingway but rarely visited by sports fishermen because of the remoteness of the waters. We are now about 80 nm from the western tip of Cuba, and about 200 nm from Grand Cayman, in the Yucatan Channel, and getting a boost from the Northern Equatorial Current as we roll along at almost nine knots at 1,600 rpm. Tonight, *Always Friday* will enter the Gulf of Mexico for the first time in her life. Things are starting to sound more like home now, and in fact we will cross the 1,000 nm range ring from Virginia Beach this afternoon!

It would be hard to improve upon this day. I have finally found a XM station that is not playing "It's Beginning to Look a Lot Like Christmas," and the fragrance of the annual Christmas tree has been replaced by that of suntan lotion. If Santa knew about this, he would dump that sack and drop by here. Did I say that life is *very* good on *Always Friday*? I did, but it's worth repeating!

12/07/2007, Friday

After last night's dinner of freshly caught dolphin cooked very well by pseudo-chef Jeff, it was another quiet, uneventful, and beautiful night of split watches among the three of us. The day was dedicated to direct travel to Key West with the hope of making landfall during daylight early Saturday, since I had not taken a boat into Key West before.

But the ocean gods did not allow for that luxury. As we turned the corner at the tip of Cuba, we picked up a strong boost from the current that dictated our arrival about midnight Friday rather than daybreak the next morning. We throttled back to 1,000 rpm and still made 7.5 knots over the ground. At our usual setting of 1,750 rpm, we were making over ten knots. So about 11 PM, we arrived at the "A" buoy off Key West and began the challenging radar run into town. An uneventful hour later, we were safely anchored off the Coast Guard station near downtown Key West!

Always Friday was back in the USA! Another important milestone in our trip was in the log. A call to customs confirmed that we could check in Saturday morning, so it was off to bed with a feeling of satisfaction that our trip of a lifetime continues to go smoothly.

BACK IN THE USA

12/08/2007, Saturday Morning (8 AM)

A BEAUTIFUL DAY in Key West! We plan to spend a few days here before moving north to Marathon Key where a new friend has offered us a slip as we move towards Virginia.

12/09/2007, Sunday

The last several days have been an enjoyable break from the responsibilities of at-sea travel. Jeff and Lee left for Texas and Grand Cayman respectively after adding much pleasure to our Cayman–Key West passage. Saturday night, Jeff treated us to a goodbye dinner at Lee's favorite Key West restaurant, Blue Heaven. Both the food and atmosphere were excellent, and it was a fantastic way to say thanks for the opportunity to share three great days on the Caribbean Sea with good friends. Both Kathy and I look forward to seeing them again somewhere down the line.

What has invariably happened this summer happened again. Both Jeff and Lee now have their hearts set on getting a Nordhavn at some time in their future. You simply can't experience how well they handle the sea in such comfort and not dream of someday doing just what Kathy and I have done this year.

We spent the first night here at anchor and the last two in a slip at Conch Harbor. The harbor is very nice, and right in the middle of Key West itself, but the slip fees of $3.50 per foot per night overshadow the convenience of the place. The winds are forecast to be quite strong until Thursday, so we plan to leave the harbor tomorrow and anchor out for the next several days here in Key West before leaving for Marathon Key. Slip fees of over $200 per night reawaken my love for Alaska where we could have stayed for over a week for one night's fee in Key West. At least we don't need any of their $4 per gallon diesel fuel!

But the good has easily outweighed the bad, as the scenery, food, and people are all genuinely nice. The fried cracked conch down here is worth a trip in itself.

Tomorrow we again attack the challenge of activating the satellite TV. We had assumed it would come to life at about the same sixteen-degree northern latitude where we lost it on the Pacific side of Mexico, but it is still a no-show in Key West. I assume that we will have to change to an East Coast satellite, but the owner's manual lost a lot in translation from Japanese to English, and I have not been able to get the Food Network back up for Kathy.

The oil has been changed in both the main engine and generator, and the fuel tanks still hold almost 1,200 gallons of the fuel bought at the Panama Canal. *Always Friday* is now mechanically prepared to get to Virginia Beach without further stops for fuel or oil changes, but we don't plan to take advantage of that capability. Too much to see and do here in South Florida, and more new friends to invite on board before the radar finally reflects the Chesapeake Bay entrance.

Our magic carpet continues to take us places in comfort that most people never see in their lifetimes. What an experience this has been.

More over the next few days, but the truth is that there just isn't as much of interest to tell you about here as there was when we were in Alaska. There is nothing on earth like Alaska!

12/10/2007, Monday

Good fortune has shined down on us again, as we are tied up in Conch Harbor next to two new friends, Oliver and Sally Miller from Wisconsin. They have retired onto their forty-seven-foot Sabre cruiser (http://www.oneoliverii.com) and have come to Key West by way of the Mississippi River across the Gulf of Mexico. Their next stop is the Bahama Islands where they will spend the winter. We have exchanged boat visits and shared several meals together in the restaurants of Key West with cruising experiences bouncing back and forth like ping-pong balls. It is a frequently proven fact that the world is full of fascinating, nice people you will never meet while watching HBO in your den.

Yesterday's email offered us another South Florida opportunity when Jerry Wert wrote that he had been following our exploits this summer from his home in Marathon, FL, and would be happy to help us with any challenges while in the Key West area. With his phone number from the email, I soon had him on the line with an invitation to join us for dinner here at Conch Harbor. So tonight, Jerry, his wife, Jeanette, and Oliver, Sally, Kathy, and I had dinner together at an outside restaurant on the harbor where our new friends from Marathon enlightened us on the details of the local waters and the Bahamas (where they have been cruising for the past fifteen years).

Jerry has arranged for us to dock at a friend's waterfront home in Marathon where we will visit with them for several days after Key West. The combination of *Always Friday* and our website continues to yield great dividends in terms of new and fascinating acquaintances along the way home.

It was blowing too hard to safely leave the harbor and anchor after dinner tonight, so we will absorb another $215 nightly docking charge to diminish the chance of an even larger repair bill should we try to maneuver out of the harbor in these winds.

It has been the strangest holiday season of our lives with eighty-five-degree days and Christmas carols replaced by calypso music, but the excitement of the ongoing adventure dilutes the nostalgia of missing friends and family who usually share the season with us.

But don't feel sorry for us. We are having a truly wonderful time down here!

12/11/2007–12/12/2007, Tuesday–Wednesday (795 nm from VA Beach)

Yesterday (Tuesday) was a lazy day around Key West with boat washing consuming much of the day. We left Conch Harbor about 2 PM and anchored off the city of Key West, made quite popular by the ridiculous slip fees charged by the local marinas. For safety's sake, I wanted to go through a tide swing at anchor before leaving the boat in Binky's paws while we went ashore for dinner by tender.

All went well on the hook, and around 6 PM, Oliver and Sally from M/V *One Oliver II* came from the dock to pick us up for dinner. They have become good friends very quickly, and we have commented more than once that they are the kind of people that make these harbor visits so rewarding. Their boat, a forty-seven-foot Sabre, is as pretty a boat as we have seen on our trip and was great for their trip down the Mississippi River. However, with the stories and pictures of our exploits as ammunition, we have been trying to talk them into broadening their horizons to include the longer distances we have enjoyed so much this year. In fact, Oliver said that after seeing what *Always Friday* had done for us, a Nordhavn might be in their future as well! This stuff is contagious.

After a great seafood dinner in one of the local Key West establishments, it was back to *Always Friday* by Oliver and Sally's eleven-foot Caribe tender for the night. We are hoping to meet up with them somewhere in South Florida before they break for the Bahamas, and they have promised to stay with us in Virginia when the Intracoastal Waterway takes them home from the islands next June.

This morning (Wednesday) I awoke at daybreak to get underway to Marathon Key to stay a few days as the guests of Jerry and Jeanette. The weather was fine but a little windy from the north, producing three-to-four-foot seas on the nose—no problem other than the task of washing the boat of salt spray after arrival. The trip was as uneventful as sixty miles through hundreds of stone crab traps can be, and we arrived unscathed with no traps in tow.

Jerry was there to meet us in his boat to lead us through the shallow waters, which can be treacherous to those without local knowledge. We are now safely tied up to a private dock with all the amenities of a Florida Keys home. We will be here for a few days before resuming our trek to the north. This is a lifestyle that everyone with an adventurous spirit should experience. Unless, of course, you just can't live without shopping malls and the local opera!

12/13/2007–12/14/2007

Yesterday (Thursday) was a very windy day in Marathon, and because of low tides conflicting with our six-and-a-half-foot draft, we planned to move the boat to Boot Key so we could get out early in the morning during low tide for our next stop near Key Largo. As we threaded the needle through several marinas, multiple anchorages, and under a drawbridge, the wind made it a challenging passage (completed without a problem). But a surprise awaited us when we checked in by VHF for our previously arranged mooring-ball assignment.

The dockmaster called to question our contention that *Always Friday*'s overall length was fifty-nine feet—from his vantage point, he was sure she was much bigger! Then he asked (for the first time!) if our displacement was less than fifty tons. Well, we missed that by only *ten tons*. He then apologetically informed us that we were too big for the mooring balls, although they are rated for a category-five hurricane for the standard sixty-footers that were there. So, in twenty-five-knot winds, we had no choice but to reverse our course and head back out to sea.

It wasn't all bad. The people that had so enthusiastically lined the docks to see the big yellow boat come in took to rails again to wave goodbye to us. Everywhere we go, the boat is the star of the marina. Apparently, they don't see many oceangoing power boats here. So, we dropped our 175-pound anchor off the island in about fifteen feet of water with almost 100 feet of four-inch chain on the bottom. We didn't move an inch through eighteen hours of fifteen-to-twenty-five-knot winds! This anchoring system has been perfect through almost sixty nights on the hook, through every set of conditions you can imagine, from Alaska through Canada, the US West Coast, Central America, and now the Keys! We sleep just as comfortably at anchor as we do in the marinas (especially when it rains).

So, this morning (Friday), I was up at dawn to begin our trip eastward to Miami. That leg is about 90 nm, and with only ten and a half hours of daylight, the possibility of an after-dark arrival is very real. Night passages in new waters, into a marginally charted anchorage in the heart of stone crab season, is not a prudent plan, so our plan was to break the leg in half with a night at anchor near Key Largo behind Rodriguez Key.

The trip is down what is euphemistically called Hawk Channel, although it has few of the characteristics one usually associates with a channel . . . like standard channel markers, deep water, and no obstructions to passage. Hawk Channel is an occasionally marked, eight-to-fifteen-foot-deep pathway from Key West to Miami that is almost wall-to-wall stone crab traps. You would never expect an accepted marine highway between two Florida meccas like Key

West and Miami to be nothing less than a continual minefield for boats susceptible to the lines securing the traps.

We guided *Always Friday* through the "channel" for 46 nm with the autopilot never seeing the "nav" mode. You had to have your hand on the rudder control constantly to avoid the ever-present traps. At times there would be a half dozen traps in an area the size of our boat. In twenty-knot winds, it is impossible to dodge every one of them when they are so randomly concentrated. Occasionally a group would pop up from behind the waves, yielding no time for an effective change in course. Your only option is to pull the boat into neutral and hope nothing catches on the stabilizers (nothing did). Trying to steer a Nordhavn 55 with the rudder when a trap pops up unexpectedly is like trying to steer a helium balloon with the string. It just doesn't respond fast enough. But we made it unscathed and are now anchored in beautiful, azure-green waters off Rodriguez Key in seventy-eight-degree, windy conditions that make for a perfect tropical evening. XM Radio is playing nonstop Christmas carols, which leads me to believe that this is what Christmas would have been like if little baby Jesus had been born on July 4 rather than December 25. Just the luck of the draw, I guess.

Tomorrow morning, we will be off to Biscayne Bay for an anchorage called No Name Harbor. It is a popular spot for boats waiting for a weather window to cross the Gulf Stream to the Bahamas. Tonight, we are going to resurrect a touch of Alaska with a salmon dinner from our stock in the freezer. Christmas dinner may be Dungeness crab from Glacier Bay. That beats turkey from Farm Fresh any day.

After almost 11,000 nm, we are now less than 750 from Virginia Beach. It's sad to think that our odyssey is winding down, but the fun is not yet over, and the freezer still holds halibut, tuna, dolphin, and wahoo!

12/15/2007, Saturday

The weather has been blustery here as remnants of Tropical Storm Olga move through the area. It was a deadly storm as it passed through the middle of the Caribbean, right where we had been several weeks earlier, but it has now weakened to just an inconvenience. The winds have been twenty to twenty-five knots moving from the NE to SE.

Yesterday we were within a mile of a plane crash that I understand made national news. A private plane left the Marathon airport and several minutes later fell into the sea very close to our position (less than a mile). Another boat was closer and reported the mayday to the Coast Guard. We heard it all as it unfolded on the VHF radio and watched as the CG rescue teams swung into action. Both occupants got out on their own and were picked up in good shape. Apparently, it was the second crash for the pilot!

Today, while underway for Miami, we heard four separate emergencies handled by the Coast Guard. Two were boats that had capsized in heavy seas, the third was a boat taking on water, and the fourth a sailboat that had literally sunk. All crews were pulled to safety, but the seas clearly prevailed over small boats today. *Always Friday*, on the other hand, wasn't appreciably affected by the wind and brought us safely and comfortably into Miami.

Upon arrival, our plans to anchor in Hurricane Harbor were precluded by a shoal with a controlling depth of five feet. Both Florida and Bahamian waters are notoriously shallow, but we are now so comfortable anchoring out that we really haven't been inconvenienced by *Always Friday*'s draft of six and a half feet. We are anchored on the other side of Government Cut with a great view of the Miami skyline. The multiple colors in the lights of the tall buildings form a scene as beautiful as any city we have seen in our travels.

We may be here for several days as NOAA says a high-pressure area on its way here will rile the seas to an uncomfortable level. Based on the number of super yachts anchored near here, everyone is expecting quite a blow.

The stormy skies and troubled seas are quite beautiful when you are safely anchored. We will sleep well tonight with rain and winds singing nature's songs all night long, while Nobletec's anchor watch does its job to guard against any variation of the anchor's position on the bottom. Technology never sleeps so that we can.

We will be off to West Palm Beach when conditions allow.

12/17/2007, Monday

As is so often the case, the weather has dictated an alteration in our plans. For the past two days, we have been on the "rode" again—that's r-o-d-e as in anchor rode! Saturday afternoon we left the Atlantic with a ninety-degree turn to port to enter Biscayne Bay with plans to anchor in Hurricane Harbor until the frontal system generating wind of up to thirty knots passed through. A secondary anchorage was to be No Name Harbor if for some reason the first did not work out.

As we moved down the Biscayne Channel, it was obvious that the weather was going to be a factor that night, as the winds had shifted ninety degrees, and the seas were swirling in a state of confusion. As we came upon the entrances to both of our anchoring alternatives, the depth sounder advised us to go no further, as the depth of our boat was about to exceed the depth of the bay. That would be, obviously, the definition of the word *aground*. So, we stopped, reorganized our approach, and moved towards the AIS signal of a super yacht anchored about a mile away, knowing that if she could anchor there, so could we.

It worked as hoped. There in about thirteen feet of water was anchored M/Y *Copasetic*, a yacht at least three times our size. We dropped anchor about a quarter mile away, yielding plenty of swing room for both of us as the forecasted winds arrived on schedule. We put out a 5:1 scope and confirmed that the anchor had a good bite on the bottom before relaxing for the evening. The Nobeltec plotter confirmed for the next two days a swinging semicircle around the anchor, which never moved an inch. It was another great performance by the anchor that has served us so well for the last 11,000 miles. As we always do, the strain of the anchor and chain was taken from the windlass and bow pulpit using an anchor snubber that hooks onto the chain at water level and then is run back to both sides of the bow of the boat with heavy rope.

For the next fourteen hours the winds blew constantly at twenty to thirty knots while *Always Friday* rode it out well, and we slept very comfortably in air-conditioned comfort. On arising this morning, the temperature had dropped to under sixty degrees, and the air conditioner was superseded by the heater. The front was through in style. All was well with one exception: the anchor snubber, which is rated for "Max 20 Kn," whatever that means, had structurally failed at both shackles and the main chain grabber. The lines held—everything else failed! So, the lesson learned is that "Max 20 Kn" is not big enough for a NH 55 in twenty-five-knot winds. Thankfully, I had backed it up with the chain lock, so the integrity of the boat's position was never threatened. Just another example of how Mother Nature can mangle anything put in her way if she so chooses.

The weather forecasts told of a short break in the winds after the passage of the front, followed by again increasing winds later in the day, so we took advantage of that brief respite in the winds to run from Miami to Fort Lauderdale—about 35 nm. The trip was beautiful with the seas about six feet but no problem at all.

The scenery from Miami to Fort Lauderdale is a monument to the success of the free enterprise system. Discretionary income by the billions spent on condo after condo and yacht after yacht. Once the turn into the Port Everglades Channel towards Fort Lauderdale is made, the opulence becomes even more obvious. Two-to-three-hundred-foot yachts are not rare, and 150-footers are seemingly everywhere. But a funny thing happened on the way to Los Olas Yacht Harbor, our home for the next several days. The same people who didn't turn their heads when a 150-foot yacht passed stood up and waved, or even took pictures, when *Always Friday* floated down the channel. We have seen this all year. There is something unique about the appearance of a Nordhavn that strikes at the heart of boat lovers.

By the time we had her docked, the usual crowd had gathered to see the "big yellow boat." There was a time when Virginia Beach on the stern drew crowds and questions, but no more now that we have left the Pacific and are within 700 miles of home. Now it is just the boat itself, and what an attraction it has been! When they hear that we are returning from Alaska, their unspoken question of "Can it go anywhere?" has been answered without being asked. As I sit on the bridge, writing this update at 10 PM, I just heard voices on the dock, with one proclaiming, "It's a Nordhavn!" I don't think that happens very often with other builder's boats. I must admit that the interest shown in the boat and its capabilities by knowledgeable mariners adds considerably to the pride of ownership that all Nordhavn drivers share.

So, tonight, we will sleep surrounded by the rich and famous and all their toys. This is an amazing place, and many would say it is the yachting capital of the world. It certainly gets my vote.

Tomorrow, Kathy and I are going out to find her a little Christmas tree to make the boat a little more in tune with the season. Tonight, our holidays were made memorable by a phone call from a Virginia Beach Christmas party attended by many of our best friends. When we became a topic of conversation at the party, they called us on board the boat to tell us that we were missed at home. The phone there was passed around among our friends, and after the call, we felt like we had been there with them. A warm feeling for us here in Florida on a cold night in Virginia.

Tomorrow, Bill and Mindy, who joined us in Alaska, will again join us here from their home in Naples, FL. Having two of our closest friends here for the holiday season will be very nice.

So, tomorrow, it is off to the malls. It has been my turn a lot this year; the next few days are all Kathy's!

12/20/2007, Thursday

We have found a place that will be our temporary home for Christmas and could be a great retirement site as well—Fort Lauderdale! It is beautiful, dynamic, and thoroughly entertaining Our slip at Las Olas Yacht Marina is right on the main waterway at the Las Olas drawbridge, so we have a constant parade of super yachts hovering beside us, waiting for a bridge lift. It's like being a judge at the Miss America pageant, with the beautiful contestants constantly filing by for your review and approval. From my present vantage point, I can see at least a dozen yachts of over 120 feet, and multiple waterfront homes that sell for tens of millions of dollars. Yesterday one of the captains of a nearby yacht visited *Always Friday* and proclaimed the NH 55 to be his personal dreamboat. Quite a compliment from someone who lives in a world of the highest-quality yachts.

Bill and Mindy Young have joined us for a few days on board. They last saw us almost half a world away in Auke Bay where they joined us for a visit to Taku Harbor, Tracy Arm, and the glaciers there. It is hard to believe that we have come so far on *Always Friday* since they last saw us. That was in Alaska's July, which felt like Virginia's December—now it is December in South Florida, and it feels like Virginia's July. New experiences and sensations abound in the world that *Always Friday* has opened for us.

Kathy and Mindy spent the early afternoon decorating a two-foot, live Norfolk pine that will be this year's Christmas tree for us.

That, in addition to the colored lights we have hung from the fly bridge, has injected the Christmas spirit into the season that hardly comes automatically in sunny, eighty-degree temperatures while wearing shorts and sunglasses.

So, the next few days will be with Bill and Mindy, then after Christmas, we will be off to West Palm Beach, then Stuart, FL, for some minor warranty work at the NH facility there. As the weather allows, we will continue up the coast with nightly stops along the way. We plan to stop in Brunswick, GA, to see Billy and Sandra Brunson, our lifelong best friends with memories that date back to our elementary school years, then Savannah, Hilton Head, Charleston, and wherever the setting sun dictates we anchor or moor until Virginia Beach appears on the bow.

Although geographically the trip is ending, the next few weeks should hold many pleasant experiences that will be added to the hundreds of great memories the past year has made possible for us. It is not often that you can say unequivocally that a particular year has been one of the best of your life, but *Always Friday* has clearly made 2007 just that, and it's not over yet!

12/24/2007, Christmas Eve!

Tis the night before Christmas on *Always Friday*, and today we traveled up the Florida coast to take advantage of offers from four of our friends from Virginia Beach. Debbie and Ray Breeden arranged for us to dock at the Palm Beach Yacht Club, right in the heart of the action here, and Martha and Ben Wiley offered us the use of their condo and car while in Palm Beach. What a difference friends make in life!

We are once again surrounded by beautiful yachts, Rybovich and Merritt sport fishermen, as well as two beautiful Hinckley

Picnic Boats (among my very favorite boats). Kathy is in heaven with the shopping, and I have offered to take her to all the stores tomorrow. (Surely, they will be closed.)

Our week in Fort Lauderdale was as nice as you could hope for. Times with Bill and Mindy always yield great enjoyment and appreciation for great friends. The city is a great combination of big and fun. I could spend every day just watching the yachts of the world move in and out of the city from some of the most famous marinas in the world. However, if you have a big ego, this is not the place for you or your boat. Some of the yachts here have tenders bigger than *Always Friday*. However, all factors considered, I would not trade boats with any of them. I don't think any of them have had a better year than we have on board *Always Friday* in 2007.

This afternoon, we hit the big grocery store here so Kathy could gather all the ingredients required for our traditional family Christmas breakfast tomorrow. Of course, there will be a big void since our children are not here with us, but an hour on the phone will hopefully at least dilute the disappointment of their absence. Kathy noted tonight that this will be the first Christmas we have spent without family since 1972 when we reported to Carrier Airwing One on board the USS *Kennedy* on Christmas Eve. That day was made even more memorable by the fact that the officer we reported to was Lieutenant Ed Andrews (now a retired Navy captain), who to this day remains one of the best friends of my life, and our commanding officer of Fighter Squadron 32 was Commander Zeke Burns, who remained a lifelong close friend until his death at too young an age just last week.

So, like almost everyone at Christmas, the day will be filled with much joy and a few tears. On *Always Friday*, the joy will predominate. Merry Christmas from all four of us on *Always Friday* to all of you who have vicariously traveled with us this magical year!

—Buddy, Kathy, Raleigh, and Binky!

12/31/2007, Monday, New Year's Eve!

Christmas Day was a quiet one on board *Always Friday*. Kathy made our traditional Christmas morning meal of eggs and sausage with apple butter; then we opened the few small presents we had under the wee Christmas tree on the shelf. The past year itself was our agreed-upon gift to each other, and nothing in the prior thirty-five years of our marriage has equaled that gift in either magnitude or excitement. The telephone rang throughout the day with family and friends from everywhere checking on us and our Florida Christmas. We had planned to have a nice Christmas dinner in a local restaurant but found them all to be closed tight . . . except for a Chinese restaurant that welcomed us for our big holiday meal. An unusual meal, but no regrets on *Always Friday*!

On Friday, Cameron Kimball flew us to Ginn sur Mer on Grand Bahama Island to see the progress being made on the development of the world-class resort that should open there within the next few years. It looks as if it is going to be truly spectacular, and less than fifty miles from West Palm Beach!

By late afternoon we were back at the yacht club and welcomed our good friends from Virginia Beach, Ray and Debbie Breeden, Ray's son, Torrey, and their guests on board *Always Friday* for a visit. Afterwards, it was off to Morton's The Steakhouse in style in their Rolls Royce for a classic Palm Beach night. The next day, we were guests in their magnificent new oceanfront home, followed by lunch at Mar-a-Largo, the mansion built by E. F. Hutton and Marjorie Merriweather Post about seventy-five years ago, now an exclusive private club owned by Donald Trump.

The beauty and opulence of the place is almost beyond imagination, as are most of the exclusive areas of Palm Beach. Ray and Debbie are living life as it should be lived after years of hard work and well-deserved success. It is great to see stress now defined as the pressure of getting the ballroom dancing steps right as they glide through the Palm Beach scene. My observation that he needs to get back into boating now that he lives here in South Florida has so far fallen on deaf ears... but don't count the idea out!

Tomorrow, we leave Palm Beach ahead of a cold front with nine-foot seas for Stuart, FL, for the few warranty items to be addressed by NH's commissioning team there. Afterwards, we plan to stop for a few days in St. Augustine with a night or so at anchor somewhere in between. After that, our next significant stop will be Brunswick, GA, to see Billy and Sandra with a planned stay of about six weeks. I'm sure that they will entertain us royally.

(I just wanted to see if Billy was reading the updates. We are really staying for just a few days!)

So, New Year's Eve in Palm Beach will be celebrated with fireworks over the river just off our bow. It's nice that they would arrange that on such short notice after our arrival last week. Palm Beach has been quite an enjoyable experience. Stuart will soon be off the bow!

1/01/2008, New Year's Day!

If you have ever wondered what America's supremely successful businessmen and women do with their discretionary income when they move to Palm Beach for the last one or two quarters of their lives, come down here on New Year's Eve, and you will see for yourselves!

They buy *fireworks*... and certainly *not* the $20 package peddled from house trailers along the highways of the South. Last night at midnight, Kathy and I were treated to a firework display unlike any I have seen since Gerald Ford presided over the bicentennial celebration of our country with a massive show of pyrotechnical excess in 1976 from New York harbor.

Raleigh and Binky chose to sit out the show inside *Always Friday*, surviving what in their minds was the canine equivalent of the Tet Offensive. Outside, centered just over the bow of *Always Friday* and about a thousand yards away in the center of the river, someone in Palm Beach put on a show to be remembered. For almost a half hour, every class, form, and style of firework was ignited on the water and over our heads, accompanied by sonic booms, whistles, and pops yielding every color and pattern imaginable. The docks of the Palm Beach Yacht Club were lined with celebrants of the New Year, but none had as good a seat as the two of us. It was quite a way to either celebrate the end of a great 2007 (our choice!), or to welcome 2008 as a pretender of as great a year as the last one (little chance of that).

We did end the year with a minimally painful loss, however. It seems that my Blackberry is now "sleeping with the fishes." The amazing little machine that has kept us in touch with the world for the last 13,000 miles when nothing else worked from sites as far away as Glacier Bay, the San Blas Islands, Cuba, and all points in between, was inadvertently buried at sea in an untimely demise when Binky kicked it off my belt while attempting to escape the attack of the fireworks.

Our 40 nm trip from Palm Beach to Stuart was over calm seas (for now) in warm, seventy-four-degree (for now!) weather no more than a mile offshore. The scenery was beautiful, even including a sailfish that surfaced right beside the boat. Kathy asked why we didn't throw out a few lines. The answer was that we might catch another sailfish, and the dozen or so billfish we have released from *Always Friday* has satisfied my curiosity as to whether we could catch fish as well from here as we did from our Hatteras sport fisherman we had for years. Clearly, we can. When there is room in the freezer, we will have baits out for dolphin and wahoo, but for now, the rods are in the racks.

We arrived at St. Lucie Inlet, the entrance to Stuart, just as the predicted front began to show itself with rain and wind. The run to Stuart from the ocean is about six miles, and none of the water is deep enough to allow you to relax as you follow the buoys through the "channels" of seven to eight feet in depth. When *Always Friday* requires six and a half feet to float, such depths keep you alert, to say the least. But we made it in one piece, surrounded by calls for sea tow assistance from those that may not have heeded the channel markers as carefully as they will next time.

I must admit that both Kathy and I questioned the rationale behind placing the Nordhavn commissioning center in a harbor whose depths are frequently less than the draft of the boats they build. Anyway, we are here and in one piece! A storm is due in tonight with gale-force winds, falling temperatures, and heavy seas that is to last for several days. We should be finished with our little warranty projects around the time Neptune allows us back onto his playground.

Once again, our website has borne the fruit of friends on the boat. About an hour after our arrival, a knock on the hull signaled the arrival of an unexpected guest. Doug Perry, our friend from Virginia Beach and a winter resident of Stuart, had read of our plans to stop here and saw our boat in the marina as he was crossing the bridge. So, he came down to see us! Pat is in Virginia, so he is alone for a few days, but not now. We plan to get together several times while here, maybe even show him the 1,500-plus pictures of our trip of a lifetime. Even though *Always Friday* is best known for bringing us new friends, when she does the same with old friends, it is even better.

Tomorrow we begin to knock off the minimal list of warranty items. None are major; perhaps the most important one is our inability to get the Sea Tel TV antenna to talk to East Coast satellites. So far it has been easier to get Santa Claus to drop by than the Sea Tel people! We have an appointment (again!) tomorrow—we will see how that works out. We still get TV from the local channels of the bigger cities.

Tonight, my team (UGA Bulldogs!) plays in the Sugar Bowl. We will be watching in shorts while the rest of the country shivers. Not a bad way to start the New Year!

1/08/2008, Tuesday

Stuart has been a very good experience. The Nordhavn people have been efficient, effective, and responsive—a very nice combination that has led to a rapid resolution of our few warranty items. The Sea Tel people have come through as hoped for and will be replacing the entire satellite antenna with a newer model designed to eliminate the very problem that led to the failure of our antenna. The winter weather of our first few days in Stuart has given way to the more usual pattern of warm and sunny days with temperatures in the mid-seventies. The morning after our arrival here, we turned on the boat's heaters for the first time when we awoke to a thermometer reading of thirty-eight degrees with a wind chill factor below freezing. The Chamber of Commerce would probably refute this, but we were colder in Stuart than we ever were in Alaska!

However, the greatest source of enjoyment has been our friend from Virginia Beach, Doug Perry, and friends he has introduced us to. Their community of Harbour Ridge is made up of some of the nicest people you could hope to meet, and we have spent every night enjoying their company at great restaurants and in their homes. Doug reintroduced us to the world of aquatic rapid transit when we scooted all over the local waters at 40 mph in his new thirty-one-foot Intrepid! Stuart is yet another South Florida location that could easily entice you into staying for your active retirement years.

We also had the pleasure of meeting Dick and Carol Rosenberg, who are here on board their sixty-five-foot Fleming, M/V *Carrousel*. They are considering a Nordhavn 55 for their next boat, and we had the pleasure of showing them around *Always Friday*. As a result, we are joining them for dinner in downtown Stuart this evening.

Again, *Always Friday* is the main attraction at the docks. Since we have been here at Harbour Ridge Marina, quite a few of the residents have walked down to see the "big yellow boat," and each has received the tour. Everyone has so far been very impressed with the quality and sturdiness of the NH, and more than one has expressed an interest in NH as their next boat. I remain of the opinion that no boat could have served us better this year.

How long we will be in Stuart will be dictated by Sea Tel's ability to get our new satellite TV antenna installed. There are plenty of very nice people here, and much to do, so a reasonable delay can be made into a positive rather easily. Somehow, we will make it through this challenge.

1/11/2007, Friday

We are still in Stuart, even though we once again have satellite TV, thanks to Mike and Dave from IMS American. They have been our sunlight in the depths of a well as we sought the assistance of Sea Tel representatives from Mexico to Palm Beach to restore Kathy's lifeline to sanity: her TV. Until we found them, no one had any inclination to assist us with the warranty work of replacing the failed antenna, but once they were on the scene, it all came together nicely.

We have some real news for a change. We are still here in Stuart because Nordhavn has asked us to delay our trek to Virginia Beach and return to Miami as a Nordhavn display boat in the Miami Boat Show in mid-February. They feel that *Always Friday* will represent a unique example of a new NH 55 that has gone almost 13,000 miles in the past nine months, from Southern California to northernmost North America (Alaska), down the NW US coast, through Mexico and Central America, the San Blas Islands, and up the Caribbean Sea to Florida. They feel that a boat that has done what they build them for is a better example of their boat's capabilities than one straight from the factory that just proclaims it can make such a trip.

From our standpoint, we hope that it will give us an opportunity to meet some of the people who have generated almost 60,000 hits on the *Always Friday* homepage and over half a million page views on our website. So, we have again altered our float plan to enjoy this unique opportunity to participate in perhaps the premier boat show in the world. You have heard us say it many times, but *Always Friday* continues to offer us opportunities that we never dreamed of just a few years ago.

Stuart is a great place to spend winter days in South Florida. Doug and Pat Perry's community of Harbour Ridge has allowed us into their fold in a way no one would ever expect. The people here are friendly beyond all expectations and have welcomed us into their homes in a way that would make anyone consider seeking the opportunity to spend years here rather than days. Just today, a half dozen visitors came down to our dock to see the boat and welcome us to the Harbour Ridge community. According to their words, *Always Friday* has become the "talk of the town," and we have had the real pleasure of an unending procession of interested visitors to see our boat.

Kathy has announced that the shopping opportunities here meet her needs nicely, so my biggest hurdle is behind me. I am in heaven in eighty-degree January temperatures here in the self-proclaimed "sailfish capital of the world," and Raleigh and Binky love their walks through the trails that wind through this community, laced with rabbits that have replaced their favorite quarry, Virginia squirrels! It is no wonder we are moving so slowly towards the winter of Virginia.

Tomorrow evening, we will again have the pleasure of dinner with Dick and Carol Rosenberg after they show us around their beautiful boat, M/Y *Carrousel*. Kathy and I both feel that we will see them again and again in our mutual travels over the coming years.

Saturday is the same song but a different verse, as Scott Jacobson from New York emailed us from Palm Beach to invite us to dinner to discuss his dream of following in our Nordhavn footsteps to Alaska in the future. Of course, we took him up on the offer, so another pleasant experience is about to spring from the "big yellow boat."

The incredible adventure continues, although at a much slower pace than our fantastic days in Alaska. The Miami Boat Show will be a memorable way to crown one of the best years of our lives. To answer the question that continues to come from Virginia Beach— *yes*, we *are* coming home . . . just not quite yet!

1/29/2008, Tuesday

It has been about three weeks since our last update, simply because we are stashed here in beautiful South Florida, awaiting the day (February 9) we will backtrack to Miami for the opportunity to be a part of the Nordhavn presentation at the biggest boat show in the world. Since NH announced that *Always Friday* would be a part of the show, we have been surprised by the number of people who have emailed us with the message that they are coming to the show to see the "big yellow boat" that has brought us so much enjoyment over the past year. In fact, two of our old friends by virtue of our boat (John and Debbie Marshall of *Serendipity*, NH 55-20) and two of our new friends (Dick and Carol Rosenberg, who are considering a new NH 55) will be joining us for the trip back to Miami. Rounding out our crew will be Dave Balfour, our Nordhavn East Coast sales representative, and Ben Sprague, Dick and Carol's Nordhavn sales rep. We have been trying all year to get Dave to join us on the boat, and finally it looks as if it will happen!

Our stay in Stuart at Harbour Ridge Country Club has been one of the nicest surprises of the trip. Doug and Pat Perry's friends here have made us feel as welcome as if we had lived here with them for years. The people here are from fascinating backgrounds, including some of the most successful business leaders in the country, but friendly beyond words and universally interested in the recent travels and adventures of *Always Friday*. They have invited us into their homes, introduced us to the nicest restaurants in the area, and even included us in the plans for their Super Bowl party this Sunday. Not a day goes by without visitors to the dock to see the boat, all of whom are welcomed on board for a tour. This never happened in our Hatteras. There is something about a Nordhavn that ignites the interest of boaters and non-boaters alike.

The happy challenge of having time on our hands has given us the opportunity to travel to Jupiter to spend several days with our good friends Bill and Margaret Gunter, who spend the winters here escaping the cold weather now gripping Virginia Beach, as well a weekend in Naples with our friends of many years, Bill and Mindy Young. Since their escape from the winters of Pennsylvania after Bill's retirement, they have never looked back to the north, and a visit to their home makes the reason for that choice obvious. It would be hard for me to believe that anyone who spent January here would not want to spend the rest of their Januarys here as well.

Back to the boat and our Miami plans. We had planned to make the run from Stuart to the boat show in one day, but two factors come into play that must be considered carefully. The depths of the outbound channel dictate that we leave on high tide, and the required shifting channel is marked by unlit day markers, precluding a safe nighttime passage into the Atlantic. The high tides on our day of departure occur at approximately 1 AM and 1 PM. The 1 AM departure is not a viable choice since it would put us in the channel marked only by day markers in the darkness. The 1 PM departure would make a single-day passage impossible, and since we don't want to arrive at the show in darkness, we will split the trip by stopping overnight in either Palm Beach or Fort Lauderdale before arrival at the staging area for the show about three days before the opening day.

Those three days will be utilized by a professional detailing company to get the boat into as close to show-room condition as possible for a veteran boat of almost 1,700 hours. Their job should be made considerably easier by the fact that we have kept it as close to spotless as possible throughout the year. The four of us (that includes Raleigh and Binky) will be staying in a hotel, although we will be on the boat for some part of each day at the show. With the recent exception of two nights with our friends in Naples, it will be the first nights we have spent off the boat since last May. *Always Friday* was truly our home for 2007!

Within the next few days, the Nordhavn home page will have a story about the decision to feature *Always Friday* in the Miami Boat Show, written by our friend and Nordhavn sales representative, Jeff Merrill. Of the many people who have contributed to the success of our last year at sea, Jeff must be at the top of our list. The many hours he spent familiarizing me with the complicated systems of the boat paid off handsomely, allowing us to successfully address every challenge that is inevitable on a boat as capable and intricate as a Nordhavn. Without a Jeff Merrill equivalent to educate you on the boat's many and varied systems, you simply cannot comfortably undertake a 13,000-mile voyage such as ours without some degree of fear and trepidation. The combination of Jeff's efforts on our behalf and the best boat we could imagine has given us the experience of a lifetime, enjoyed in comfort and safety every foot of the way.

Several magazines have contacted us about writing an article on our trip. One asked that we include on our webpage an option for visitors to our web journal to share their reaction to our trip and website. Therefore, our web master has added a visitor comment page to our home page. If you have an interest in leaving your reaction to our adventure, it is there for your use. You may even end up in a magazine!

We hope to see many of you who have traveled vicariously with us this past year in Miami! Please drop by if you are at the show. It will be our pleasure to show you *Always Friday*, our magic carpet boat!

2/09/2008, Saturday

With our departure this morning from Harbour Ridge Country Club for the Nordhavn warranty center, we left the company of wonderful new friends we will truly miss. The warm welcome we received from people we had never met makes it very easy to visualize Stuart as our home away from our Virginia home after we are fully retired. Over the past weeks, we have been invited to more dinners, Sunday brunches, parties, and informal get-togethers here in Stuart than we have ever experienced before! It is entirely possible that if we could find a qualified judge of such matters, we might even be designated Florida party animals.

We have been told many times that *Always Friday* was the talk of the club, and in fact many of our new friendships arose from members visiting the docks to see our boat. The dockmaster declared it the most interesting boat he has seen visiting Harbour Ridge, and certainly the most popular among members in recent times. Once again, *Always Friday* has taken the last few weeks and changed them into indelible memories of exceptional friendships that will endure long after resuming our northward course.

We are back at the Nordhavn Center to off-load much of the baggage, fishing equipment, spare parts, and other "stuff" that has accumulated over the past ten months. Many of our guests in Alaska opted to leave their luggage with us for the return trip to Virginia rather than toss it into the abyss of airline travel. At the time, we had no idea that we would be a part of the Miami Boat Show. Since one of the unique features of the boat is its massive storage area, NH chose to off-load our "stuff" to better show the boat to interested visitors. As a byproduct of that decision, we will stop off here in Stuart after the show to reload our baggage before resuming our trek home.

To those at home who continue to doubt our intentions of returning home, we anticipate rounding Cape Henry for Virginia

Beach in three to four weeks. Previous arrival goals of before Christmas, before New Year's, and before Valentine's Day were all considered reasonable at the time of their formulation, but unexpected factors arose to dash our plans. Taken together, those factors have forced us into the predicament of spending the winter in South Florida. What a dilemma!

The boat is now in near-perfect condition, with one exception. Over the past ten months, *Always Friday* has never slowed down for any period, and the hull remained sleek and clean. However, the last month of dockside inactivity has allowed the accumulation of a moss-like growth that we found today to have slowed the boat by several knots and rendered the thrusters sluggish at best. I'm not sure why the bottom paint did not better protect the boat from this accumulation, but it should be easy for a diver to remove before we leave for Miami. In fact, a good bit of it would probably come off with nothing more than returning to the sea at cruising speed. Tomorrow, NH will complete the loading of their display materials on board, and Sunday, Dick Rosenberg, a prospective NH owner, and John Marshall, owner of *Serendipity*, another NH 55, will accompany me on the run to Fort Lauderdale. There, Kathy, Carol Rosenberg, Debbie Marshall, and two NH sales reps will join us for the final leg into Miami and the show.

Over the next several days, NH will take control of *Always Friday* to ready her for display.

Through our website, we will attempt to take you to the show with us as we enjoy one of the closing chapters of the adventure of our lives! Not a bad way to begin to draw the curtain on the voyage that many thought to be nearly impossible for the two of us (plus Raleigh and Binky!) to complete.

2/12/2008, Tuesday

After five weeks at the Nordhavn commissioning center in Stuart, waiting for the Miami Boat Show, *Always Friday* was in perfect condition and ready to go. Although the weather in Stuart had been near perfect for the great majority of the time, departure day was a windy one with a northeaster blowing at twenty to twenty-five knots. Leaving the dock required all the magic the bow and stern thrusters could offer, but we were on our way without incident. Our friends from the West Coast and owners of NH 55-20 *Serendipity* were with us, as was Dick Rosenberg, who had spent most of his and Carol's offshore life in Hinckley and Derecktor sailboats.

It was a good day to demonstrate the seaworthiness of NHs since the seas were approximately six feet and off the stern quarter, about the worst conditions a boat's autopilot can be asked to steer into. The trip was very comfortable but not completely uneventful. About ten miles north of Fort Lauderdale, we were startled by a loud crunching sound, followed by dramatic vibrations from below the waterline. We quickly shifted to neutral and simultaneously checked both the engine room and behind the boat. All looked normal, so we went ahead slowly, only to realize that we were either dragging something or had prop problems.

After coming to a full stop, we could see something trailing the rudder. A shift to slow reverse yielded pieces of an eight-to ten-inch plastic conduit rising to the surface. After shifting into forward gear and slowly accelerating, the boat handled normally and returned to nine knots at 1,850 rpm. So, for the second time in almost 13,000 miles, we had hit and drug something that we could not see at all. The first was a thirty-foot kelp plant off Costa Rica, and the second was man-made junk that had somehow ended up several miles off Fort Lauderdale. In both cases, *Always Friday* digested them uneventfully and without damage.

We arrived Sunday night after dark and enjoyed the beautiful approach into Bahia Mar Yacht Harbor through some of the most beautiful waterfront real estate anywhere. After some good baby back ribs at the Quarterdeck Restaurant, we were off to bed for an early departure for Miami on Monday.

Monday's weather was more of the same with small-craft warnings and NE winds predicted to be even stronger at twenty-five to thirty knots. Again, *Always Friday* handled the weather with no problems and a comfortable ride in conditions that forced most boats inside to the ICW. The Intracoastal Waterway is not an option for us due to our six-and-a-half-foot draft, and the areas of shallow water in the ICW.

The ride in adverse conditions was so impressive that it led Dick to proclaim the boat's offshore performance to be "unbelievable"! Quite a compliment from someone who has traveled many thousands of miles in some of the finest sailboats in the world. However, that was not the highest compliment Dick and Carol paid to *Always Friday*. That title was reserved for their decision to make NH 55-50 their next boat!

We have an interesting string going. Don Weipert rode from Southern California to Victoria, BC, with us through some of the roughest weather you can imagine and now owns his own NH 55, *Lilly Pad*. Dick rode with us through rough seas to Miami—and will soon be the proud owner of NH 55 *Carrousel*. There is a pattern here—the rougher the water, the more likely one is to decide upon a Nordhavn. Kathy and I are certainly believers after experiencing some very rough seas in safety and relative comfort.

Our arrival in Miami underscored the effects of the bad weather. No more than a fourth of the boats had made it in for staging day, and reports of forced stops along the way for rough seas were common. So, we had the docks essentially to ourselves, and the cleaning crews were boarding the boat in droves since they had few other boats to work on. After a steak dinner, we were off to bed with excitement building as the boat show's physical plant springs to life.

This morning (Tuesday), the other two Nordhavns arrived after rough rides from the south and docked successfully despite twenty-five-knot winds directly off the beam. Today Kathy and I will be getting our "stuff" arranged for the show, then move to the hotel that NH has for us. Binky and Raleigh have been a challenge in that most hotels seem reluctant to consider them as anything other than dogs.

2/15/2008, Friday

Monday was supposed to be the initial staging day for the world's largest boat show, but the weather precluded the timely arrival of most of the participating boats. By virtue of our uneventful midday Monday arrival, we had a front-row seat as boat after boat fought the winds to get into their assigned slips, with variable degrees of success.

For the next two days, the weather remained marginal with both wind and rain, but by Wednesday night all the slips were filled, and the show was on for Thursday morning. The first day of the show (Thursday) has a ticket price twice that of the other days to discourage the masses from attending and open the docks to smaller numbers of visitors who are presumed to be the more serious potential buyers. That plan seems to be effective, as the relatively small number of visitors to the boat represented very knowledgeable boaters, who inspected *Always Friday* in detail while asking technical questions that reflected a serious interest in the capabilities of these little ships built by Nordhavn.

John and Debbie Marshall (owners of *Serendipity* NH 55-20) and Kathy and I spent the entire day answering the many questions of potential buyers, with three or four couples spending several hours on board the boat. The wives answered the questions only they could answer, while John and I dealt with inquiries of a more technical or operational nature. John is an electrical engineer and one of the most knowledgeable members of the NH owners' group. The depth of his understanding of the NH 55 is amazing and a real asset to owners and potential owners alike.

The worldwide popularity of Nordhavn was reflected in the fact that we enjoyed the company of potential buyers from Russia, Canada, Ireland, England, Panama, New Zealand, Italy, Brazil, and Sweden, many of whom came to Miami primarily to see and discuss the Nordhavn fleet. A surprising number of the foreign visitors had been following the adventures of *Always Friday* regularly over the internet and were aware of the details of our travels. The boats ordered today will not be delivered until the latter months of 2009, but the unparalleled quality of these boats makes the wait worthwhile to many.

Although we had heard by email from many who have followed our trek that they would come to see us at the show, we have been surprised at how many have done so. We have had dozens of people come by simply to offer congratulations on our trip, and a few that had their pictures taken with us at the stern of *Always Friday*, conferring temporary (very temporary!) mini-rock-star status upon us. There have been multiple inquiries as to the whereabouts of Binky and Raleigh, with expressions of disappointment when they learn that the much-traveled dogs are relaxing at the hotel before resuming their trip to the land of Virginia squirrels and their own big backyard.

Here in the land of sunny skies and eighty-five-degree temperatures, Alaska again rose to the forefront. As we walked through the booths of the Miami Beach Convention Center, a friendly-sounding voice said, "*Always Friday*, weren't you in Alaska this summer?" Alan Veys had seen the boat's name and logo above the pocket of my shirt and remembered hearing our VHF radio calls on many occasions during the summer months of last year.

Alan runs the Pybus Point Lodge south of Juneau, and we had passed the mouth of his cove several times in our travels through

Alaska. We talked about our similar Alaska experiences for about half an hour and compared our summer travel paths, which nearly crossed on multiple occasions as we traveled from Auke Bay near Juneau to many of Alaska's most scenic spots. However, we were not Alan's only experience with the Nordhavn community. Richard and Lorna Maybin, on board *Spirit of Ulysses*, a NH 76, anchored in Alan's cove, leaving him with a great interest in the NH family. In fact, he expressed the wish that one day he might retire on a smaller NH and travel the seas as the NH community so effectively does. We invited him to come see *Always Friday* during the show, and he promised to do so. It doesn't take much to bring the joys of Alaska into my thoughts, and our conversation with Alan served to do just that.

Tomorrow (Saturday) is expected to bring the biggest crowds to the show. Kathy and Debbie are taking the day off and going to the Coconut Grove Art Show, while John and I return to the boat for our opportunity to talk boats with those interested in Nordhavns—a true labor of love! Not a bad way to spend a winter's day.

Tomorrow night is the Nordhavn owners' party for not only owners but for prospective ones as well. It is always a highlight of the show, and *Always Friday*'s trip pictures will be the running slideshow during the party. It should be fun—we will let you know!

2/18/2008, Monday

The Miami Boat Show is winding down, but not before several hundred people per day had toured the boat with universally positive responses. Boat shows are Nordhavn's best friend since prospective buyers have the competition docked nearby, allowing close inspection to clearly show the differences in the boats. I wouldn't want to make a living selling the competition's boats when parked next to a Nordhavn!

We continue to be amazed at the impact our website has had on NH devotees. Perhaps the most surprising story was from the wife of a NH fan who told us that he called home every morning to have his wife read him the entry so he wouldn't have to wait to read it later after work. Scot Jacobson, the art dealer from New York who treated us to dinner when he was in Palm Beach for an art show, brought his family to see the boat in hopes that Kathy would be able to convince Susie that a NH in her future would be a good thing. Lee Aires came to see us again from Grand Cayman, renewing the friendship that arose when he greeted us upon our arrival in Georgetown last December, and then accepted our invitation to ride with us from Cayman to Key West. For the trip, Michelle had been replaced by Freddy, a boat captain and dive instructor not that many years ago, now teaching economics in a Cayman university. Both Lee and Freddy offered to crew *Always Friday* to Bermuda or Europe with us if the situation ever arose! It might—who knows?

The surprise of the day came when someone brought a cruising magazine (*Power Cruising* April issue, page 24) that had a story about us, complete with pictures, with my name listed as the author. Although we have had multiple requests from magazines to write an article on our trip, I declined each offer simply because I wanted no deadlines in my present life. But there it was . . . I had become a published author without writing a word! The explanation appeared to come to light when we noticed a little box on page one proclaiming the article to be excerpts from our website. So, the puzzle was solved. The magazine liked the website entry and passed it on to their readership. Quite a compliment! Maybe I will write a book the same way: do nothing, and then sit back and read my book. I wonder if they have a Pulitzer Prize for non-writers?

The show ends today, and tomorrow we begin the last leg of our homeward journey to Virginia Beach. It will take us at least one stop to get back to Stuart to reload all our stuff we left there for the show. Since we must approach the inlet into Stuart at high tide during daylight hours, it is impossible to make the trip in one day. Dick and Carol Rosenberg, now the future owners of NH 55-51, will ride with us for fun. We have really enjoyed their company since the boats first brought us together in Stuart earlier this year.

We plan stops in St. Augustine, Brunswick, Savannah, and Charleston before steaming around Cape Henry into the Chesapeake Bay and home in early March.

The Miami Boat Show was a perfect way to cap off the trip of a lifetime, adding even more pleasant memories and new friends to our long lists of both!

We will keep our position reports and immediate cruise plans updated on the web page; however, most of the news fit to print is behind us. We are pleased that so many enjoyed our adventures with us! It seems that the word *vicariously* was invented to describe the relationship of the many friends who accompanied us in spirit over the last 13,000 miles or so. You have added immensely to our enjoyment of the trek, and for that Kathy and I are most appreciative.

Next stop: Stuart!

2/20/2008, Wednesday

Tuesday's high tide in Miami was around 8 AM, and we needed that extra depth to get out of the temporary harbor constructed only for the boat show. Our exit was uneventful with several feet of water under the keel before entering the outbound channel to the ocean. Contrary to our arrival last week, there were no cruise ships moored in Government Cut, so it was open for the procession of the showboat's "march to the sea." For some reason, someone in Homeland Security has decided that when two or more cruise ships are tied up on Miami's cruise ship piers, the channel is closed to all other boats. Maybe the name "Government Cut" explains the basis of the decision that few can understand!

The weatherman's predictions had waffled all week between windy and calm, but their most recent promise was ten knots of wind from the north and two-foot seas. That was not far off for the first ten miles, but thereafter the winds and seas began to build to the point that 75 percent of the trip was directly into twenty-five-knot winds with building, short seas of five to six feet. *Always Friday* thrives on such conditions, but some of the smaller boats were forced to fall in behind the larger ones to get to the next exit point that allowed them to enter the protection of the Intracoastal Waterway.

Our progress through the water generated apparent winds of over thirty knots, and the resonance of the antennas generating their characteristic wail confirmed the error of the weatherman's predictions. Our prearranged slip was at the Palm Harbor Marina just south of the Flagler Bridge. We were now going south with the wind behind us, and the current of the incoming tide was boiling behind as well. To top off the challenge, we missed the Flagler Bridge opening by minutes and had to hover on the upstream side of the bridge for a half hour with both the wind and current trying to push us towards the closed drawbridge. When finally open, we passed through uneventfully with only minor course changes accomplished with the thrusters.

Then came the big challenge. *Always Friday* is most conveniently docked with the starboard side towards the dock to allow the use of the side door for access to the dock. In this case, which required a turn downwind and down current with both forces roaring from behind, the first pass failed to get us within throwing distance of the lines, and the second succeeded only in getting a single line on the dock that had to be tossed back when the current and wind laughed at our efforts. So, the obvious decision was to alter the plans for a starboard-side tie and temporarily dock to the port side, allowing a much easier approach into the wind and current but a more difficult exit from the boat. As we moved into the south end of the harbor, with the depth sounder reading five feet under the keel, the bow slid into the sand! The chart clearly suggested plenty of water, but the bow disagreed. The roaring current then pushed the boat sideways along the sandbar and we were "asand" (if there is such a word) in charted deep water. Thankfully, the boat's prop and shaft are well protected by a strong keel, so there was no real threat of damage to the boat.

Now for some good news! I am not much of a gambler, having lost five straight $20 red vs. black bets on the roulette wheel in Las Vegas when Kathy and I went there for our thirtieth wedding anniversary (which quickly exhausted my $100 maximum commitment to the world of chance). However, when we first arrived in South Florida, many fellow boaters advised us to subscribe to TowBoatUS simply because the sands shift so frequently here that hitting the bottom in the middle of a channel is not at all unusual. In fact, we went almost 13,000 miles without touching the bottom until we bumped twice at high tide in midchannel within ten miles of the Nordhavn commissioning center.

So, we gambled that we might one day need their services and put down about $130 for an unlimited membership that allows for free towing anytime you find yourself in a South Florida sandbar dilemma. So, a call on VHF channel 16 got an immediate response, and in fifteen minutes, a capable-looking craft was there to assist us.

He rode around the boat and reported that it was in no less than seven feet of water at every point. Somehow, we had become lodged on an anthill of sand deposited by the roaring current with deep water all around. With very little effort, we were extracted from the sand and minutes later were successfully moored at Palm Harbor only a short distance from the Worth Avenue shopping area, and in sight of the Breakers Hotel. The service was completely covered by our membership, and the receipt showed that had we not had the unlimited membership, the charge would have been $987! A 7:1 return on our investment, and we still have eleven months of coverage to go. We will be renewing this deal every year we have the boat.

Tied up near us was another boat show participant, a beautiful Sassa 52 Italian sports cruiser with the owner, Noel, and his friend Dan on board. You will not be surprised that we invited them on board for a tour, and they reciprocated with a visit to their beautiful boat. Noel recently sold his pharmaceutical company that specialized in orphan drugs (drugs that are used in low volume for rare diseases), and Dan has been his guide in learning to operate the new boat, as well as being a scuba instructor. They have spent the last month on board the boat in the Bahamas with their wives and children and are about to load it on board *Dockwise* (a large ship that transports yachts across long distances when the owners choose not to make the trip on their own) for shipment to Victoria, BC, for the summer in Desolation Sound. The option exists to ride their high-and-dry boat as it rides the ship, and they may well do that. It's not like taking the boat on its own hull, but it is nowhere near as demanding either. After mutual boat tours, we enjoyed a delicious Mexican meal in Palm Beach before calling it a night about 11 PM.

We must get back to Stuart to repack before resuming out trip home. Stuart's inlet and passes to the NH office are shallow at best, and essentially impassable except at high tide for boats of our draft. We are four-plus hours from Stuart, and the high tides are at 8 AM and 8 PM. We can't get there for the AM tide without traversing the five miles of the Intracoastal from Palm Harbor to the Palm Beach inlet at 3 AM, and the 8 PM Stuart high tide would require running that unpredictable inlet and the twelve miles after it in the dark. Neither are rational choices, so we are left only with the option of waiting for the high tides to advance by a half hour each day until a midafternoon high leaves us with the opportunity to leave Palm Beach in daylight and arrive on a high tide in Stuart and dock before nightfall.

South Florida is very much like Alaska where your arrival time was the determining factor for the departure time. However, it was currents, not depths, that dictated your plans in Alaska. So, for the time being, we are captive transient residents of Palm Beach—not a bad fate! We will be off to Stuart and points north when the gods allow.

2/24/2008, Sunday

The fact that we are in Stuart and have been since Friday was not an easy accomplishment. I did not feel comfortable taking *Always Friday* in under the cover of darkness, but NH had the answer. They sent their chief delivery captain, who had run the inlet at night many times, to join us in Palm Beach for the after-dark ride through the Stuart inlet. Rob's expertise was obvious as we entered the channel well to the north of the center of the channel and then varied our approach through the markers in ways dictated only by real local knowledge.

The threat of running aground was made obvious by the sailboat and motor yacht hard aground between the entry channel and Manatee Pocket, and in fact we bumped the bottom on multiple occasions as we passed through the shallow run to the Roosevelt Bridge but never became stuck. There is no doubt that if we had followed the center of the channel, we would have been among the many TowBoatUS customers of the day! But thanks to Rob, we tied up near the NH docks about an hour after dark, none the worse for wear.

Our few days here have allowed me to go over David and Debbie Sidbury's new NH 68, *Grace of Tides*, and Andy and Susan Francis's new NH 55, *Maggie May*, in considerable detail. Both are here in Stuart for commissioning, and both are beautiful.

The warranty list for *Always Friday* is now down to two simple items that should be resolved tomorrow. If that is the case, we will leave on the midday high tide for the short run (about 20 nm) to Fort Pierce. We will anchor there overnight and proceed the next morning to Port Canaveral, about 65 nm north. After that will be a 90 nm run to St. Augustine for a one- to two-day stay there to enjoy the company of two new friends met through *Always Friday*'s participation in the Miami Boat Show. By the weekend, we hope to be in Brunswick, GA, to visit Billy and Sandra Brunson, lifelong friends that were invited to Alaska but could not make it there last summer.

Kathy is excited about the prospects of visiting Charleston and Savannah, and both are on our list of probable stops over the next several weeks. At some point near Savannah, Ed Andrews, a great friend of over thirty-five years from my Navy flying days, will hopefully join us for the last leg of the trip around Cape Fear and Cape Hatteras into Virginia Beach. We will be running overnight on those legs and will choose our days on the ocean carefully as we pass through the "Graveyard of the Atlantic."

Stay with us if you like. As mentioned before, most of the excitement is behind us (we hope), but we will keep you up to date as we run the final challenges of our trip of a lifetime into Virginia Beach!

2/26/2008, Tuesday

As planned, we left Stuart at midday on the high tide to avoid the infamous shoaling that makes TowBoatUS such a successful franchise in the Stuart area. The trip from the Nordhavn service center to the Atlantic takes a little over an hour since it is most prudent to move slowly through the many areas that represent threats to boats that draw over five feet. In front of us was a yacht of approximately 150 feet moving even more slowly for obvious reasons as they attempted to avoid the embarrassment of an unexpected stop in the sand. Although we heard radio traffic pertaining to a sailboat working its way out of the sand's grasp, no other boat appeared to do more than occasionally tap the soft bottom.

As we finally entered the ocean, we were met by calm seas, beautiful clear water, and almost no wind! The trip up the coast was all that the Chamber of Commerce could ask for. In fact, it was so nice that we discussed the feasibility of running not just the twenty miles to Fort Pierce but skipping that port and running another sixty-five miles to Port Canaveral. We put it into the computer and found that we could be at Cape Marina, where they were expecting us the next day, by midnight. The charts and cruise guides confirmed that it was a wide-open commercial channel with a well-marked approach utilizing both lighted buoys and a visual range. In short, it seemed an excellent alternative to our present Fort Pierce anchorage plans, so off we went!

Kathy made us an excellent meal of roasted chicken while Binky and I drove the boat through a beautiful night with thousands of twinkling stars. After a very clear-cut radar run, complicated only by the presence of a departing cruise ship in the channel, were in the harbor by midnight with our dock space waiting for us. The prior plans to spend the night there and depart early the next morning for St. Augustine were dashed by the prediction of an aggressive cold front moving across Florida over the next few days, accompanied by near gale-force winds and rising seas, necessitating another delay of several days before again heading north. So today we spent the afternoon as Florida tourists, visiting the Kennedy Space Center and the Warbird Museum where my youth again came alive in the presence of an F-4 Phantom fighter, the jet that gave me so many exciting memories during my days in the Navy almost thirty-five years ago.

The predicted storm led us, and most everyone else in the harbor, to secure the boat with double lines at every point in anticipation of the 60 mph winds that are said to be on the way. It looks like the decisions of the past twenty-four hours made in the interest of comfort and safety at sea were sound ones. Our plans have evolved into an anticipated departure for St. Augustine on Thursday morning, and hopefully Brunswick by the weekend. But we continue to live by the aviation adage "You never have to be anywhere," so time and the weather will tell.

On a more entertaining topic, on the home page of Nordhavn, you will find in the top right corner a topic called "Calendar Girls." There Jeff Merrill of Nordhavn has written of the meeting at the Miami Boat Show of two of the wives/co-owners of Nordhavns that were featured on the 2008 Nordhavn calendar. You may recognize them. One of them is very well known to me—and now yet another one of my lifelong fantasies has been fulfilled. I have been to Alaska *and* I am married to a pin-up girl!

2/29/2008, Friday

After two nights in Port Canaveral waiting out a strong storm, we departed Cape Marina at 4 AM to ensure a daylight arrival in St. Augustine about 110 miles north. Port Canaveral is an excellent stop with a well-marked, deep, commercial channel into the marina. It requires intensive use of radar and includes a visual range to confirm your position. It is one of the few ports that I think can be safely entered at night without prior experience in a well-equipped boat with a confident (and competent) crew.

The weather forecast was for good conditions with seas of two to three feet and winds of 10 to 15 mph from the north. However, as we turned north at the entrance buoy, leaving the Cape Kennedy launch pads on our port side, it was evident that the weatherman had not looked out of his window. Over the next hour (still dark!), the winds built to thirty-plus knots from the north with the seas about six to eight feet and very close together.

Since the chairs went through the AV cabinet in the southern Caribbean, we have always prepped the boat for challenging conditions, even when the forecasts were for good weather. Once again, it paid off handsomely. For ten hours, we endured the high winds and seas in relative comfort and complete safety until about 3 PM when the weather turned much more favorable. However, the damage to our plans had been done. The seas had slowed our progress from our usual 8 to 8.5 knots to less than 7 knots. As a result, our arrival time, which should have been with two hours of daylight, was now to occur in darkness. Our rule of avoiding previously untraveled inlets at night was about to be broken by circumstances that we thought we had controlled . . . until the weather interfered.

To mitigate any concerns for entry, I called the marina dockmaster and two local friends to ask if there were any "local knowledge" bits of information that I should know before entering the inlet. The dockmaster gave us a few generic hints, one friend warned us to "be careful" as a friend had run aground there recently, and the third felt the channel was straightforward and passable. So, we headed for the Morse "A" safe water buoy, turned due west as the chart demanded, and slit the channel with the red markers on the right and green ones on the left. Routine and elementary, until the bow bumped the bottom. We stopped and reconfirmed that we were in the middle of the channel (we were) and that the depth was acceptable (the sounder read a reassuring five feet under the keel).

When we left Stuart, a fellow boater emailed us with the suggestion that we might call TowBoatUS as we approached the inlet for their advice on exit strategies. We had safely passed the Stuart inlet when the message arrived, but that advice now made good sense in the St. Augustine inlet as the bow bumped the bottom. So, rather than proceeding onward at some minor risk to the bottom of the boat, we again utilized out membership in TowBoatUS and called for local advice. The news was that they had pulled ten boats out of the "channel" in the last week! For a moderate tip, he came to our position and led us into the marina. Again, his sounder confirmed that we were in eight feet of water (we only need six and a half) all around the boat, but the bow was over an "anthill" of shoaled sand that should not be there. Twenty feet from our position, the depth was twenty-five feet.

Such is the South Florida cruising experience. One of the great benefits of the Nordhavn design is that the boat has a strong keel/skeg that protects the prop, shaft, and stabilizers very effectively. I can only guess how many props these inlets eat up on unprotected boats. The lesson again for all following in our wake: get the TowBoatUS unlimited policy before you get to Florida. It will probably be a very good investment.

Upon arrival at the Municipal Marina, our friends Cameron and Pam Kimball and Tim Kings were waiting for us for dinner. Cameron is with Ginn Development Corporation, and Tim met us at the Miami Boat Show when he accompanied a prospective Nordhavn buyer on a tour of *Always Friday*. He has been a project manager for some of the biggest yachts in the world and knows boats like no one I have ever met before. His admiration for Nordhavns speaks volumes for the quality of the boats!

After a day of crackers and Gatorade on the high seas, a real meal with great company was a real pleasure. On Friday Tim will show us around a 165-foot yacht being built for a wealthy Floridian at Newcastle Yachts here in St. Augustine that, although begun three years ago, is still several years from delivery. Ernie and Mary Martinez, present owners of a NH 40 and prospective owners of a 55, are coming to the marina to visit this afternoon, then join us for dinner downtown, so *Always Friday* continues the tradition of filling our days in port with new friends and admirers of the boat.

Our tentative plans are to make the short run of about thirty miles to Jacksonville tomorrow, anchor out there, and arrive during daylight in Brunswick on Sunday evening. As always, all plans are weather dependent, but that schedule looks good right now. We will tell you what really happens!

3/01/2008, Saturday

We left St. Augustine after a very pleasant early morning walk through the city with Kathy, Raleigh, and Binky. It is a fascinating city, filled with history from the sixteenth century on, and a place that you could easily spend a week. Yesterday was an enthralling day thanks to the generous offer from Tim Kings while in Miami to show us the 164-foot Newcastle yacht for which he is the project manager.

We spent the first hour in his office, looking at the boat's plans and system descriptions, and then went through every level of the massive yacht. You won't believe how much bigger a 164-foot yacht is than our 55-foot boat. There is about the same difference as between a Volkswagen and an eighteen-wheeler! The boat will be staffed by a crew of twelve dedicated to serving the owners and their ten guests while remaining as close to invisible as possible. The owner's stateroom has multiple windows looking out over the bow, yielding a magnificent view of the ocean . . . unless someone inadvertently walks in front of the windows while the owners are in their quarters. If such a forbidden act were to occur, pressure sensors in the teak deck immediately energize an electrostatically charged laminate within the window, rendering it opaque. When the offending crew member passes, the window is again gloriously transparent. We don't have anything like that on *Always Friday*.

The final price will be between $35 and $40 million (*Always Friday* was less), based upon furnishings; in fact, just painting the hull is a multimillion-dollar contract. With the money it takes just to staff and maintain the boat, you could buy a new Nordhavn 55 every six months. It is another world that without Tim's invitation we never would have seen. After the tour, it was off to Hammock Beach Resort with Biff Kimball, Cameron's brother, for lunch overlooking the golf course that will soon host an event of the PGA Senior Tour. Quite an enjoyable day with great company and unique experiences.

Upon our return to *Always Friday*, Ernie and Mary Martinez were waiting for us at the dock. We met them in Miami at the show, where Ernie crawled over every inch of our boat. They have used their NH 40 extensively but now feel they are ready to move to a 55 and take more challenging trips than they felt comfortable pursuing in their smaller boat. They live in Ocala, FL, and know the St. Augustine area well, so we followed them about town, enjoying the high points best known to locals (or near-locals like Ernie and Mary). Their choice of restaurants was superb, as we had a very memorable dinner at the century-old Columbia Restaurant on St. George Street. I don't recall ever eating at a "Spanish-style" restaurant in this country, but it was an experience you should not miss if you are ever in St. Augustine. After a final glass of wine on *Always Friday*, Ernie and Mary returned to their boat with the promise to call us when they pass through Virginia on their boat this summer. It is amazing how many new friends *Always Friday* has brought us this year spent on the oceans.

As if to reemphasize that point, I received an email this morning from Tom Crabbs, the captain of the Coast Guard Cutter *Thetis*. We first met him in Georgetown, Grand Cayman, when he came to the customs docks to admire our boat and later joined us on board for a prolonged visit and tour. We have stayed in touch with him via email since, and today's message was that he hoped we could get together again tomorrow in Jacksonville, as he was inbounding with his ship for a noon arrival. Unfortunately, we plan to weigh anchor about 7 AM for the run to Brunswick, GA, so we will not be able to take him up on his invitation. We considered staying in Jacksonville an extra day to again enjoy his company, but the weather is forecast to deteriorate significantly Sunday night, making that alternative quite unattractive.

So, we are now moving north about five miles off the coast with Jacksonville about ten miles off the bow. The Duke game is on TV, the seas are calm, the winds less than five knots, and the temperature sixty-five degrees. Not a bad way to spend the afternoon.

Kathy has grilled lamb chops planned for supper on the anchor off Jacksonville. Then tomorrow it is off to Brunswick for a rendezvous with our friends of many years, Billy and Sandra Brunson. It also looks like more of our friends from Georgia will join us there for a visit. *Plus*, my sister, who was invited to join us in Alaska, Panama, Key West, Miami, Fort Lauderdale, Palm Beach, Stuart, and Brunswick, may finally take us up on our offer

It seems like all the people who said we would never make it from Alaska to Virginia are changing their minds!

We crossed the 30th northern parallel this morning with 13,000 miles now behind us. Home is closer every minute. That's not all bad . . . or all good. Frankly, part of me would like to just keep on going.

3/05/2008, Wednesday

Our arrival in Jacksonville confirmed that the port is the easiest and safest one to enter we have seen on the East Coast. The channel is straightforward, well marked for day or night entry, wide and deep—in short, everything that you could ask for in an all-weather, day/night port! We arrived at midafternoon and discussed the options for the night as we motored down the channel in total comfort and perfect weather. The Jacksonville Marina was easily accessible on the port side, with nothing but a dock as motivation for stopping there. So, we continued our joy ride down the river towards the city.

About five miles from the jetties, a commercial dry dock on the starboard shore offered an excellent source of shelter from the current and any potential weather, so we dropped *Always Friday*'s anchor in about sixteen feet of water and were rewarded with good holding on the first try. We set the anchor watch and settled in for the night on the river with the hundred-dollar marina fee still safely in our hands. With XM Radio serenading us from all over the boat, Kathy began her magic with the lamb chops destined to be our dinner on the river.

But Kathy noticed we had visitors circling the area, looking at our boat in admiration. The boat was a beautiful one like a Hinckley Picnic boat but made in Turkey by what were obviously very talented builders. M/V *Blue Guitar* had become another of our fascinating contacts that have characterized our trip over the last year. Among those on board was the owner, a Navy veteran with prior duty on board an aircraft carrier and current knowledge on the status of my old carrier, USS *John F. Kennedy*. After further discussion of our mutual contacts in the naval aviation community, they were off into the setting sun with a promise to contact us by email after reviewing our adventures on the website.

The next morning, we were on our way to St. Simon's Island, adjacent to Brunswick, GA, at sunup. Another beautiful day on the Atlantic with calm seas and very light winds. We arrived at midafternoon to the very attentive staff of Golden Isle Marina and some of our very best friends of many years. Billy and Sandra got the royal tour of *Always Friday* since they had missed the opportunity to join us while in Alaska. Upon completion of the tour, we were off to the Sea Island Club for dinner in surroundings that would impress a sheik.

Over dinner, Billy offered the opportunity to take a sightseeing flight in his plane the next day to get a better idea of the local geography. Even better, he offered me the left seat, which put me in control of an airplane for the first time in over a year. It was a welcome experience, not unlike riding a bicycle. After flying around the local area for about thirty minutes, we nailed a practice instrument (ILS) approach to top off a great time in the air. There are few things more satisfying than seeing the world through the cockpit of an airplane, and that afternoon was a very enjoyable experience.

On Monday, Phil and Susan Greene, who joined us in Alaska, and my sister, Tina, with our cousin Beverly joined us for several days on board the boat, adding the warmth of great friends and family to the chilly air of Georgia's early spring.

They have all left for home now, and tomorrow we are leaving in the early morning for Hilton Head, SC. Billy and Sandra's son, Trey, is going to join us for the run to Hilton Head. He is an adventure lover who has been very impressed with the boat at the dock. My offer to see it in action at sea was quickly accepted, and he will be a welcome addition to *Always Friday*'s crew for the day. The weather should be nice for at least one day, and then a gale is expected to dictate our plans over the next several days. We will let you know how it turns out.

3/08/2008, Saturday

The trip to Hilton Head was a very pleasant one with winds of less than ten knots and seas of about three feet, both of which go unnoticed by *Always Friday*. The morning was spent showing Trey the boat's electronic systems, which he quickly learned, at least in part because his profession is the design and installation of computer-controlled smart homes. We arrived at the Savanna entrance buoy exactly at our predicted time and followed the channel to the point of exit that leads to the Harbour Town Yacht Basin.

Once again, in keeping with East Coast yachting tradition, the channel was shallow, poorly marked, and tricky to follow. We had by plan hit the shallow area at high tide, so our passage was challenging but uneventful. With the famous red-and-white lighthouse of Hilton Head prominent at the entrance, we entered the harbor and were welcomed by a harbor tender who led us to our slip. After mooring the boat, they presented us with a bottle of wine, which kindled my concerns that we were about to spend a lot more money for dockage than we usually do!

The harbor is modern, beautifully equipped, and, on this day, the home of several beautiful yachts of more than 100 feet. However, the day of our arrival was one of mystery and concern for the staff, as evidenced by a significant police presence and a flurry of law-enforcement activity. Before long, we heard some of the lurid details: A couple that lived aboard a yacht in the harbor had simply disappeared without a trace, leaving the TV on and the cat on board. One of their two cars was gone, and neither had shown up for work for a day or two. The harbor was buzzing with a body-sniffing dog working the surface for gases emitting from a decomposing body while divers scoured the bottom for either evidence or remains—all to no avail. So, we have sailed into a mystery with no answers to many questions.

In contrast to that situation, a very nice surprise was docked adjacent to our slip—the M/Y *Breakaway* owned by Tony and Renee Russell of California! We share mutual friends in Alex and CeCe Cook, who have an NH 55 on order, and Alex emailed both of us as an introduction. Once again, we had new friends within minutes of arriving at a new destination. Over the next several days, we ate several meals together, toured the island, and enjoyed their company before they headed south to Port Canaveral to watch the shuttle launch next week. They have completed the great loop circuit up the East Coast, across to the Mississippi River, down to the Gulf of Mexico, and across to the East Coast again in their beautiful forty-nine-foot Hampton motor yacht and have plans for more extensive cruising this summer. Their boat and journey can be seen in detail on their website.

As if that were not enough, Walter and Beth Howell, whom we first met at the Miami Boat Show, again came by the boat and entertained us for the day with an extensive tour of their beautiful home and community of Wexford. Wexford will be the site of Alex and CeCe's new home for both them and their new Nordhavn. Walter retired from Coca-Cola, left Atlanta for Wexford, and is now actively involved in the real estate business of Hilton Head. Tony and Renee are retired from professions in California and are contemplating a home here as well. So, with six new friends on Hilton Head Island, we are sure to stop here again on our next trip south—no matter what the cost for docking.

As has been the case so often since leaving Alaska, the weather is the determining factor in our schedule. Today it has been blowing thirty-five to forty knots all day, and temperatures are in the high forties. Although she is a veteran of far worse conditions, I have promised Kathy to keep her out of rough seas on our last legs to Virginia. We have tentative plans for a departure for Charleston tomorrow, but the actual conditions in the morning will dictate our final decision. The weather forecasts are often very much at odds with reality, and we don't make a final decision until we look out the window just before casting off the lines. We will see how it looks in the morning.

3/10/2008, Monday

Saturday in Hilton Head was a day predominated by the weather. The winds blew from the west all day at thirty-five knots, playing havoc with the seas to the degree that there was no decision to be made other than to spend the day in Harbour Town Marina. Were you so foolish as to attempt to venture out into the Atlantic, King Neptune did you a favor and blew almost all the water out of Calibogue Sound, making it impossible to leave. *Always Friday* and all the boats around us were mired in the chocolate-pudding bottom to the extent that moving was not an option.

Sunday was better, but Kathy so enjoyed Hilton Head, and so does not enjoy rough seas, that we decided to spend another day there and wait for the calm after the storm. Our strategy worked well, and this morning at daybreak we left Hilton Head for Charleston.

The mystery of the missing live-aboard couple, now making national news, remained unsolved as we left. I saw an interview on Fox TV that included *Always Friday* in the background, but that was as close to being involved as we came. Most seem to think that they left on their own free will—why they would do so, nobody seemed to know.

The ride to Charleston was very good, although once again the weatherman was way off on wind direction. His southerly prediction gave way to the reality of ten knots out of the NE. The trip up the coast led us to the commercial shipping channel with depths of thirty-plus feet, wide channels, and easily seen channel markers. An easy entry into Charleston took us right by Fort Sumter, so close you could almost hear the "Star-Spangled Banner" riding on the wind. A slight delay came when the Coast Guard called and asked us to stand off while they lifted a swimmer from the water into their helicopter. It looked as if they were practicing ocean pickups, but we couldn't tell if it was for real or not. Whatever the case, it went well, and the helicopter headed off into the sunset.

The Charleston City Marina is one of the nicest we have seen anywhere. It is a massive facility with many impressive yachts and a dozen or so long-range boats of our class. We got in too late for me to meet any of the many boaters here, at least tonight, but I'll be talking to them in the morning. Charleston has been one of Kathy's most anticipated stops, so we will stay here for a few days and take in the sights and experiences of the city.

After our departure from Charleston, Cape Fear, 115 nm NE of here, will be our next stop. We are hoping that Ed Andrews, a friend of three decades from my naval aviation days, will join us for the ride around Cape Hatteras, the "Graveyard of the Atlantic." He has had a standing invitation on board since we left California for Alaska, but so far it has not worked out.

It looks like we will be home before too long. Under different circumstances, I would much prefer to just keep going, but it is a few years too early for that.

Tonight, Kathy is cooking halibut from our freezer. I could almost hear Craig and Greg saying, "Nice fish" as we hauled it over the side from the cold Alaskan waters. The term *priceless memories* takes on a new meaning after a year like our last one.

It's not quite over yet, but the fat lady is backstage, warming up!

3/12/2008, Wednesday

Our time in Charleston was everything that we had hoped for. In fact, it was one of Kathy's favorite stops of the year. The Charleston Municipal Marina was an excellent choice for our base while in the area. It is a true mega yacht center, and the quarter-mile-long, main deepwater dock was essentially filled with very serious boats of many kinds. The big sport fishing boats are here in numbers as they head back north after wintering in Mexico or Central America. The cruising boats are well represented too, with many that are confining their cruising to the Intracoastal Waterway and a few that stay in the ocean as we have. Most are returning from the Bahamas or South Florida. None that we have talked to have been as far as *Always Friday* has safely taken us!

Shortly after setting our dock lines, Kathy had a gourmet meal ready for our first night in the city. The next morning, the marina's shuttle took us downtown where we became the ultimate tourists, wandering the markets and looking in amazement at the prices they asked for the famous Charleston woven baskets. Little baskets that you might expect to pay $50 for were ten times that much; even placemats were over $500 each! We left them for someone more impressed with them than we were.

The website answered our question of "Where for lunch?" One of our office managers read that we were in Charleston and emailed us her recommendation of Café Cru. Annette had been there many times before and always found it memorable. So, noon found us there, but without reservations. It was obvious that this was not just any little lunch place. On the wall was a receipt for catering the staff lunch when the president visited Charleston (over a thousand taxpayer dollars, by the way).

Since we had beat the rush, we were seated quickly and enjoyed a truly memorable experience that we would recommend heartedly for anyone following in our wake. Having taken great pleasure in mingling with the locals as a non-tourist in Alaska, the next event left us with no option other than to admit to present status as visitors to the city: we bought a ticket for a buggy ride through the city.

So, there we were, riding behind two mules with quintessential tourists from Canada, California, and Pennsylvania. We even had cameras draped around our necks. It was quite enjoyable and very informative. Charleston is indeed a beautiful city. Earlier today, we again hit the tourist circuit as we visited the City of Charleston Museum and two historic homes filled with priceless antiques. Even though my interest in antique furniture is not great, and my knowledge of the subject even less, the great beauty of the old cabinet makers' art is very easily appreciated. Since they are owned by the Charleston Museum, they will never come on the market, but if they were ever sold, the best pieces would easily bring seven-figure prices.

Following two full days of sightseeing, it was time to move on to the north. After many rejected invitations over the past year, our old friend from our naval aviation days of thirty-five years ago, Ed Andrews, joined us tonight for the ride to Virginia. He arrived at 8 PM, and within a half hour, we had thrown off the lines and left Charleston under the cover of darkness. The nighttime departure was chosen to put us into Cape Fear, NC, tomorrow afternoon before sunset. Having come into Charleston during daylight on Monday, we now had an electronic chart of our inbound course of two days ago. That information made a night departure much easier and very safe.

It is now the middle of the night, Kathy and the dogs are sound asleep, and we are twenty-nine miles off the coast on the way to Cape Fear's Bald Head Island Marina. If you ever wonder why this area is called Cape Fear, just look at the chart. Within ten miles of our present position are twenty-one charted shipwrecks sitting on the bottom! In fact, we just deviated around a beacon marking the final resting place for the M/V *City of Richmond*. The lighted beacon is essential since the wreck sits as high as forty feet from the bottom, with only nineteen feet of clearance for ships passing over her. Since many of the commercial ships plying these waters draw over twenty-five feet, a collision with the wreck would be a significant threat without the marker.

However, tonight the seas are friendly, and the wind less than ten knots. The nighttime offshore skies are again filled with the millions of stars that land dwellers are never privileged to witness, and the sound of the seas parted by the bow lull you into a state of relaxation usually limited to the vibrating chairs in Brookstone's showrooms. This is our forty-sixth overnight run on *Always Friday* this year, and few have been nicer than this one. After Cape Fear, we will make a sort run of less than a hundred miles to Beaufort, NC, and then wait for a weather window to challenge the Graveyard of the Atlantic as we make the trip around Cape Hatteras into the home stretch for Virginia Beach. Almost 14,000 miles behind us, and less than 300 miles before home.

The reality that we are on the last pages of the last chapter of our trip of a lifetime conjures up mixed emotions. It will be nice to see our friends and family that we have missed so much, but I will greatly miss our life at sea, which I have grown to love and enjoy greatly. I must admit that the same profound sadness I felt as we left Alaska in our wake is beginning to raise its head again as the reality of once again centering our lives on solid ground presents itself as inevitable. Virginia is a truly great place to call home, if you can't live in Alaska.

3/15/2008, Saturday

Our arrival at Cape Fear's Bald Head Island Marina on Thursday was uneventful, and the marina quite nice. After a flounder sandwich for each of us at Eb & Floes, a nice walk around the marina took us to the old lighthouse and the resort town where it seemed that everyone had seen the "big yellow boat" come into the harbor. After answering the many questions from the locals gathered around the post office about our trip and offering the obligatory boat tours to several admiring locals (including Joe the harbor master, who pronounced *Always Friday* to be the best boat to go through the marina in recent times), we returned to the boat to consider the options for our continued northerly progress towards Virginia.

One option was to get a good night's sleep and leave for Beaufort early the next morning, but that would put us into a new harbor after nightfall—a situation we have always made every effort to avoid. The second option was to take a nap to offset the fact that we had run the boat all night and leave on the rising tide about 9:30 PM for Beaufort. By running all night, we would arrive about noon for an easy entry into a deep and well-marked commercial channel.

We decided on choice number two, and with the rising tide, we were on the way to Beaufort. By virtue of the extensive shoals surrounding the entry channel, we were forced to run almost due south for over an hour to reach deep water before turning to the northwest for our next port. The radar, electronic charts, and FLIR again showed their mettle in a very demanding and potentially hostile environment of a dark night and extensive areas of very shallow water (less than six feet). The seas were about three feet and the wind behind us, yielding a very comfortable trip into Beaufort.

The course into the City Marina of Beaufort was a serpentine one with depths that varied on the chart from a foot to fifteen or more feet—not a situation that engenders great trust in the available data. So, I called TowBoatUS on the VHF for some very valuable "local information." After a very prompt and friendly reply from their local boat, we had priceless advice as to the best approach into the marina and enjoyed an uneventful trip to the dock with no less than ten feet of water under our keel the whole way. A very nice way to finish our second all-night run in as many days.

Our inability to contact the city marina over the past two days by both cell phone and VHF was easier to understand when the personality of the dockmaster came to light. He seemed to have a definite dislike for all three of us, and probably for Raleigh and Binky too, had they not been confined to the shower (their usual station for our arrivals). It seemed unusual for someone to dislike us so intensely after having known us for only a few minutes, but he appeared to have perfected instantaneous animosity. We were later reassured that he doesn't seem to like anyone, at least leaving us in good company with others on the dock.

Not long after our arrival, a friendly knock on the side of the boat signaled the arrival of Billy Page, the owner of the Nordhavn 40 M/V *Southern Comfort* docked in Morehead City. He had emailed us an invitation to call him if we came to Beaufort but saw on the website that we had just arrived, so he came by with a bottle of wine to welcome us to town. Although he lives several hours away, he had come to Beaufort primarily to meet us and hear more of our adventure. After a very enjoyable visit and a tour of *Always Friday*, he left with plans for all of us to get together for dinner tomorrow night after a tour of their boat. Another new friend thanks to *Always Friday*, and another enjoyable night to look forward to.

Beaufort is a very interesting little town filled with very friendly people, almost all of whom enjoy the boating scene. Most of the shops are nautically oriented, and seafood restaurants abound among the twenty-four eating establishments that line the harbor. The long seafaring history of the town is proven by the many homes facing the water that date back to the late 1700s to mid-1800s. The local graveyard is the final resting place for veterans of the War of 1812 and the Civil War, as well as dozens of citizens whose lives spanned the eighteenth century and later. A truly fascinating little town, and well worth a two- or three-day stop.

Our protracted runs of the past several days were dictated by a weather system that earlier today played havoc with the Southeast. This evening we tracked the storm on our seventy-two-mile radar as it moved towards us, accompanied by tornado watches and rising winds. About 9:30 PM, it hit with a vengeance, with 50 mph winds, torrential rains, and one of the biggest drops in barometric pressure we have seen all year, but nothing of a destructive nature. In fact, the five of us enjoyed dinner in the salon as the rain beat down on the deck. Kathy's sister and her husband, Susanne and Hugo, who joined us in Alaska for ten days, again joined us today for a short overnight visit from Raleigh, NC, to welcome us back to the East Coast.

The talk today has been how best to head north again in a day or so. The Atlantic is forecast to be quite unfriendly for the next week, with seas as high as seventeen feet and winds of gale force intermittently. We could pick our time and run the thirty hours to Virginia Beach through eight-foot seas, or we could consider riding the Intracoastal Waterway (ICW) through North Carolina and into Virginia. The ICW has not been a viable option until now because the depths are either too shallow or unpredictable through Florida, Georgia, and South Carolina. However, the Coast Guard, TowBoatUS, and the local watermen confirm that boats considerably larger than ours can now safely traverse the waterway north of us if navigation is careful and accurate.

I gave Kathy the option of thirty hours in six-plus-foot seas through the Graveyard of the Atlantic, or a slower trip through the ICW in much calmer conditions. Since she had been asking to see the ICW since South Florida, I had a good idea of what her response would be, so today we will be deep into the paper charts as we prepare for a ride down the "ditch" to Norfolk. It will be the first time we have not been in an ocean since we turned south into the Pacific from Canada last fall. From the standpoint of running the boat, it will be a much more challenging trip. In the ocean, it is usually a "set it and forget it" scenario with the autopilot and chart plotter. However, in the confined channel of the ICW, the boat's direction requires the constant attention of the helmsman, or the bottom will rise and smite you.

The wind here in the harbor is about fifteen knots out of the north, and XM WeatherWx reports gale warnings and challenging seas just offshore. So today will be a lazy day with Susanne, Hugo, and Ed before we join Billy and Linda for dinner in Morehead City tonight. Then tomorrow we will be off on a new adventure up the ICW to home in Virginia!

3/17/2008, Monday

Last night was a most enjoyable night. Billy and Linda Page of NH 40 *Southern Comfort* treated us to a night on the town of Morehead City. They picked us up from the boat, and after a tour of *Always Friday* for Linda, we were off to one of their favorite restaurants, Windansea. Not a place you would find on your own, but well worth the trouble of finding it if you are ever hungry for an excellent dinner and in Morehead City.

The food, although excellent, played second fiddle to the superb company of Billy and Linda. They live about sixty miles from Morehead City but have had a waterfront cottage for years that has evolved into a great vacation home with their Nordhavn moored in their front yard. After dinner we went to their home for a tour of both it and *Southern Comfort*. Both are beautiful. Bill is an electrical engineer, CPA, and Wharton graduate, so every facet of their lives is organized and efficient. Their boat is the second-generation forty-foot NH, and the workmanship and design are excellent. Billy has taken it to an even higher level with his knowledge of electronics and electrical circuitry. Billy is one of those people you could talk to all night and learn something from him with every sentence.

So, by about 11 PM, we had said good night to Billy and Linda and were back on board *Always Friday*, preparing for an early departure up the ICW for Belhaven. Around 7:30 AM, we were underway with an adverse tide not only rolling against us but also stealing the water under our keel as low tide progressed. We had been told by many that we would have plenty of depth with occasional exceptions at dead low tide. You guessed it! At dead low tide, with the depth sounder announcing four feet under the keel, we bumped the soft bottom from well within the channel.

In no time a shrimp boat came over with an offer to assist us off the shoaled sand. Before we could thank them for their kindness, they demanded $200 for their benevolent services. Thankfully, their prophecy that we would never get off without their help proved inaccurate, and much to their disappointment, we were soon off and again headed north. For the next 65 nm, the narrow channel required our full-time attention, with almost no use of the autopilot's nav mode and constant use of the jog lever, which is basically an electronic steering wheel.

Our original plan was to spend the night in Belhaven, NC, but our arrival there at 5 PM would have been a waste of two hours better used for getting closer to Coinjock, NC, tomorrow. So, we canceled our plans for Belhaven and continued another hour down the road to the Alligator River-Pungo River Canal area. There we picked an acceptable area for anchoring for the night and dropped the hook about a quarter mile off the ICW in twelve feet of water. The anchor held beautifully, and we are now set for an evening under the stars, with a pork tenderloin on the grill preceded by a real treat of smoked moose, courtesy of our good friend in Alaska, Craig Forgaard. Our Alaskan friends continue to be stars of our conversations daily as the memories of last summer flood our thoughts. Tomorrow, we hope to be in Coinjock for the night where our friends from NC, the Goddards, will join us for dinner at the Coinjock Docks, famous for their seafood and prime rib. If all goes well, we may be in Virginia Beach by Wednesday evening.

It is almost over. Judging by distance traveled, we have completed 99.3 percent of our planned trip, with the remaining fraction of a percent just off the bow. I can hear the fat lady warming up in the dressing room. Although all good things must come to an end, we can relish the fact that it has been a truly fantastic show . . . and one hell of a trip.

3/18/2008, Tuesday

Last night was an excellent one at anchor with little wind and no problems at all and the anchor rock steady with a 3:1 scope in twelve feet of water. A sailboat and shrimper followed us into our chosen anchorage, although the cruising guide would lead you to believe that no decent anchoring sites existed within miles. Before sunrise this morning, I was up to make sure that we were underway at first light.

As we entered the Pungo Canal, we were met with fog that required radar for a safe passage. I knew that the sailboat that anchored with us did not have radar, so I called him to warn him of the conditions he was about to encounter. What followed was yet another delayed reward of our Alaskan adventure. Another boat had heard the call of *Always Friday* to the sailboat, and that boat was M/V *Emerald Lady*, the same *Emerald Lady* that had shared Alaska's Glacier Bay with us last summer! Dick and Nancy White had shared the experience of Marjorie Glacier with us and called on the VHF there when they saw our home port of Virginia Beach, since theirs was the same. We talked at length of Virginia and

Alaska, then went our separate ways. We last crossed paths south of Ketchikan. The VHF came alive this morning with the question, "*Always Friday*, this is *Emerald Lady*! Remember us?"

With great memories of Alaska bubbling to the surface, I quickly answered, "Sure do! Great to see you again!" It took us almost 12,000 miles to cross paths again, but it happened. After a few more pleasantries, we agreed to meet at the Coinjock Marina for dinner later for our first face-to-face meeting ever.

But before that was to be, we had about sixty miles of very challenging ICW travel to safely complete. The decision to take the ICW option over the outside passage around Cape Hatteras has turned out to be a very sound one. The weather system offshore runs from Maine to Cuba and is associated with winds as high as sixty-five knots and seas as high as forty-five feet. Just offshore, the seas are eight to twelve feet! *Always Friday* has been through worse than what Hatteras would throw at us today, but there is no reason to subject ourselves to that when the ICW option is available.

The challenge switches from that of a rough sea passage to one of limited visibility through tight channels and shallow waters. Twice today we were stopped by soft sand blocking the very center of the channel. On both occasions, we were able to back out of the dilemma and find an acceptable area for passage outside of the published channel. Just tonight, I received this message from a seasoned delivery captain suggesting that we will see more of the same tomorrow:

> Buddy,
>
> I've been following your trip like many others and had a chance to meet you in Miami. Great trip. As I'm sure others have told you—you will exercise caution in Currituck Sound. I've been through there delivering boats with 6ft draft and bumped bottom many times in mid channel. It's a miserable stretch of markers to follow. Once past the open sound you

are in good shape, but expect a little bottom paint to rub off.
—Mike

But it is far better than being punished by seas that would make the two-day, nonstop passage around the cape into a miserable experience, impossible to justify when an acceptable alternative was available.

About 4:30 PM, we completed this leg of our ICW journey and tied up at Coinjock Marina with *Emerald Lady* at our bow. My recollection of their green-hulled boat as a truly beautiful one was borne out by closer inspection. The layout is excellent, and the roominess of her interior would lead you to believe that she is much larger than her forty-one feet. They have equipped her as a live-aboard boat in a way that would make you think about giving up your shore-based home too.

As proof that we were almost home, we were joined for dinner by Mark and Jacqueline Goddard and their son, Mark Jr., who came over from their home in Currituck. They have been great friends for years, as shown by the fact that among the most excited to see them were Raleigh and Binky. Their tails could not stop wagging after seeing one of their best people friends, Mark Jr. After tours of both *Always Friday* and *Emerald Lady*, all eight of us gathered at the Coinjock Marina Restaurant for a dinner featuring their specialty—prime rib.

The conversations centered around our many adventures in Alaska and the Inside Passage through British Columbia, with the surface only scratched in three hours of nonstop recollections. Dick and Nancy chose to ship *Emerald Lady* from Victoria, BC, to Fort Lauderdale, FL, rather than subject their forty-one-foot boat to the uncertainties of a long ocean passage. Their boat certainly could have made the voyage, but at about one fourth the displacement of *Always Friday*, it would not have been a pleasant experience.

With two more good friends added to our list of Alaskan treasures, we are about to go to bed in anticipation of one of the highlights of our trip—our arrival home after over a year away. During that year, we have experienced adventures that, although in the reach of many, are experienced by only a very few. We were asked many times by those who work with me in our water-view office, "When will you be home?" On each occasion, I have answered that we will be home when you hear *AF*'s horn blast out the news of our arrival! Well, the office has been told that our arrival is eminent, and the horn should blow tomorrow afternoon, barring unforeseen challenges in the shallow waters of Currituck Sound. They have promised to be leaning out of the windows as we pass by the Norfolk harbor on our way to East Beach Marina in Virginia Beach.

Tomorrow, the fat lady will sing at the top of her lungs ... and we should be home in our old beds for the first time in more than a year tomorrow night.

The term *ambivalent feelings* will take on a very personal meaning to me as I step off *Always Friday* and into our car for the short ride "home" from the marina.

For the past year, the word *home* has meant *Always Friday*. In a way, it still does in my dreams.

3/21/2008, Friday

We awoke before sunrise for the final chapter of our trip of a lifetime. With the dawn, we were on our way north through the challenges of the unpredictable depths of the ICW. We began the trip with *Emerald Lady* leading the way with her five-foot draft, calling the depths for us. Just as predicted, we often crossed areas that were marginal for *Always Friday* even though we were in the center of the channel. Although we were never "aground" in the strictest sense of the word, it was frequently necessary to slow to a crawl or even reverse course as we sought deeper water.

The weather that had dictated our entry into the ICW system was a challenge even within those protected waters. The winds that were about twenty knots in the morning increased throughout the day to as high as forty knots, confirming the appropriateness of our decision to avoid the fury of the Atlantic for the final 130 miles of our trip! As we approached Norfolk, our progress was slowed significantly by the bridges that opened on a schedule that was not made with boaters in mind, but by early afternoon, we were passing landmarks that confirmed our arrival in home territory. Messages from friends confirmed that they were awaiting our arrival at various points along our route to welcome us home.

As we arrived at Hospital Point, which is mile marker 1 of the ICW, *Emerald Lady*, whom we first met in Glacier Bay, left us for her slip in Portsmouth, symbolically ending our Alaskan trek. There is no doubt that we will see Dick and Nancy again somewhere, sometime.

Then the Wainwright Building where I have practiced medicine for the past thirty-one years came into view! The windows of the top floor were open and filled with our friends and staff waving their welcome to us after a year away from home. A very touching scene that reemphasized the ambivalent feelings associated with the end of such an adventure as we have had the privilege to experience together. The last time I recall experiencing such feelings was my last flight in fighter jets as I was about to leave the Navy after three of the best years of my life.

An email from Scott Dungan, who has been following our trip via the internet, predicted that we would have feelings like those he felt as a high school football player during the final minutes of the last game of his senior year. He was right. The wonderful memories were flooding our thoughts, mixed with regrets that it was about to come to an end. The last ten miles of our journey took us by Pier 12 of the Norfolk Navy Base, which I'd left thirty-six years ago on board the aircraft carrier USS *Kennedy* to prepare for our anticipated time on Yankee Station off Vietnam. It was fitting that one of my very best friends and a fighter pilot from those days, Ed Andrews, was with me on the bridge as we passed that milestone in our lives and this journey.

With the winds howling at near-gale-force levels, *Always Friday* took us safely and comfortably into Little Creek Harbor where some of our best friends were waiting to welcome us home and take our lines. As I turned the engine off for the final time of our journey, the realization that Kathy, Raleigh, Binky, and I had traveled almost 14,000 miles around the North American continent together on the greatest adventure of our lives came welling to the surface with a sense of accomplishment, happiness, and sorrow that is hard to describe.

There is no way to overstate the happiness that *Always Friday* has brought into our lives. It is no longer an inanimate floating work of the boat builder's art. It's a part of our family's lives that can never be taken from us. At some point in the distant future, someone else may own and enjoy our boat, but no one else will ever possess her soul. *Always Friday* is an indelible part of our being, and that cannot be changed.

What has the last year meant to me? Maybe it can be summed up by the fact that no matter what the circumstances in the future, I will always be able to close my eyes and relive many of the most memorable moments of my life, until my mind no longer knows my name.

To all of you who have added so much in so many ways to the journey of *Always Friday*, we thank you from the bottom of our hearts.

We loved having you with us!

—*Buddy, Kathy, Raleigh and Binky*

SOME PERSONAL THOUGHTS ON ALASKA

WITH ALASKA NOW almost 400 nm behind us and a lazy day here at anchorage in Pruth Bay while waiting out a gale in Queen Charlotte Sound, I find myself trying to understand how Alaska could have so thoroughly captivated me this summer, the most memorable one of my six decades. I had been to Alaska before, hunting and fishing in the Brooks Range north of the Arctic Circle, so it wasn't just the uniqueness of the geography, although Alaska's unparalleled beauty certainly played a major role.

It wasn't just the boat, either. There could not be a better boat for what we did than our Nordhavn 55, *Always Friday*, and the summer would have been impossible without her. In many ways she was the catalyst that made it all come together. She has certainly afforded us fantastic opportunities that would not have been possible in her absence . . . but we had enjoyed the boat in Southern California, Catalina Island, the Pacific Coast, and the Inland Passage through Canada without generating the excitement that later permeated every minute of my summer in Alaska. So, *Always Friday* was important and essential, but it was something else as well.

Was it our best friends and family who joined us along the way, enjoying the sights, sounds, and experiences of this wonderland with us? They all certainly played a major role, but I had spent multiple summers of my life with them without the resultant impact of this summer. However, there was one very notable exception. I distinctly remember when we first crossed the border into Alaska. It was one of the great memories of the trip for a reason you would not guess.

We had gotten behind schedule in meeting our friends Jim and

Monica in Ketchikan, and Frank had been scheduled to leave for home from Port Hardy, BC, after joining us in Victoria, CA. Kathy and I found ourselves 450 nm away from our rendezvous in Ketchikan with no way to make it on time with day trips through the Inside Passage. So, in a gesture of friendship which would not surprise you if you knew him as I do, Frank said, "I can't leave you like this," cancelled his reservations home, altered his busy work schedule, and extended his trip to Ketchikan! He and I then ran the boat through the open Pacific for fifty-four straight hours through a weather window that allowed us to meet the Harts on time and in Ketchikan.

That personal commitment by Frank began the Alaskan experience at a personal level few close friends ever could experience. It was a return trip for both of us, as Frank was with me on my first Alaskan adventure when we were dropped off by float plane in the northern Alaskan wilderness for ten days of moose and bear hunting about ten years ago. Life doesn't offer you many friends like Frank, and he will always be among the brightest memories of the friends in my life and our trip.

So, what else was the chemistry that came together from June through August 2007 to yield the unique experience that has certainly changed my life, and quite possibly a significant portion of my future?

After pondering this question all summer, I think that I may have a possible answer. It was a combination of all those things mentioned above, plus an ingredient new to my life... the wonderful people of Alaska! Here, in the rough order that we met them, are some of my new friends who turned a journey into an indelible, fantastic memory.

It all began at the beginning! On our first day in Ketchikan, we met Bill and Mary Pfiefer through her sister in California, whom we had met during the commissioning of *Always Friday*. We knew nothing of each other until that day, but within hours of our first meeting, they had dedicated their next several days to seeing that we all (the Harts included!) enjoyed Ketchikan to the maximum.

If you have read our journal, you will recall that Bill is one-eighth native Alaskan of the Tlingit tribe, and a real student of his (and therefore Alaska's) past. His pride in his heritage generated a respect in me for Alaskan history that led me to read all I could find about the history of this magnificent state. Their warm welcome at the beginning of our trip, as well a repeat performance of their hospitality on the homebound leg, left us with the sincere hope that we will once again enjoy the company of two of the nicest, most gracious people you could ever hope to meet. It was just the first of many brief associations that quickly led to friendships that will endure far longer than the image of Alaska in the rear-view mirror.

Next up on our Alaskan all-star team was Craig Forgaard of Gustavus, AK. If you have followed our trip, you already know him well. Craig's pictures are all over our internet picture albums simply because he made many of our most vivid memories possible. We met him shortly after our initial arrival in Auke Bay Harbor near Juneau as he endeared himself to Kathy by guarding Raleigh from the eagles when we inadvertently left her a pathway to the front of the boat where eagles had enough "swoop room" to take Raleigh out for lunch! From that day on, Craig went out of his way to make us feel at home in his home state. In fact, it was Craig that took me for my first shopping spree at Western Auto and Marine where I walked in as a tourist and walked out as a local. Remember the Carhart pants and red suspenders? All Craig's work!

And his education of me didn't stop with our mutual sartorial splendor. He taught me how to tie the rigs for halibut after giving me a dozen 12/0 circle hooks that later yielded such success that we were routinely throwing seventy-five-pound fish back into the bay. He showed up on the boat one day with a newly purchased navigational chart of Glacier Bay marking all the "secret" spots known only to locals . As a direct result of that effort, Lauren and Nathan (our daughter and her husband) each caught their first halibut, and Nathan took the lead for *Always Friday*'s largest fish contest with a fifty-pounder (later bested by fish of sixty, seventy-five, and one hundred thirty-five pounds—all taken at spots recommended by Craig!).

He taught us the techniques for Dungeness crabbing, and then loaned us the equipment to do so. When we were successful beyond our expectations, he took the crabs home to boil them since we didn't have a pot large enough to cook our catch. He not only showed us how to catch prawns (shrimp to us), but he also actually went with us, set out all his traps for us, and gave us the shrimp. And sockeye salmon! We probably caught more than all the other tourists combined. How? You guessed it: Craig! And when Kathy's father, Charles, said that he had always wanted to catch a salmon, Craig took me to get the correct lures and showed me how to rig them most effectively. Did it work? Fifteen minutes after the lures went into the water at Three Hill Island, Charlie had landed a ten-pound Coho salmon, the first of his eighty-seven years. Within an hour, ten more were on board, and waiting for the freezer.

When we asked questions about his hometown of Gustavus, he responded by picking us all up at Bartlett Cove in his fuel truck and showing us everything there was to see in the town (including their home). The few times we had Craig and Marylyn over for dinner on *Always Friday* paled in comparison to what he did for our Alaskan experience. I sadly recall the image of our final departure from Auke Bay on *Always Friday* with Craig waving goodbye from his boat *Jonathan*. My thoughts then, and my thoughts now, are that I sure hope I get to see him again in his world. I have never enjoyed the company of a new friend as much as I did Craig's during this summer of a lifetime. And I think I may have talked him into putting the Camels down.

A few days after our initial arrival in Auke Bay (Juneau), I had the good fortune to cross paths with Greg Gallant on the dock adjacent to *Always Friday*'s berth. Greg had just returned from a fishing trip in his skiff *Stormy Seas* and was cleaning seven beautiful king salmon. These were the first ones I had seen in Alaska, and of course I introduced myself and began asking all the fishing questions: where, how, what bait—all the usual stuff. Greg patiently answered all my questions, and then had several of his own about our boat, the trip north, and our plans for the summer. After knowing me for about ten minutes, he offered us a king salmon fillet, made even more special by the fact that it was a white king salmon, the ultimate delicacy of the salmon family. I offered him a tour of our boat, and several days later he and his wife, Terri, joined us on board *Always Friday* for a visit. His fascinating life as a king crab fisherman out of Dutch Harbor in his younger days could be made into a movie.

From that day on, Greg was an important part of our Alaska experience. He took me for my first king crab experience, then cleaned the crabs, boiled them on the dock by *Always Friday*, and gave them to us. Among my many pleasant memories of Alaska, our days together in his skiff, halibut and salmon fishing in the rain, stand out vividly as high points. If you were to ask Lauren and Nathan (our daughter and her husband) the high point of their visit with us, you would almost certainly hear of the day Greg picked us all up in *Stormy Seas* during a chilly rain squall and took us with him to check his king crab traps. When someone from Virginia is given the opportunity to see a trap pulled up from 300 feet beneath the surface filled with crabs measuring three feet across, it becomes a lifetime memory. When they were then presented to us as a gift, it became even more memorable.

It was always welcome when retuning from one of our many trips out of Auke Bay to hear a call from *Stormy Seas* on the VHF welcoming us back "home." It was a sad occasion when on our last departure from Auke Bay, beginning our southward trek to Virginia, I heard our last call from Greg's boat as he said goodbye and good luck to *Always Friday* from his favorite halibut hole. If I ever get back to Alaska, he will be among the first of my calls to my great Alaskan friends. I *really* miss these guys!

The most unique experience of my summer gave us priceless memories of three new close friends—Glen and Jean Carroll and their skiff man, Ian. You could never ask to meet nicer people, but for a tourist from Virginia to find them in Alaska on a commercial fishing boat from Homer was a long shot at best! The memories of the night they invited us to a sockeye salmon and prawn dinner on board F/V *Hadassah* in Auke Bay Harbor would have been enough to make our all-star list, but to then take me with them on a salmon-seining trip to Tenakee Springs catapulted my time with them to the "priceless" list. To spend three days with quintessential commercial fishermen (or fisherpersons, since Jean was an essential part of the fishing team) while they practiced their profession was a thrill no one could expect in a lifetime. Not only did they allow me to intrude into their world, but somehow, they made me feel truly welcome in their company. No part of the fishing process went unexplained; no question went unanswered, and Glen even left me on the bridge to take a turn at *Hadassah*'s wheel. Ian not only made sure that I understood the essential role of the skiff man in the seining process but also took me with him on several sets so I could see the process from that point of view.

To show you better why we have such strong feelings for our Alaskan friends, I'll tell you of the night that *Always Friday* was returning to Auke Bay in fog and rain after a great week in Glacier Bay. I called the harbormaster on the VHF radio for a slip assignment, but there was no answer. A few minutes later, Ian came up on his handheld VHF to tell us that he would meet us at the harbor and find a place for us to dock. He had heard our unanswered call while eating dinner at a local restaurant and left to help us tie up at night in the wind and rain!

Why would Glen and Jean let me into their fascinating world and make me feel so welcome? Why would Ian go out of his way so many times to make our Alaskan visit as pleasant and as memorable as possible? I don't know, but maybe you are beginning to see why I think Alaskans are the best people on earth. I would sleep even better if I knew that I would see these special friends again one day in Alaska.

Then there were two young men who added significantly to our days in Auke Bay. Both were younger than our children—salmon fishing guides with charter services out of Auke Bay. James Mothershead took Kathy and me for our first successful king salmon trip and made every minute of it into a special day. You have never seen anyone try harder to make the day rewarding for his fishermen! It was with James that we saw the bald eagle attack the salmon and almost drown in the effort. It was James who stayed out an extra hour and a half until Kathy caught a king salmon. Although she had caught several nice chum salmon, he wanted her to have a king, and he got her one. We fished with him twice more: once with Phil, then with the Taylors. On every trip, his personality and perseverance made the trip more than expected. If he represents the next generation of Alaskans, the state will remain a wonderland of wonderful people.

Eddie Kelly's part in our experience sprang from Susan Greene's amazement at his ability to catch king salmon from the Auke Bay Harbor docks. As she watched him bring in several, she offered to take one off his hands if he ever found himself with too many to use. Susan is a really helpful person! A day or so later, Eddie showed up at the boat with a cleaned white king salmon for our pleasure. After a tour of *Always Friday*, Eddie was officially our friend. He took Kathy to the grocery store and took me to Western Auto and Marine—each guaranteed to cement a tight relationship with our family. The night before we left, he joined us in Juneau for pizza and promised to join us again in his hometown of Seattle when we passed through there in September.

Why would two young men less than half my age make such efforts to ensure our enjoyment of Alaska? It's more of that magic of the North that I have been speaking of all summer.

Next, if you know me and you met Paul Johnson of Gull Cove, you would know that he would be a "best friend for life" type for me. Paul was born in Alaska before it was a state, a fact which he laments precludes his running for president of the United States! Not unlike my dilemma that I can't run for pope since I was born a Methodist. However, I remain a fan of the pope's big hat. To offset that cruel twist of fate, Paul has spent his life in Alaska hunting, fishing, and living off the land. Note that I did not say "his adult life"; he explained that he has not yet grown up.

He and Tami now run a guide service near Idaho Inlet, the site of our serendipitous meeting when that dramatic fog bank at the entrance to Elfin Cove forced us into the inlet for the night. Paul and Tami were among the guests on Steve's boat when we and the Walkers, our guests on board *Always Friday* for the week, were invited to join the party going on there. Over the next six weeks, *Always Friday* made two stops at Gull Cove, welcomed Paul and Tami on our boat at Elfin Cove, and joined Paul and John (his guide in the business) at the restaurant at Bartlett Cove when we met at Glacier Bay.

On every occasion, it was if I were playing with my good friend of many years. His infectious smile and irreverent humor, coupled with his grizzly bear appearance, makes him a memorable character, even among the many unique personalities of the Alaskan scene. There is nothing I would rather do than spend several weeks in the wilderness with Paul. We would be safe from the bears, but we might laugh ourselves to death. Maybe one day we will get to see. I very much hope so!

By the way, the last time I talked to Paul, he was planning to go to Hawaii for the winter to lounge on a nude beach. If any of you are in the market for property in Hawaii, follow Paul to that beach. His bright-white presence there will instantly deflate property values to about $0.50 per acre.

What are the chances that when a thousand-foot cruise ship pulled up next to us at Marjorie Glacier in Glacier Bay, the pilot on board would become a good friend we would see in person twice before leaving Alaska, even joining him and his wife in their Ketchikan home for an afternoon? Well, that is exactly what happened. Doug McPherson was on board the *Noordham* as a bar pilot when we both witnessed the calving of an office-building-sized iceberg from the glacier—the largest one Doug had seen in his twenty-year career! His admiration for Nordhavn had precipitated the first VHF conversation between us, but many others by email, phone, and in person followed that eventful day. He and Jean came to the dock in Ketchikan to see us off, and Doug and I discussed the possibility of the two of them joining us on *Always Friday* for part of our southerly trip.

It is amazing how events in Alaska spawn such friendships in so little time, but I saw it happen more times than I would have guessed possible. Maybe it is because so many in Alaska have such similar interests or they simply wouldn't be there. Maybe the oddest part of the equation is that my interests exactly parallel so many of those who have found Alaska to be their home for life. Whatever the case, Doug and the experiences we shared together have become very meaningful memories of our summer.

Ken, the captain of the *Fairweather Express II*, a tour boat in Glacier Bay, and his son, Luck, a mate on the boat, are yet more great memories of our northern adventure. *Always Friday* again started the friendship when they expressed an interest in our boat. After the obligatory tour, Ken and Luck became a wealth of information about Glacier Bay and its sights. Their expertise was no surprise since they spend eight hours a day on the waters of the bay, searching for bears, wolves, orcas, and humpbacks to amaze the tour boat crowd. It was Ken who told me exactly where and when to be at Three Hill Island to ensure that Kathy's father caught a coho salmon. Ten minutes after our arrival there on the rising tide, Charlie had a ten-pound trophy in the box, thanks to Ken. Both Ken and Luck were on the dock when we brought in our 135-pound halibut, and it was Ken's daughter who jumped aboard and finished the filleting job I had begun.

Our last bright memory of Ken was when he called us on our way out of Glacier Bay for the last time to thank us for the times we spent together over the summer. Imagine that—he was thanking us. What a role reversal! If I am ever in Glacier Bay again, I will not leave without seeking them out for fond recollections of the summer of my life, with significant contributions by my friends Ken and Luck.

Then there was Doug and Donna Nolder. Doug is a retired Alaskan Airlines 737 pilot, and Donna is the expert fisherwoman of the family. Doug wandered by the boat one afternoon and fell into my web of a boat tour. Several days later, they came by for a visit, and the friendships were begun. Before we left, Doug and Donna had taught us much about Juneau and Douglas (its bedroom community); best of all, they had taken me coho salmon fishing on their boat at Hand Trollers Cove, a famous hot spot this time of year. How was it possible to meet so many nice people in such a short time? It wasn't me—it was Alaska, home of the nicest group of people you could ever hope to meet.

Do any of you remember Doug, the commercial fisherman and owner of F/V *Oracle*? I'm sure that Phil and Susan do, as he was the fisherman sharing the dock with us at Taku Harbor when, for no good reason, he walked up, introduced himself, and gave us a sockeye and coho salmon from the hold of his boat. He had just caught them that day, and the fish represented cash in his pocket—until he gave them to four strangers from a foreign land (the East Coast!). His admiration for *Always Friday* was the catalyst for his visit, but his kind heart was the reason for his gift of the salmon.

We ate the salmon that night in a memorable meal docked in a landmark of Alaska. The next morning, as we passed the fishing fleet on our way to Tracy Arm, he hailed us on the VHF to say that he was taking our picture as we passed and would email them to us later (and I am sure that he will). But that was not the end of the story. On our final exit from Juneau, I heard Doug on the radio, again fishing from *Oracle*. I called him to once again thank him for his contribution to our great time in his home state. He remembered us well and offered us his best wishes for a safe trip home. I have fished for thirty-five years in Virginia and never had anything like our experience with Doug. Our memories of him are just another reason that Alaska was so special during this summer of so many men's dreams.

So, there is my case! I think the reason that I so hate to leave this place after such a wonderful summer is not a geographical one but a personal one. The kind of people who have been drawn to Alaska are my kind of people, and I hate beyond words to be leaving them. Maybe one day I will see them again—or maybe they can come see me . . . in my little log cabin on Shelter Island, the one with the little aluminum boat and the float plane tied up out front!

—*Buddy*

AN HONOR BESTOWED

TODAY I RECEIVED the following email from my good friends in Ketchikan, Bill and Mary Pfiefer! The title of "sourdough" bestowed upon me by a true native Alaskan is a high honor that I cherish greatly. You may find his letter interesting. Here it is:

Buddy

You do a great job of writing as usual, and I am sure that all your friends and Alaskans appreciate your thoughts as much as we do. One small correction is that I am 1/8th Tlingit. Your story about the Carharts and coming out a local reminds me of a story.

I had just finished power trolling in the summer out of Hoonah with my uncle Adam Greenewald and had started high school in La Conner, Washington, during the time that Alaska was considering the Alaska Pipeline. I decided to do a report on the pipeline for school and requested information from several firsthand people, including the governor of Alaska, William A. Egan. I of course received information from the office of the governor with a letter on state printed stationary.

The letter began "Dear Cheechako . . ." (I have pasted definitions below at the end.) I subsequently showed my uncle Albert Greenewald the letter from the governor since our families would get together every Sunday. He was born in Hoonah, AK, and was a commercial fisherman that lived in Mount Vernon, Washington, in the winter when he wasn't fishing. He laughed when he read that the governor called me a cheechako. He explained to me what it was and said that he, my grandmother, and grandfather were all close friends with Governor Egan. He suggested I write a follow-up letter to the governor thanking him for the information. He said to include the fact that I was Tlingit, born in Juneau, Alaska, and fished with my uncle Adam Greenewald (who served on the Alaska State Board of Fish and Game) in the summer. He told me to write that if the governor considered me a cheechako, could he also please write my uncle Albert to let him know that he was also a cheechako since while he was born in Alaska and commercial fishes in Alaska, he winters in Washington State.

So, I wrote the letter as my uncle advised and I am sure the governor had a good chuckle. I subsequently received a letter from the governor, which this time had a gold-embossed seal of the state of Alaska, stating that indeed I was not a cheechako and was a sourdough. He also sent a certificate making me a member of the Order of the Walrus with a little walrus-head stick pin. I still have the letters packed away some place.

So, I would consider you leaving Alaska as a sourdough, even though you have not spent all four seasons in Alaska, and I would challenge anyone that would call you simply a cheechako. You had many new friends to help you get to this point along with several adventures that you had to push forward on your own, having limited knowledge of what lies ahead. Alaska is a great land, filled with adventure, and will build a spirit that bonds all those who have shared in the adventures and challenges Alaska brings.

You now have shared in that legacy that bonds Alaskans. Don't let too much time pass to where you forget that spirit that brought life into your soul. Visit Alaska and your friends often.

Until our paths cross again,
Dr. Bill Pfeifer Ketchikan, AK

Welcome to Alaska, cheechako!

If that's the greeting you get up north, don't be insulted. In Alaska and the Canadian Yukon, cheechako means nothing more sinister than "newcomer" or "tenderfoot," a stage you will outgrow if you stay around. The harsh climate and terrain of Alaska do make greater demands on newcomers than the lower forty-eight, and that is why there is a special northern word for them. The word was imported from Chinook Jargon into the English of that region during the Yukon gold rush that began in 1896 and is chronicled in the stories of Jack London and the poems of Robert Service. In *White Fang* (1906), London takes time at the beginning of a chapter to explain:

Service's third book of Yukon poems, published in 1909, is called *Ballads of a Cheechako*. Chinook Jargon was a trade language spoken in the Pacific Northwest by as many as 100,000 Indians and the white traders and settlers who dealt with them. It was based on the language of the Chinook Indians of the lower Columbia River, but its vocabulary had many additions from English. Today there are just a few speakers of Chinook Jargon left. The Chinook language itself is extinct. In Chinook Jargon, cheechako means "new comer," the two parts of the word deriving from Lower Chinook and Nootka, respectively. English has gained half a dozen other words from Chinook Jargon, including camas (plant with edible bulb, 1805), eulachon (fish, 1807), salal (shrub, 1825), and chum (salmon, 1902). The motto of Washington State is the Chinook Jargon al-ki, meaning "by and by." But the name Chinook, used for a wind and a kind of salmon as well as the tribe, is not from Chinook Jargon but from the Chehalis Indigenous language.

Alaska sourdough (or simply sourdough) is a colloquial title for an Alaskan "old-timer." The term originated during the Klondike

Gold Rush when settlers began to flood into Alaska. Due to the limited availability of leavening in the remote bush of Alaska, settlers made their bread using a sourdough starter, which uses flour, water, and sugar to naturally collect yeast from the air. The use and consumption of this bread was so widespread that these settlers began to be known as "sourdoughs."

This term is also used within Canada's Yukon territory to refer to permanent residents of the territory, sometimes defined as persons who have lived in the Yukon during all four seasons.

www.ingramcontent.com/pod-product-compliance
Lightning Source LLC
Chambersburg PA
CBHW020518080526
44583CB00013B/641